D0411968

WITHDRAWN

19 NOV 2011

56006423

WELSH COLLEGE OF
MUSIC & DRAMA
LIBRARY

Howard Brenton

HOT IRONS

Also by Howard Brenton

Plays

Berlin Bertie
Bloody Poetry
The Churchill Play
Epsom Downs
The Genius
Greenland
H.I.D.
Hitler Dances
Magnificence
Revenge
The Romans in Britain
Sore Throats
Thirteenth Night
Weapons of Happiness

Screenplay

Dead Head

Translations

Bertolt Brecht's
    Life of Galileo
Georg Büchner's
    Danton's Death

Collections

Plays: One (Christie in Love,
    Magnificence, The Churchill
    Play, Weapons of Happiness,
    Epsom Downs, Sore Throats)
Plays: Two (The Romans in
    Britain, Thirteenth Night,
    The Genius, Bloody Poetry,
    Greenland)
Plays for the Poor Theatre (The
    Saliva Milkshake, Christie in
    Love, Gum and Goo, Heads,
    The Education of Skinny Spew)

Collaborations

Brassneck (with David Hare)
Pravda (with David Hare)
Iranian Nights (with Tariq Ali)
Moscow Gold (with Tariq Ali)
A Short Sharp Shock
    (with Tony Howard)
Sleeping Policemen
    (with Tunde Ikoli)

Novel

Diving for Pearls

LIBRARY

Howard Brenton

HOT IRONS

Diaries, Essays, Journalism

NICK HERN BOOKS
London

E
BRE
82
(Archive Room

A Nick Hern Book

Hot Irons was first published in 1995 by Nick Hern Books Limited, 14 Larden Road, London W3 7ST

Copyright © Howard Brenton, 1995

Howard Brenton has asserted his right to be identified as author of this work

Lines from 'New Year Letter' in *Collected Poems* by W.H. Auden, edited by Edward Mendelson, reproduced by courtesy of Faber and Faber Ltd and Random House Inc, USA

Lines from 'Changing the Wheel' by Bertolt Brecht in *Poems 1913–1956* published by Methuen London, reproduced by courtesy of Reed Consumer Books and Routledge, Chapman and Hall Inc

Lines from Julian Jaynes's *The Origin of Consciousness in the Breakdown of the Bicameral Mind* reproduced by courtesy of Penguin Books Ltd

'Tea and 7-Up' reproduced by courtesy of Times Newspapers Ltd

A CIP catalogue record for this book is available from the British Library

ISBN 1 85459 123 1

Typeset by Country Setting, Woodchurch, Kent TN26 3TB and printed in Great Britain by the Bath Press, Avon

In memory of
Donald Brenton

Contents

Note

The first part of this book is a selection of articles and lectures: the articles, with the exception of a report of a visit to Beirut, are about plays that were in rehearsal at the time of writing, or written at moments of excitement, for example Margaret Thatcher's fall from government; the lectures are about enthusiasms, or taken as opportunities to buzz bees in my bonnet. I have rewritten the articles here and there, sometimes cavalierly, when I felt there was more to say.

The second part consists of four diaries: three are travel diaries, one kept while on tour in England doing a reading of *The Romans in Britain*, one while travelling in Australia in Far North Queensland's rain forests and one while visiting the Soviet Union towards the end of the Gorbachev era. The fourth diary is, I suppose, a kind of travel piece also: it is the headlong rush through a rehearsal period of a play of mine at the Royal Court in 1992. I made some cuts in the diaries, but they stand as they were written.

'Hot Irons': strike while the iron is hot, keep as many irons in the fire as you can . . .

H.B.

Part I

Essays

1. Masks and Us

There are some great mad books, like Frazer's The Golden Bough *or Graves's* The White Goddess, *which writers love because of their heretical ideas and their powerful imagery. One of the great mad books of recent years must be Julian Jaynes's* The Origin of Consciousness in the Breakdown of the Bicameral Mind: *though I suspect it is not mad at all but terrifyingly true. In January 1994, I was asked to give the T.R. Henn Memorial Lecture at St Catharine's College, Cambridge: I took the opportunity to try to sketch something of Jaynes's majestic theory.*

When I was a young playwright, struggling to find my voice let alone a living, I had the romantic notion of getting a job in the theatre, any theatre, to 'learn about the craft'. So I spent a year as what was called an 'acting assistant stage manager,' then as a stage manager, in weekly rep. The acting experience was limited: I played corpses discovered behind sofas, postmen delivering death threats, and I have a memory of standing in fisherman's thigh-length waders and sou'-wester, holding a three-foot-long *papier mâché* salmon in my hand and saying the line, 'The old lady's dead'.

The weekly repertory was a bizarre artistic form now, perhaps happily, no longer with us: a new play was offered each week. This was our routine: Tuesday, read through the play and 'block' it, that is give the actors their moves; Wednesday, Thursday and Friday, rehearse; Saturdays were matinée days, an afternoon and an evening performance of the play that had been going on each evening; Saturday nights we on the technical side worked late, striking the old play's set and setting up the next; Sunday was for lying in bed, exhausted; then on Monday we finished work on the set in the morning, dress rehearsed in the afternoon and opened in the evening. Exhausting though it was to work in, I look back with unabashed affection on what I suppose was a sub-genre of professional theatre, with its dusty stages, with its acting companies of despairing alcoholics doing the 'character parts' and bright young 'juvenile leads' fresh with ambition from drama school, and with its flimsy box sets of old canvas, heavy with repainted patterns of wallpaper, usually still wet on opening nights.

The theatres were almost all in seaside resorts. They survived, dowdy and near bankruptcy, into the mid-sixties, despised by the profession but loved by their audiences of predominantly lower middle-class, middle-aged to elderly women. The plays were thrillers and light comedies, Agatha Christies and old, 'dated' commercial hits from the thirties and forties. The texts came in furry grey books published by Samuel French, with the moves all marked out in the text (such as XUSL, meaning cross upstage left). The director had only to ensure the actors followed the directions in the Samuel French edition. The set was invariably a 'drawing room', a sofa with a drinks table behind it and a set of french windows stage left or stage right, through which, also invariably, the leading character, made his or her first entrance.

What did I 'learn about the craft'? Well, my work's been called 'difficult', 'political', 'avant-garde' or, oh little death, 'serious', but, because I worked in weekly rep, I've never felt the divide between seriousness and entertainment that many seem hung up about in cultural life. I'm comfortable with my tacky theatrical roots. Glamour and tat are inextricable in the theatre, as are the comic and the tragic, the silly and the profound.

And, while I was at the Connaught Theatre, Worthing, one evening there was an incident that I've often pondered and which, I think, I've only recently understood.

Weekly rep plays had rules as strict as the eighteenth-century sonata form. One of those rules was that, in a thriller, the name of the murderer is revealed in the last line. One night, after I had risen to stage manager, with a team of two ASM's, I was in a little kitchen just off the stage. One of my ASM's was 'on the book', that is sitting in the wings following the text in case a prompt to an actor was needed and calling the lighting cues. A thriller, with the murderer's name in the last line, was in progress.

Suddenly over the tannoy I heard an odd, strangled noise. I rushed down upon the stage and found an extraordinary state of affairs. The ASM had, for some reason, brought the curtain down three pages too early. Actors stood before the curtain in a state of shock, cut off in mid-flow.

But this was the most extraordinary thing: the audience applauded warmly and were happily leaving the theatre, even though the name of the murderer remained unrevealed. The front of house manager rushed to the stage and called the stragglers back, the curtain was raised and the last three pages performed.

But . . . but . . . *what were they watching?* What were they there for? How were they following the play? The plot had no meaning to them, clearly. They were 'reading' the performance in some utterly different way. Whatever they were getting from the play, it was not its story.

I've often thought of this incident over the years, and tried to explain it. There's a bitter remark by the comic, Frankie Howerd, about audiences: 'People don't know what they like, they like what they know.' (Comics are naturally depressives; the misery of clowns runs deep.) But that's too cynical. Audiences can be manipulated to a degree, but they aren't automatons. For some time my reading of this incident of 'the premature curtain' was that the audience was using the theatre not to follow a story, the play was not important to them: they were there to dream. Any audience has a Utopian impulse, they want an affirmation from the stage. Perhaps that elderly, decent, unsophisticated audience wanted an affirmation that the world was young and beautiful and happy, and got it from the presence of the rep. company, consisting largely of good-looking young actors at the start of their careers. They wanted to see 'their darlings' do well, each week, in whatever comedy or thriller they were acting.

*

But in the late eighties, twenty or so years into writing plays for a living, and still romantic about 'the craft', another sense of strangeness began to preoccupy me. It was to do with acting and what actually happens in rehearsals.

I think I now know what this 'strangeness' is . . . but I'll try to explain what it was that began to so upset me.

In rehearsals you discuss the motivation of characters; the social world of the play, how, hopefully, it connects with real life; the purpose of a scene. And the writer, rewriting, worries about the meaning of the play: we want to be reassured that we are engaged on a rational, humanist activity.

But in reality we make judgements about what we're doing in irrational ways. We say: 'Does it work?' And say yes or no, for no reason except that we all know 'it works' or it doesn't; we say, 'She' – meaning a character – 'was there, present, then not'; we say, 'He had it in act one, he lost it in scene two'; we say, 'It suddenly came alive.' And, during the run of a show, actors will say, 'I was on auto-pilot tonight', even, 'I look forward to getting this on auto-pilot'.

Also the rehearsal of a play is ridden with rituals. In order to get themselves to act, actors have to go through certain things that are obsessive, mantra-like, and nothing to do with learning the part or understanding the character. Some start from 'inside', talking of psychological landscapes. Others are technical, starting from the outside. I remember one excellent actor saying on the first day of rehearsal, 'What teeth do you want?' He opened a briefcase to display a wide range of dentures. We proceeded to find the character's correct teeth.

So it's my experience that rehearsals are not so much 'preparing a role', as 'working yourself up into a state to do it'.

The basic acting ability is mimicry, replacing your voice with another. But there is something deeper involved, which a simple mask exercise demonstrates.

The exercise is done with an actor and someone as a monitor. You need a mirror, small enough to be held in one hand, and a paper bag with holes for eyes and mouth cut out: the bag should be plain, the shape of the eyes and mouth should be as neutral as possible (tricky, the most bland mask can set a mood; it is very easy for the actor to be imprinted. When the exercise is finished, it's fun to try it with, say, a Venetian or a Chinese mask: the result can be spectacular).

The actor sits cross-legged in front of the monitor and puts the paper bag on. They have eye contact.

The monitor makes wordless sounds, which the actor repeats: whoops, clicks, whispers, screams. After a while, the monitor chooses a moment to stop and breaks eye contact.

The actor continues making the wordless sounds alone, until relaxed and comfortable. The notion is to 'empty the mind' as much as possible, to have nothing planned.

The actor then makes a hand-signal. The monitor shows the actor his or her face in the mirror for five seconds, no more, then says 'Hello,' and 'Who are you?'

At once, without fail, it seems out of nowhere, a character appears, with a name, personality, history, family.

Try this, but be careful: sometimes the 'characters' who appear by spontaneous invention can be fierce, it can be a disturbing experience for the actor, for whom the experience feels like a kind of possession.

It is as if the mask itself is alive and speaks, independent of its wearer. When an actor stands upon the stage, the whole body is a mask. But where does the mask's voice come from? I write the text, the actor walks upon the stage – but the voice of 'the character' belongs to neither of us. What is the source? Yeats tried to describe it:

Where got I that truth?
Out of a medium's mouth,
Out of nothing it came,
Out of the forest loam,
Out of dark night where lay
The crowns of Nineveh.

Ah, nothing quite like that old Celtic-mist bullshit! But it does describe the moment a mask speaks. But I don't believe in spirits, I said to myself, or mediums or possession. What is a good atheistical, humanistical, Marxist-leaning lad like me getting mixed up with all this stuff for?

I've found an explanation in a book, *The Origin of Consciousness in the Breakdown of the Bicameral Mind*, by the American psychologist Julian Jaynes.

I got to the book through chance.

I was on my way to see the people at the Deutsches Theater in Berlin to discuss a production of an old play of mine that was in rehearsal. The plane was late and I bought a book, Italo Calvino's stories, *Our Ancestors*. I read the wonderful medieval one about a man split in half, 'The Divided Viscount'. I got off the plane, the theatre said write us a new play if you have an idea. I do have an idea, I said. Have you read Calvino's story? 'It is my favourite,' exclaims the Artistic Director and three days later they make me an offer. Serendipity . . . Back in England, thinking about writing such a play of two halves of the same man at war with each other, I was mooching around in a bookshop, there was a big fat Penguin with the word 'Bi' in an incomprehensible title . . . and I was on board the Jaynesian roller-coaster.

The book kicks off with a magnificent paragraph describing the glory of what it is simply to be awake.

> O, what a world of unseen visions and heard silences, this insubstantial country of the mind! What ineffable essences, these touchless rememberings and unshowable reveries! And the privacy of it all! A secret theatre of speechless monologue and prevenient council, an invisible mansion of all moods, musings, and mysteries, an infinite resort of disappointments and discoveries. A whole kingdom where each of us reigns reclusively alone, questioning what we will, commanding what we can. A hidden hermitage where we may study the troubled book of what we have done and yet may do. An introcosm that is more myself than anything I can find in a mirror. The consciousness that is myself of selves, that is everything, and yet nothing at all – what is it?

> And where did it come from?

> And why?

Before he answers that with a startling, even repugnant and frightening hypothesis, Jaynes goes on a long tour of what consciousness is and is not. It's a fascinating read. You check what he is saying with your own head . . .

Jaynes points out that each age describes consciousness in terms of its own themes and concerns. St Augustine among the cavernous hills of Carthage was astonished at the 'mountains and hills of my high imaginations', 'the plains and caves and caverns of my memory', with its recesses of 'manifold and spacious chambers, wonderfully furnished with unnumberable stores'. In the early nineteenth century, there came the great geological discoveries of the past, written in layers of the earth's crust; this led to the popularisation of the idea of consciousness as being in *layers,* recording an individual's past, there being deeper and deeper layers until the record can no longer be read. By 1875 most psychologists were insisting that consciousness was but a small part of mental life and that unconscious sensations, ideas and judgements made up the majority of mental processes. In the middle of the nineteenth century, chemistry succeeded geology as the fashionable science; so consciousness for John Stuart Mill was a compound structure that could be analysed in the laboratory into precise elements of sensations and feelings. Then as steam locomotives chugged their way into the pattern of everyday life, so they puffed their way into psychology: the subconscious became a boiler of straining energy which demanded manifest outlets and, when repressed, burst valves and shot out as neurotic behaviour.

Note, says Jaynes, how the *metaphors of mind are the world it perceives.*

The difficulty is that we feel it is the most self-evident thing imaginable to be conscious of consciousness:

> We feel it is the defining attribute of all our waking states, our moods and affections, our memories, our thoughts, attentions, and volitions. We feel comfortably certain that consciousness is the basis of concepts, of learning and reasoning, of thought and judgement, and that it is so because it records and stores our experiences as they happen, allowing us to introspect on them and learn from them at will. We are also quite conscious that all this wonderful set of operations and contents that we call consciousness is located somewhere in the head.

And Jaynes delivers the first of many direct head-butts:

> On critical examination, all of these statements are false. They
> are the costume that consciousness has been masquerading in
> for centuries.

Jaynes sets out to show that consciousness is a far smaller part of
our mental life than we know, we are caught in a Wittgensteinian
tautology: *we cannot be conscious of what we are not conscious.*

Don't panic, it gets even more difficult.

Like a flashlight in the dark, consciousness is only conscious of
being on, when it is on. And since, from a flashlight's point of
view, there is light in a darkened room in whatever direction it
turns, the flashlight would have to conclude that there is light
everywhere. And so *consciousness seems to pervade all mentality when
actually it does not.*

Jaynes goes on to take a hammer to assumptions about consciousness. To rattle through some of his points:

Consciousness is not a copy of experience. When you swim, you
see yourself swimming; Nijinsky said that when he danced, it was
as if he were in the orchestra pit, looking back on himself; when
you play the piano, if you become too aware of what your hands
are doing, you can make a mistake.

Consciousness is not necessary for concepts or for learning; it is
a helpless spectator, for example when you learn to juggle: indeed
it can impede learning.

It's easy to bristle at all this . . . Jaynes also argues that consciousness is not necessary for thinking. He devotes some pages to
this: thinking is a matter of reaction to a stimulus, an instruction;
once the stimulus for a spate of thinking has come, the thinking is
automatic. A way of saying this is: *one does one's thinking before one
knows what one is to think about.*

Nor is consciousness necessary for reason. The long tradition of
homo sapiens, the rational animal, 'in all its pontifical generality'
(Jaynes), rests on the assumption that consciousness is the seat of
reason. But, Jaynes writes, there has been great confusion: reasoning and logic have been confused with each other just as health is

with medicine – or better – as conduct is with morality. Logic is the science of the justification of conclusions we have reached by natural reasoning. Jaynes's point is that for such natural reasoning to occur, consciousness is not necessary. The very reason we need logic at all is because most reason is not conscious at all.

Indeed, great reasoning does seem to just arrive. Einstein told a friend that his greatest ideas came while shaving; he had to move the blade very carefully every morning, lest he cut himself with surprise. A famous physicist once said 'We often talk about the three Bs: the bus, the bath and the bed. That's where the great discoveries are made . . .'

Ideas 'seem to appear' because their thinkers are not conscious of having thought them. I can testify to the writer's uncanny sense of being dictated to on occasion, usually the best stuff. 'Where got I that truth . . . out of nothing it came . . .'

No, not out of nothing. You thought it. You reasoned it. You made it. Perhaps over minutes, hours, days, years. You are just *not aware* that you did.

What is Jaynes up to? By chiselling away at our conceptions of what consciousness is, he lays the ground for the notion that a *human civilisation is possible without consciousness.*

Jaynes is one of many psychologists who believes that consciousness came from language; that language came first *then* consciousness.

He coins some hybrid terms to help us in a complex argument about the nature of metaphor. A thing to be described he calls *the metaphrand*; the thing – or relation – used to elucidate it – the *metaphier*. For example: 'The snow blankets the fields.' The metaphrand, the thing to be described, is the snow, the thing used to elucidate it, the metaphier, is the blanket of a bed.

The 'grand and vigorous function of metaphor' is the generating of new language as it is needed, as human culture becomes more and more complex, for example, the naming of plants – lady's slipper, bluebell, darning needle, Queen Anne's lace, buttercup. The human body is a particularly generative metaphier: the *head* of an army, table, page, bed, ship, household or nail, of steam; the *face* of a clock, cliff, card or crystal; the *eyes* of needles, winds, storms, targets, flowers, potatoes; the *teeth* of cogs or combs; the *tongues* of shoes, the *arms* of chairs; the *leg* of a table, compass, sailor's voyage, or semi-final of the European cup; and so on and on.

All of these concrete metaphors greatly increase our powers of perception of the world about us and our understanding of it. *Language*, Jaynes concludes, *is an organ of perception, not simply a means of communication.* Language moves out into the space of the world to describe it and perceive it.

Just think (or catch yourself thinking!) how even in human relationships our concepts are generated by concrete metaphors. The skin is a particularly important metaphier. We get or stay 'in touch' with others who may be 'thick' or 'thin' skinned or perhaps 'touchy', in which case they have to be 'handled' carefully in case we 'rub them up' the wrong way.

Even the verb 'to be' was generated from a metaphor. It comes from the Sanskrit 'bhu', 'to grow, make grow', while the English forms 'am' and 'is' have evolved from the same root as the Sanskrit asci, which means 'to breathe'. It is . . .

> . . . something of a lovely surprise that the irregular
> conjunction of our most nondescript verb is thus a record of a
> time when man had no independent word for existence and
> could only say that something 'grows' or that it 'breathes'. . . .
> Abstract words are ancient coins whose concrete images in
> the busy give-and-take of talk have worn away with use.

Our understanding is an extension of metaphor. In the phrase 'the blanket of snow' the blanket, the metaphier, carries many associations: warmth, the bed, un-snowness, an image of a blanket on a bed now, or on a childhood bed many years ago. It is in that way we understand the snow, that we are *conscious* of the snow.

What I call 'me', this 'I', is itself a metaphor. I use the complex, subtle, accrued metaphor of the language that flows in me and in which I swim, to narratise, to project the analogue 'I' forward. I imagine finishing typing up this lecture. I can then go out for a drink with my wife and our good friends D. and J. I see myself, at a pub table in the Grove Tavern. I see myself lifting the telephone to check the friends are free . . . and do it.

That is what consciousness is for Jaynes. It is the invention of an analogue world on the basis of language; we live, and call ourselves awake, and make decisions, by telling ourselves stories about what the 'I' – the 'me' – is going to do next.

And now things get really freaky.

If consciousness is based on language, then it follows that it is of much more recent origin than has been supposed.

And Jaynes argues that until recently, some three to three and a half thousand years ago, our consciousness was radically different. We literally walked with gods, heard gods, saw them and obeyed them. Constantly, in moments of stress, of choice, we heard a god's voice. Jaynes believes that that was the everyday experience of the men and women who lived and died in the kingdoms of the Tigris and Euphrates rivers, Anatolia, the valley of the Nile, Cyprus, Thessaly and Crete, the Indus river valley and beyond, along the Yangtse river, and in Central America and in the Andean highlands. These ancestors, the first city dwellers, were not what we would call conscious at all. Their will came to them as the commands of gods.

Can we imagine this radically different state of mind, our nervous systems speaking to us directly, in the hallucinated form of a god or goddess by our side, can we reach back to our long dead brothers and sisters who may have lived it?

Jaynes calls this 'non-conscious' mind 'bicameral'. Perhaps we have literary evidence of what it was like. In a splendidly contentious chapter, Jaynes argues that the *Iliad* – though partly composed and then written down by conscious hands – is an account of the bicameral mind. It is, indeed, not sung or recited by a man at all, but by an immortal: 'Of wrath, sing goddess . . .'

The characters in the *Iliad* do not sit down and decide what to do. They have no conscious minds such as we have, and certainly no introspections. When Agamemnon robs Achilles of his mistress it is a goddess who appears to instruct him –

Rearing behind him Pallas seized his fiery hair –
Only Achilles saw her, none of the other fighters –
Struck with wonder he spun around, he knew her at once

Pallas Athena! the terrible blazing of those eyes –

It is a god who whispers to Helen to sweep her heart with home-sick longing, a god who hides Paris in a mist in front of the attacking Menelaus, a god who leads the armies into battle, who speaks to each soldier at the turning points, who tells Hector what to do, who urges soldiers on or defeats them by casting spells over them or drawing mists about their eyes. It is the gods who start quarrels among men –

> Ares drove them, fiery-eyed Athena drove the Argives,
> And Terror and Rout and relentless Strife stormed too,
> Sister of manslaughtering Ares, Ares comrade-in-arms –
> Strife, only a slight thing when she first rears her head
> But her head soon hits the sky as she strides across the earth.
> Now Strife hurled down the leveller Hate amidst both sides,
> Wading into the onslaught, flooding men with pain.

'It is one god', writes Jaynes, 'who makes Achilles promise not to go into battle, another who urges him to go, and another who then clothes him in a golden fire reaching up to heaven and screams through his throat across the bloodied trench at the Trojans, rousing in them ungovernable panic. The gods take the place of consciousness.'

*

How did the bicameral mind begin?

There is an excavation of a town called Eynan ten miles north of the Sea of Galilee. The site dates from 9000 BC; it's of a town of 50 stone houses.

Here is a change in human affairs. Instead of a nomadic tribe of about 20 hunters living in the mouths of caves, we have a town with a population of 200 to 300 persons. At the centre of Eynan, is the king's tomb. It is circular, like the other houses; inside lie two corpses, lying on their back, legs detached after death. One wore a headdress of shells, the other, an adult male, was propped on stones, his upright head facing the snow-covered peaks of Mount

Hermon, thirty miles away. At some time later the tomb was surrounded by a red-ochred wall, or parapet; then large stones were
laid over the top, roofing it in; then, on the roof, a hearth was
built.

Jaynes suggests that in the hallucinations of his people, the dead
king, propped on his pillow of stones, was still giving forth his
commands; that the red painted parapet was a response to the de-
composition of the body and that the smoke rising from the hearth
was a source for hallucinations of the king's voice.

The king's tomb as the god's house continues through the
millennia as a feature of many civilisations, particularly Egypt. But
more often the king's tomb becomes a temple. The successor continues to hear the hallucinated voice of his predecessor during his
reign, and designates himself as the dead king's priest or servant.
And in place of the corpse is a statue, enjoying even more service
and reverence.

The gods were not 'figments of the imagination'. They *were
human volition.* Each person had a part of his or her nervous system
which was divine, by which he or she was ordered about, by a
voice or voices which we would call 'the will'. It was divine
government by hallucinated voices, related in carefully established
patterns, in a hierarchy.

Jaynes was trained as a neurologist. He explains how he thinks
the nervous system once spoke to us, in the form of hallucinated
Pallas Athena out of the mist to the bronze age warrior whose faint
trace comes to us as the name Achilles. For most of us (left-
handers, like this author, are wired the other way round) speech
areas are on the left-hand side of the brain; language function is in
only one hemisphere. The right hemisphere seems to have no
function; and there's where, says Jaynes, the gods used to live.
There is a connecting bridge between the two hemispheres called
an 'anterior commissure'; across it one half of the brain 'heard' – a
metaphor, note – the other half's commands.

In the bicameral era, the bicameral mind *was* the instrument of
social control, not fear or repression or even law. There were no
private ambitions, no private grudges, no private anything, since
bicameral people had no internal 'space' in which to be private,

and no analogue 'I' to be private with. All initiative was in the voices of gods. Within each bicameral state, therefore, the people were probably more peaceful and friendly than in any civilisation since. But at the interfaces between different civilisations, the problems were complex and quite different.

Then, in Mesopotamia and Europe, around the end of the second millennium, there was a terrifying 'change of mind'. The gods died on us. We could no longer hear them. We began to narratise our own fates, in great pain.

Listen to these Hittite fragments of the last three centuries of the second millennium BC:

One who has no god, as he walks along the street,
Headache envelopes him like a garment.

And this from Babylon –

My god has forsaken me and disappeared
My goddess has failed me and keeps at a distance
The good angel who walked beside me has departed
My god has not come to the rescue in taking me by the hand
Nor has my goddess shown pity on me by going at my side.

The bicameral mind was weakened by trade and by writing; the analogue mind grew, the gods fell silent. When I first read Jaynes's book I rushed to the British Museum; there was the great divide. Go through the Egyptian rooms, it's the imagery of a bicameral culture: then go to the Assyrian collection and you are hit by the change, the terrible shock: the tyranny of a ruling clique – that is, the world as we know it – has arrived. Instead of the voices of the gods controlling society, there is fear and repression. The long march of our era toward democracy and community, being conscious of ourselves and what we share, begins in terror and war.

And the bicameral mind lingers on in our cultures and in the ways we think. Jaynes, who has a doctor's experience, believes that schizophrenic voices are throwbacks to what was once universal; their hearers suffer, with the voices often turned against them, because there is no longer a social structure, the dead god king and the goddess and all their idols, to give the voices coherence and order. And the vestiges are everywhere; it's common, when tired or stressed, to hear your name called out in a night-time street. Lines for plays just come, or don't come. Our religions are full of bicameral incidents: St Paul saw Christ on the road to Damascus, Mohammed went up to heaven to talk with God. We yearn to hear and follow the voices of the political leader, the artistic guru, to be given orders or, in effect the same thing, for someone 'to speak for us'; authoritarian regimes exploit a bicameral longing to hear 'the voice of the nation'.

*

So now I believe I know why the masks speak, how they tell the story of a life that appears from nowhere. It's the nervous system speaking to us. Acting opens a door to a profound recess of our being. And the audience of 'the premature curtain', with which I began this speculation, were there to hear the voices of the actors, just the voices, of their darlings. They were in a sense worshipping the actors; the play didn't matter.

I don't approve of that. I want plays and entertainments I'm involved with to have meaning, to be awake and to wake the audience up, not slur them into the old bicameral miasma. But Jaynes's book has made me realise that the theatre is archaic; that practitioners must come to terms with its ancient, hidden, irrational power. Jaynes argues that consciousness is new. His wonderful book isn't grounded in an eighteenth–century or Darwinian folly that we are the centre of nature, but in the frightening realisation that we are animals with something fragile, painful, and sometimes dangerous in our heads, which can drive us to terrible excesses and self-destruction but which we must nevertheless nurture to survive. The old controls went three thousand years ago; we're finally going to have to accept that the gods died, and live without them.

There's a strange new humanism for the millennium in this. Perhaps Jaynes's extraordinary book, which is creating powerful research programmes, particularly at Princeton University, is the harbinger of a new enlightenment.

Also I admit it was a wonderful mine of fantastical notions while I was writing a play about half a man hopping around with only half his head! Buy the book. For myself, I owe Professor Jaynes a pizza and a beer.

2. Tea and 7-Up

At the end of July 1982, at the invitation of the Bertrand Russell Foundation, I went to Beirut with a group of young people – an idealistic deputation of 'socialist youth' organised by the Spanish Socialist Party. At that time, the PLO were in the western part of the city, under siege by the Israelis.

We crossed on foot to West Beirut at 2 pm at the 'Museum Gate', ignored by the Israeli soldiers. After a Lebanese checkpoint we hired a taxi. Commerce in all its forms is flourishing, so much money is being made by the Alexandre Hotel that there is a notice in reception saying, 'Cash only. We do not take American Express.'

We asked for the office of Mr Mahmood Lebady; the driver dumped us at the Commodore Hotel: the office was far away in a heavily shelled area. Another driver told us we were mad and agreed to take us for 100 Lebanese pounds, about 10 pounds sterling. On our way an air raid began.

Our cheerful, Muslim Lebanese driver swore mightily in English and drove at hair-raising speed to each intersection of the smashed streets, where he would brake to stop, sliding the car in the rubble, judge where the planes were and shoot off in the other direction. 'Too dangerous,' he said and, with great kindness, took us to his own house to sit out the raid.

His street was half destroyed. Those who had remained had set up an electricity supply of sorts, wires hanging in the gardens. He had sent his wife and three daughters away and stayed to look after the house with his elderly father and brother-in-law. As the raid continued they gave us tea and cans of 7-Up.

The driver's humour, courtesy and resourcefulness were typical of the 'Blitz spirit' we met from both Lebanese and Palestinians. My parents have told me of the effortless courage and self-control in the Blitz during the last war but I had doubted that it was humanly possible. (Why are we who are fortunate enough not to have had to survive in a war zone or with an army, so know-all and cynical about simple courage?)

'Everything is abnormal here,' a PLO guide warned. We saw the façade of an apartment block, deserted by its wealthy residents, packed with refugees from Southern Lebanon, the families on the balconies hanging out washing, watching TV (later, the Israelis turned the electricity off), the children playing, and all the time bombs falling not far away, the building humming with voices like a football crowd.

Late at night, against the crump of shells from the tanks and ships and the whoosh of PLO rocket fire, the eerie cries of cockerels echoed in the streets – a lot of people were keeping chickens in strange places. In daylight, between raids, cars drove about furiously, civilians visiting, shopping, carrying water; we saw wells being drilled; as we were driving, a girl called to the PLO guide from a window. In the appalling conditions, daily life seemed irrepressible.

We visited three hospitals. The first, the Dar El Ajazah El Islam mental hospital, had been hit twice. Its top storey had been blown away, Red Cross flags hung in the air amid the jagged concrete.

The two hospitals for the wounded that we saw were set up in the Triumph Hotel and in what was once the French School. We saw terrible injuries: a PLO fighter whose skin had been burnt off all over his body; an old man in great pain with both legs gone; a PLO fighter with a leg and an arm gone, blind in one eye, who was so grateful for a halting conversation he gave us each a biscuit; a child with an arm gone; another child with his lower stomach and genitals blown away – I cannot continue the list.

After seeing the wards of the French School hospital, we were in a little garden with children playing. I was talking to the hospital secretary; her two eldest children were in the north, her three-year-old daughter was with her. A plane screeched and a bomb fell a hundred yards away. Uncannily the children barely reacted as they were shooed into the school.

'You see how we have lived for two months,' the woman said. The plane screeched; another bomb fell; the blast rattled the windows. We ran through the garden into the corridor of the main building, now full of patients and staff sheltering. The guide said, 'We go,' and we made for the main entrance and ran out. Into the hospital ran three men, each carrying a child covered with blood.

Later that afternoon, four of us went down to the PLO fighters. They made us coffee on a Calor gas stove. We sat round a table in a smashed room. The wine bottles and vine leaves printed on the tablecloth are indelibly stamped on my mind. There was an atmosphere of terrible concentration: it was a most dangerous place.

The PLO fighters were utterly still. We spoke to them in Spanish: they did not seem to know English. Then suddenly one said: 'I have lived in England,' in a near perfect accent. He was a doctor who had trained at Kent University. 'I love England,' he said; 'there is stability there.' I gave him my address. He said, 'If I live through this war, I will visit you,' then added, with conviction beyond any political slogan or party line, 'and one day you will come, with your family, for a holiday in Palestine.' The shells began to fall nearby. We shook hands and were rushed away.

I was no more than a tourist passing through the overwhelming suffering and courage of the siege of Beirut. What I saw was beyond grief, beyond tears, beyond human sense. As I write, the radio gives news that Israeli tanks are fighting in the streets. It seems that Israel will do its worst and America will do nothing to stop it.

Two points, one inhumanly political, one simply human. In conversations with PLO officials we heard some wild voices, checked up to now by the PLO leadership's policy of an international settlement, in the end, with an Israeli state and a Palestinian state recognised internationally. But I fear a total massacre in West Beirut will sweep Yasser Arafat's policies away, and a new generation could wreak a terrible revenge of international terrorism against Israel, Western and also Arab countries, which will be as insane and inhuman as the present Israeli assault. All hope of peace in the Middle East will be lost and the region will become the theatre for a third world war.

And the human point: I thought I would meet a bunch of thugs in West Beirut. Instead I met the Palestinians, an attractive, witty, endlessly resourceful lot, with a love of story-telling and argument; in short, so like Jewish friends I have in England. A line kept coming to me from Georg Büchner: 'We are all very like each other. All villains and angels, idiots and geniuses, all things in one.' That human reality overpowered everything in West Beirut.

3. A Crazy Optimism

In 1982 I worked with my wife Jane, who is a translator, on a version of Büchner's Danton's Death *for the National Theatre.*

There is always a question you are asked about a play you've worked on that gives rise to murderous thoughts. With Georg Büchner's *Danton's Death* the question is, 'But was he for or against the Revolution?' We are so simplistic and childish in our 'cultural life' in England. For all the sophistication, the arts columns, the arts courses, the measure of free speech and relative lack of censorship, the 'cultured' among us can, it seems, only ask, 'Who is the goody, who is the baddy, and what does the writer want me to think?' Be it the Falklands War or a play in the theatre, the pundits debate politics or art in terms of a third-rate TV crime series. In *Danton's Death* Camille Desmoulins, the brilliant journalist loved by both Danton and Robespierre, lets fly at this reduction of everything to an artificial 'good' and 'bad', a grammar of thought and feeling in which the real cannot be described or discussed. The historical Desmoulins did actually write such an article; but you can, as with Hamlet on acting, catch the dramatist's rage about the misrepresentation he knew his work was in for:

> I tell you, if they don't get everything in wooden reproductions in their theatres, concerts, art exhibitions, they won't even listen. But if they get a ridiculous marionette and they can see the strings moving it up and down and they can see its legs creaking along in iambic pentameters, they say 'What truth! What understanding of human nature, how profound!' Take any tiny insight, any fatuous notion or tin-pot aphorism, dress it up and paint it in bright colours and parade it about three acts until it gets married or shoots itself, and they cry

'What idealism!' But turn them out of the theatre into the street and, oh dear, reality is just too sordid. They forget God himself, they prefer his bad imitators. Creation is being newly born every minute, within them and all around them, a storm glittering with lightning, but they hear and see nothing. They go to the theatre, read poems and novels and praise the caricatures. To creation itself they say 'How ugly, how boring.'

To answer the question. Büchner was more than *for* the Revolution, he was, though writing forty-one years after the events of the play, in a very real *sense in* it. His father was a prosperous doctor in the service of the autocratic ruler of the Grand Duchy of Darmstadt, a state with a population of 700,000. The young man opened his eyes and saw the inhuman, half-feudal society he was born into and raged at it. While at the small University of Giessen he joined a revolutionary group, 'The Society For Human Rights'. He wrote, in a letter to a friend, 'The relationship between the poor and the rich is the only revolutionary element in the world.' He composed a pamphlet, 'The Hessian Messenger', addressed to the peasants, exhorting them to insurrection: 'With their drums the soldiers drown the sound of your sighs, with their rifle butts they smash your skulls . . . They are the lawful murderers who protect the lawful robbers.' The pamphlet had a famous slogan: 'Peace to the hovels! Death to the palaces!' But the conspirators were betrayed to the police (Büchner suspected a close friend). One, Pastor Weidig, the group's mentor, was tortured in prison and committed suicide two years after being arrested. Another was released, insane, after three years; another was in prison for four years. Büchner fled to Darmstadt and his family house where, forbidden to write anything by his father and under constant police surveillance, tormented with fear for his arrested comrades and for himself, he wrote *Danton's Death* secretly in five weeks, then fled to France. He was twenty-one.

The play he wrote is not (as is often said) a tragedy, but a comedy, a celebration of what we are; like all the great comedies it sings, it does not judge. That is why they who rummage about in the play for the goodies and the baddies get so thoroughly lost. All the people in the play made the Revolution, from the royalist General Dillon to the idealist Saint-Just with his fiercely egalitarian vision. They are all given their voice and they are all responsible. 'The lava of the Revolution flows' is a line twice used in the play. For Büchner, the play was what the world was going to be like, the Revolution was never going to go away.

Because it was written by a revolutionary from within, the play depicts horror and despair with great accuracy. In one extraordinary scene Büchner cracks into Robespierre's skull and dramatises the great man's conscience: he knows that if he is wrong, he is damned.

Dickens' *A Tale of Two Cities* pales beside such intensity. The comparison is shaming: Dickens is fantastical, ignorant and shoddily propagandistic. To illustrate the complexity of Büchner's writing about the Terror, here are two passages. First, a letter he wrote to his fiancée:

I have been reading the history of the Revolution. I felt as though crushed by the hideous fatalism of history, I find in human nature a terrifying sameness, in human institutions an irresistible power, bestowed on all and on none. The individual mere foam on the wave, greatness a mere accident, the sovereignty of genius only a puppet-play, a ridiculous struggling against an iron law, to recognise it is our highest achievement, to control it impossible. Never again shall I feel inclined to bow down before the performing houses and the corner boys of history. My eyes have grown accustomed to the bloodshed. But I am no guillotine blade. 'Must' is one of the execrations pronounced at the baptism of mankind. The dictum 'It must needs be that scandal cometh; but woe to him through who scandal cometh!' is terrible. What is it in us that lies, murders, steals? I cannot bear to pursue the thought.

This is often quoted to show that Büchner had despaired and turned reactionary, but in *Danton's Death* the thoughts of that letter mutate into something else. Danton and his friends are in their cell, about to leave for the tumbrel. The Dantonists are like peacocks, working themselves up to flash their tails at the waiting crowd outside:

DANTON: When history comes to open its tombs, despots may
    yet choke on the stench of our corpses.
HÉRAULT: We stank pretty high in our lives, too. You're talking
    to posterity, Danton, not to us at all.
CAMILLE: He puts on a face to be dug up by the archaeologists
    of the future. All that effort, pursing your lips, painting your
    face, putting on a good accent. We should take off our masks.
    Then we'll see, like in a room of mirrors, only the infinitely
    repeated, age-old image of the fool, the joker's head. We are
    very like each other. All villains and angels, idiots and
    geniuses, all things in one. We all sleep, digest food, make
    children, we are all variations in different keys on the same
    tune. That's why we strut about, put on faces: we embarrass
    one another because we know each other so well. And now
    that we've all eaten ourselves sick at the same time don't let's
    hold napkins up to our mouths and pretend we've not got
    belly-ache. Yell and groan as it takes you. No heroic gestures,
    no witty sallies. Spare yourselves the trouble. We all know
    each other.
HÉRAULT: Yes, Camille, let's sit down and scream. Why be tight-
    lipped when you're in pain? Greeks and Gods screamed
    aloud, Romans and Stoics pulled the heroic faces.
DANTON: Greek or Roman, they were all Epicureans, like the
    rest of us. They did what made them feel impressive. Why
    not drape your toga about you and cast a long shadow? Why
    torment ourselves?

I would not pretend the play is a barrel of laughs. But the comic structure, the under-cutting, the unexpected twisting and lifting of scenes, struck the actors increasingly in rehearsal. They had expected to be depressed performing it; instead a gaiety overtook everyone working on it. Jokes flew constantly in the rehearsal room. You can see why from the passage quoted.

The intellectual despair of the letter has changed into a crazy optimism. Once you cease to be frightened of the content of the play, encouraged, perhaps, by the way the characters are not frightened to be living their dangerous lives, the whole map of the socialist and communist tradition unfurls itself with all the marshes, volcanoes and precipices clearly marked. In Danton, we see the difficulties true libertarians have always had with bad conscience, indulgence and general disorganisation; with Robespierre there is the classic difficulty of 'holding the centre', against Left and Right; in the second tier of the members of the Committee Of Public Safety there are corrupt cadres saying one thing to the leadership and another thing among themselves; in Saint-Just there is the danger of trying to turn a wholly impersonal and determinist view of history into a political policy; and again and again in the street-scenes there is the insistence that, good, let death come to the palaces, but if peace does not come to the hovels then the exercise is meaningless.

4. Writing in Thatcherland: Five of My Plays

This is the introduction to the second volume of my plays, published by Methuen. 'Thatcherland' is, I think, a coinage by Alan Bennett; if it is, it's stolen here without shame. It's the perfect name for the era of the British 1980s, which in retrospect certainly looks socially destructive, but also cranky, tinpot, even silly, a kind of moral Legoland.

When I was a boy, I wanted to be an archaeologist. What the Freudian explanation is of this childhood fascination with what is buried, hidden under-foot, leaving upon the surface of the landscape a kind of cloud shadow in reverse from deep below, I don't think I want to know. (Henry Moore was once given a weighty, German psychological analysis of his sculpture. He refused to read it, saying, with Yorkshire phlegm, that if he knew too much about why he sculpted, he might not need to sculpt.) But the memory of this childhood interest in the buried past did, I must admit, give me the idea for *The Romans in Britain*.

Along with dinosaurs, the Roman occupation of Britain used to be something of an obsession with primary teachers in our schools. I remember a picture of 'Caesar's legions crossing the Thames' pinned on the classroom wall when I was nine. So the play takes a rooted, popular myth from the British national consciousness. Everyone knows the Romans came to Britain. This is vaguely felt to be 'a good thing', because they built straight roads and 'brought law'. The play was called an 'anti-imperialist epic', but the subject is really 'culture shock'. For the Romans, Caesar's second raid on Britain is a minor operation which is not that successful. It is a small war on the edge of the known world that gets bogged down, a wretched summer of little achievement and, to Julius Caesar, of little interest. The scene in which he appears is titled 'Caesar's tooth'. He has toothache and, irritably, removes the offending tooth and throws it away. That sums up what he thinks of Britain. He notes a few local customs for his memoirs, orders the fields to be salted 'as a reminder', and leaves the stage and these shores for greater things.

But for the Celts, the appearance of the Roman army is the end of their culture, its touch is death. I tried to imagine what it must have been like for three young Celts, seeing Roman soldiers for the first time. I titled the scene 'Two Worlds Touch'. The Celts have been swimming on a fine summer's day. On the river bank they fool about, brag and laugh, then stretch out in the sun. From out of the trees come three Roman soldiers. They have had a bad day, losing touch with their platoon in a confused skirmish in the trees, and want a swim. The Celts are between them and the river. To the Romans it's nothing, there are three natives, three 'wogs', between them and a much-needed swim. The Romans kill two of the Celts and grossly abuse the third, who runs off. To the soldiers it is nothing, nothing at all. To the Celts it is worse than death, it is the end of their world.

My scene shocked many, for it is profoundly shocking. What is so hard to take is the flippancy of the soldiers, their jokey indifference, the fact that they 'know not what they do'. The play took three years to write, through three versions. It was a most difficult undertaking. Ten years on, I think I've forgotten the heartache of writing it. It seems quite simple and straightforward to read. It does break many of the received theatrical rules of 'the well-made play'. There is no lead character. There are no 'goodies' and 'baddies'. There is no obvious, or usual, 'moral message'. The scenes of the past are haunted by the 1980s with another army, the British, blundering around in another foreign country, Ireland. And the play's dramatic shape is perverse, for it goes from 'dark' to 'light', with a first half that is violent, dynamic and tragic, while the second half is elegiac, still and flooded with an hysterical, light-hearted, comic spirit. You were faced in the theatre with the problem of an audience in the interval saying, 'My God! If that was Part One, what the hell is going to happen in Part Two?' For it is a received notion that a funny play should be funniest at its end, and a violent, angry play should end at its highest pitch of mayhem. It is deeply perverse to fly in the face of that expectation. Indeed, the play ends with a perverse joke – one evening, in a time of civil war, a century after the Empire abandoned these islands, two cooks are hiding in a ditch. It is not a good time for cooks. There is famine, and the big houses, with their kitchens, have been burnt down. The cooks realise they need another profession and decide to be storytellers, inventing, there and then, the story of King Arthur . . . which has done rather well since.

The first difficulty was to construct an account of the Celtic society the Romans found. There are some thirteen accounts of the ancient Celts by classical authors, including Caesar's disapproving observation of what he took to be gross sexual immorality (was he looking at a quasi-matriarchal society, in which women had several husbands, his imperial mentality making him assume he had come across tribes of female sluts?). It was something of a shock to realise how thin the written record is, how rocky the pillars are upon which volumes of scholarship have been built. So, since in a play people have to say and do *something* while they are on the stage, my account of the ancient Celts is highly speculative and academically suspect, though I did find after a few months of research I could hold my own in an argument with a professor about whether the eaves of Celtic roundhouses were, or were not, painted and decorated with gods . . . the academic world is as full of bullshit as any other, including mine!

When Peter Hall commissioned the play, he said one thing: 'How are they going to talk?' Since, as a rough and ready rule of thumb, the Romans in the play are nearer to us and they are soldiers, I was able, without too much trouble, to develop an anachronistic prose for them. Julius Caesar was a religious man, his family believed they were descended from the Goddess Venus. Historians have puzzled over Caesar's religious reforms, to which he devoted enormous energy when he came to power in Rome. Some see this as power-broking between powerful families, elevating the cults of friends, downgrading the cults of enemies. But one suspects it was from an impulse lost to us. The paganism of the classical world, viewed through Christianised eyes, is dim and difficult to read. Nevertheless, in many respects Caesar in my play thinks like us, that is dialectically, in terms of cause and effect. His mental world is symmetrical, four-square, logical. Writing the Celts, I kept staring at the few examples of their decoration we have, which is off-centre, curled, triangular. In the British Museum there is a remarkable relic, a Celtic game. It looks like solitaire, but no one is sure how it was played. A simple game, which any British Celt's child would know, that melts our best archaeological minds . . . Then there were the Welsh triads (again, thinking in threes), which are the nearest thing we have to their sense of poetry and, therefore, to their mentality. The triads are, to us, infuriating. They mention heroes and battles, but without any sense of what we call history. An 'asymmetrical view of the world'?

From puzzling at these cryptic traces in the archaeological record and at the triads, and from visiting some sites of Celtic camps – again, triangular, maze-like, once hidden in woods, unlike the square Roman camps dominating ridges and hill tops – I began to find a language for them. A triple-rhythmed speech, fiery, full of a kind of self-display and relish, an unabashed bodily self-love (nearly every Roman author could not get over what they did to their hair . . .), and a language hopelessly ill-equipped to even describe the Romans. An emissary from another family in the play attempts to do so. He cannot find the words.

But the greatest difficulty I had, when I began to try to write the play, is a weighty matter. It was what to do about a sense of overwhelming sorrow, a grief for the nameless dead, with which the material of the play is drenched. This is, itself, difficult to express. It was what Blake addressed in the terrifying 'Proverb from Hell': 'Drive your cart and plough over the bones of the dead.' If you do not, you will go mad with grief. But cruelty is hard to dramatise. What you must never do is pretend, by stagecraft sleight of hand, that the cruelty is not as bad as it is. If you are not prepared to show humanity at its worst, why should you be believed when you show it at its best, in a play that attempts to do both in equal measure. You must not sell human suffering short.

*

While the *Romans in Britain* scandal (see 'On Tour' in the diary section of this book) was in train, I was working on *Thirteenth Night*. I remember sitting in Horseferry Road magistrates' court, with the director of *The Romans*, Michael Bogdanov, for one of his three appearances there, the morning after *Thirteenth Night's* first preview at the RSC. The theatrical chit-chat of 'How was your preview?' . . . 'Pretty rough, Michael . . . ' seemed curiously out of phase with the massed cameramen on the pavement outside and the bustle of lawyers and policemen. In the courtroom that day, before Michael 'came on', there was a request from an undercover policeman, disguised in long hair for which he apologised, for a warrant. The purpose of the warrant was not revealed in open court. It was granted in seconds and the policeman was hurried away. It was as if he had wandered out of my play of the night before.

From one nightmare into another . . . For *Thirteenth Night* is, literally, a dream play. At the end of its prologue the lead character, Jack Beaty, is hit over the head. As he falls to the ground, the play is what streams through his brain. It is, I suppose, 'a Shakespearean derivative', since, cheekily, it plays ducks and drakes with the plot of *Macbeth*. Its title is a code for the play's theme.

This is the play for when the celebrations have to stop. A critic accused me of 'having my cake and eating it' by writing a dream play. It is an open licence for improbability. Quite so. That is what I wanted. You can only do something really good, perhaps in the end really profound, in the theatre, if you do not take the theatre too seriously.

Thirteenth Night is addressed 'to the troops', that is to fellow socialists. I make no apology for once, just once, writing a play that dramatises an internal row, hanging up the Left's dirty, indeed bloodstained, linen in public. I became fed up with the unreality of some of us on the Left, who would not address the Stalinist horrors, the repression in what were called socialist countries in Eastern Europe. The play is an assault on their Orwellian double-think. Tyranny is tyranny. To quote Mohammed, 'When oppression exists, even the bird dies in the nest.' That is true whether a country be nominally socialist or not. The play is, of course, pre-Glasnost, pre-Gorbachev, pre-the fall of the Berlin Wall and the 'disappearance' of the Soviet Union. Watching a revival in 1992 at the Lyric Hammersmith's Studio was curious; the political meaning of the play was dim, the tide being, for now, out on its issues. What was left was a study of fanaticism, of horrible un-reason, which drives friends to kill each other. Büchner under-stood all this, as I was to discover working on a version of *Danton's Death* the year after *Thirteenth Night* was first performed.

In 1980, I wrote an English version of Brecht's masterpiece, *The Life of Galileo*, which John Dexter directed at the National Theatre with Michael Gambon in the lead – a production of great clarity and force. I had a somewhat grandiose scheme to write a modern parallel, a *Galileo* of our time, and to talk the National into performing it in their smaller auditorium, the Cottesloe, while Brecht's mighty play was running on the big Olivier Theatre stage. The scheme came to nothing, for a number of reasons. I was locked into preparations for the production of *The Romans in Britain*, and was embroiled in another mini-scandal over a little 'knockabout' satire on Margaret Thatcher's first Government, *A Short Sharp Shock*, which I'd written with the 'rough theatre' specialist Tony Howard. Then the Mary Whitehouse brouhaha began. The 'Galileo' play was shelved. The spirit is always willing but sometimes you just can't get the flesh to the typewriter . . .

I eventually got down to it in 1982, writing the play very slowly, five lines a day, and the Royal Court Theatre put it on in 1983. Its first title was *Galileo's Goose*. Playing around with the question of who would a modern Galileo be, I thought, 'he'd be an American . . . ' glamorous, brilliant and articulate, a man who seems to have everything, the good looks of a film star, the brain of an Einstein . . . He should be a 1980s' 'Renaissance man', univer-sally admired and a light in people's lives. But like Brecht's Galileo, my genius, Leo Lehrer, cannot deal with the moral dilemmas his work forces him to confront. And, again like Brecht's character, this golden human being falls apart and becomes gross, in a 1980s' manner. He is a dangerous man to know – arrogant, promiscuous, cruel and self-indulgent, a wrecker of the lives around him. I try to dramatise his reformation. *The Genius* is, though, about two bril-liant people, Leo Lehrer and a student, Gilly Brown. They struggle with a dangerous idea – that nuclear science is a profoundly malign pursuit and that, for the first time in human history, we must deny ourselves a technological 'advance'. It was a strange play to write, trying to dramatise the intellectual love affair between two characters whose intelligence was light years ahead of their author's.

*

In the early 1980s, I wrote three shows for the small touring company, Foco Novo. The first, in 1982, was an adaptation of Brecht's long, discursive dialogue *Conversations in Exile*. Roland Rees, Foco Novo's artistic director, had a one-act play by the Jamaican playwright, Alfred Fagon, *Four Hundred Pounds*.

Roland Rees is an unsung hero of the contemporary theatre, the most daring producer (that is, dreamer-up of ideas for plays and shows) I've had the privilege to work for. Roland's second, madcap scheme was to commission a collaborative play between myself and Tunde Ikoli, *Sleeping Policeman*, which we did in 1983. Roland wanted a play about Peckham in South London, not one of the more poetic places to draw poetry and drama from. The three of us met off and on for a year, discussing characters. We invented, from observations made on the Peckham streets, six people, three white and three black. We set a rule – the action would take place on one particular weekend. Tunde and I went away swearing, on Roland's insistence, that we would have no contact and, separately, each wrote our two plays, each scripts of some seventy pages' length. Then we sat down and did a William Burroughs-style, 'cut up' job, in one long session, slicing the two plays together. Roland's point in setting up this bizarre process, was to keep the sharpness of the voices of two very different playwrights, one white and middle-aged, living a middle-class life, and one young, black and working-class. The result was extraordinary, a kind of cubist *Under Milk Wood*, with a most strange dramaturgy, which had a 'singing' quality about everyday life in a London hinterland where writers do not usually travel with their pens.

The third show dreamt up by Roland for me to write was *Bloody Poetry*. I resisted his idea for some time. He wanted a play about the poet Shelley for Foco Novo to tour. My resistance was because I am wary of 'Art about Art' and plays about writers. I had only tried it once before, when I was beginning to write, with a play about Maxim Gorky called *A Sky-Blue Life*, and that was more a dramatisation of some of his short stories than a stage biography. I suspect that Roland's impulse was to present Shelley as a revolutionary hero. But I said 'yes' to the project when I saw a different way of handling it, writing not just about Shelley, but about the quartet of Shelley, Byron, Mary Shelley and Claire Clairemont, Byron's mistress. Throughout the eighties I had been wrestling with the notion of writing a Utopian play, a version of William Morris's *News from Nowhere*. Several attempts at doing so had broken down – I was building up a 'bottom drawer' of half-completed Utopias . . . *Bloody Poetry*, which was premiered by Foco Novo in 1984 and has been widely performed since, with a revival by the Royal Court Theatre in 1988, became a way of broaching the subject, for the quartet are determined to invent a new way of living, free of sexual repression. They make a terrible mess of it. Some found the 'morality' of the play bewildering. I was not concerned with saying whether these people were 'good' or 'bad', I wanted to salute their Utopian aspirations for which, in different ways, they gave their lives. It is a celebration of a magnificent failure.

*

Greenland, after an extended, bitter prologue, is an outright Utopia. It was greeted, on its first production, with incomprehension. I wanted to stage a world in which Shelley, Byron, Mary and Claire would be happy to live . . . though, thinking of Act Two of *Greenland* in that light, I think George Byron might have kicked over the traces. I know that this play was a reckless undertaking. Gentleness and peace are not meant to make good drama. The mental agony of *The Genius*, the death and defeat of *Bloody Poetry*, the dystopia of *Thirteenth Night* were praised, while the sly, quiet contentment and weird utterances of 'The Greenlanders' were derided by the critics. The first full draft of the play, which ended up on an autumn bonfire, simply went through scenes in the distant future set on one day, without comment. In the world we have it is difficult enough to understand our different cultures. A common humanity unites us in our basic needs and instincts, food, shelter, love of children, the use of language, curiosity, the pride of being alive, the love or the fear of death, but I have a suspicion that the humanist faith that 'people are the same everywhere and always have been' is too generalised a truth. Cultural Weltanschauungs, the 'mind sets' and world views we live in, vary sharply and often cruelly. Witness the confusions between Christianised and Muslim British citizens at the end of the eighties. Imagine then the folly of a writer trying to describe a new 'world culture', seven hundred years hence, free of conflict and oppression. How do you dramatise people without fear? We wouldn't understand a word they'd say.

It was not surprising that the first draft for *Greenland* was not only mad, which I didn't mind, but also totally incomprehensible even to its author. Definitely one for the bonfire. Then I realised there was a model, Shakespearean romantic comedy, *As You Like It* and *A Midsummer Night's Dream*. I took the basic joke – people like us, with all our hates, confusions and contemporary troubles hanging from them like rags, get lost in a 'magic wood', a new, alternative reality. The comedy comes from them loving or hating it, and from watching our assumptions about our 'human nature' challenged and changed. A Shakespearean scholar, Sally Homer, tells me this is now a most dated and discredited view of Shakespearean comedy, originating with Northrop Frye . . . But no matter. It helped me to write a play. I took a handful of 'travellers' and by a ludicrous device (you can do anything on a stage, and should) threw them into the Utopia I had been trying to imagine for nearly ten years. Act One introduces them, Act Two tries to dramatise how they get on 'in there'. It is a silly idea, but I wanted it to be *wonderfully* silly. The powerful advantage of our theatrical tradition is that it is profoundly comic. Serious matters can be tackled in the theatre by mucking about and having some fun with what is meant to be unstageable. Why shouldn't the exploration of the human spirit be light-hearted?

*

These five plays were written with a left-wing perspective, in opposition to the dominant political mores of 1980s' Britain. It was a nasty decade, a mean time to be a writer at last coming on song. But I'm encouraged, re-reading the plays, to realise that along with many others, I did manage to get so much on to the stage, in the teeth of fashion, cuts in the arts and a hostility to the very idea of a subsidised, that is publicly owned, theatre, putting on plays like these. The theatres and the actors who helped me with this writing held the line, though at some cost. The gallant Foco Novo Theatre Company, which initiated *Bloody Poetry*, went to the wall in 1988, murdered by the grant-cutting knife of the Arts Council.

Also I realise these five scripts could be read as one long play. The cooks at the end of *The Romans in Britain* could be Greenlanders; Jack Beaty in *Thirteenth Night* is an extension of my version of Julius Caesar, and the lovers in *Greenland* could be the 'witches' in *Thirteenth Night*; *Bloody Poetry* and *Greenland* are twinned by their Utopian themes; Leo Lehrer at the end of *The Genius* is shuffling towards Greenland, and in *The Romans in Britain* a stone is held up, then thrown, in a gesture of liberation by a slave, while at the end of *Greenland* a stone is brought back from the future and held up, shining with light . . . If these plays were to be given a Shavian title, they could be called *Five Plays for Romantics*. Or maybe: *Plays for the Bloody-Minded*. 'Better a long, slow fire than a brief explosion . . . ' said Joan Littlewood when I met her in 1980. She claimed this was a quote from Brecht. She may have made it up. But it was a motto I continually recalled, writing in the 1980s.

5. The Spaceman amongst
the Tower Blocks

Early in 1989, in the sheepish disguise of a critic, I was sent to Paris by the lively and colourful, but sadly short-lived, 20/20 magazine, in search of an idea that once inspired me. It was a spooky experience. Also, when this was written the year seemed another cold-war nothing year: 1989 was not yet 1989, the year of communist collapse.

To Paris, to attend the private view of an exhibition about the Situationist International at the Pompidou Centre. The Situationists were a group of unruly, unrulable and wildly inspiring artists, architects and theorists who gave intellectual muscle to the 'May Events' of Paris, '68, that failed Revolution of which no trace can be found today, except, perhaps, in this art exhibition.

Turning up for the show is a slightly unnerving experience. For a few moments I think something is actually going to happen. An illusion, I'm afraid. When in Paris, I become an over-excited tourist, who can't really accept that the city in which so much that is magnificent in our art and political thought exploded has become an EEC metropolis, dripping with shlock wealth and svelte well-dressed people and festering, away from the tourist's eye, with an abysmal immigrant poverty. Where are the present students, the heirs of the *enragés* of 1968? They are packed into cinemas watching old Jacques Cousteau underwater movies, the current, inexplicable Paris fashion. Meanwhile the Government can't even get a logo together to celebrate the bicentenary of the first French Revolution. What have they come up with? A seagull, with red white and blue wings. A seagull? Yup! Jean-Paul Sartre, did you see this coming? Was it despair at this trivial, eternal present that Parisians seem vacantly happy in, that made you fall down drunk in the street so often when you were an old man?

There is a bit of edge, though, outside the Situationist exhibition . . . Police sit in two buses outside the side-door that leads to the show, a door through which your correspondent cannot pass. Security men block my way. In vain I wave a letter from *20/20* magazine, in vain I drop the name of the Pompidou's English curator. I do not have a press card to prove I am a journalist. Therefore I am a loony. Since the exhibition inside is, to a policing eye, also lunatic, the patience of the security men is wearing thin. They are young and very fit. 'Au revoir, monsieur,' says the one with dead blue eyes. 'Pfft,' says another.

I stomp off for a walk in the Marais, closely followed, to my alarm, by four regular policemen dressed in high couture Fascist leather coats and conspicuous firearms. But after a hundred yards, when I'm clear of the Pompidou Centre, they turn back. Bored, no doubt. Nothing is going to happen. This background radiation of police paranoia around the show is a flicker of acknowledgement by the authorities of what was once a powerful idea. The Situationists were uncategorisable, quixotic and ferociously uncompromising. They gave coherent expression to underground and 'avantgarde' political ideas that ran through the Dadaists, Surrealism and the COBRA movement. With them, Surrealism finally had something like a political stance. 'Here then are the last outposts of CULTURE. Beyond, begins the conquest of everyday life. All is yet to be done,' runs a Situationist slogan. One of their images, in their posters and bizarre cartoons, is of a spaceman, in full space suit, wandering around the tower blocks of twentieth-century reality, saying things like 'the hacienda must be built'. Yes indeed. Feeling my oxygen is running out, I wander around the Marais, which was once the *ancien régime*'s 'no-go area', the crowded slum district in which the seagull's 1789 Revolution hatched to emerge red in beak and claw to change Europe forever. It is now a chintzy, pricey ghetto of expensive flats and twee shops, and I become mightily depressed. The Situationists attacked the 'banalisation' of city life, the 'spectacle'. Another slogan sums up their attitude, worth getting your head around – 'The spectacle is capital to such a degree that it becomes IMAGE.' In the Marais of today, there it is, five minutes' walk from the exhibition. Their texts – and with the Situationists, it's the texts that matter – are a bewildering cocktail of pretentious tosh and blinding insights. For a movement that wanted to 'relive the future' and 'transform everyday life', which stood for a popular freedom in urban life and, after it had disbanded, gave force to the brief wild fun of punk, the Sex Pistols and Jamie Reid's collages, their writing is very mandarin, very highfalutin', and bloody difficult. When I first read their strange pamphlets as a young playwright, I shouted for joy and ripped off what I took to be their ideas like crazy. I shamelessly 'co-opted' them to make plays ('co-option' is one of the Situationist sins, by the way). Two of their 'techniques' interested me. There was 'détournement', which involves the deflection of ideas, objects, behaviour, from their accepted usage. I tried to do that with dramatic language and form, in plays like *Christie in Love* and, in different ways, I've gone on doing it. 'Shock tactics', critics have tut-tutted. Not at all, I was trying to break the dead hold of the theatre on the theatre. Then there was the technique of 'dérive', which I made several attempts to get hold of. This was to set up 'situations' that are diverse, atmospheric, contradictory, which allow the spectator a mental freedom to wander about in. Performance art, at its best, gets near to it. I could never crack it, though I began to write epic plays which are looser, more open-ended, than the trad 'well-made play', which, sadly, is making a big comeback these days. I've not given up the idea of 'dérive', indeed I returned to it with a vengeance in my play *H.I.D (Hess Is Dead)*, written for the Mickery Theatre in Amsterdam.

Having more or less written my 'review' of the as yet unseen exhibition in my head, I return to the Pompidou Centre an hour later. The leather coats are back in their buses. There is an older security guard on the door. I get my pidgin French together and talk my way in. The exhibition is impossible, of course, for how can you exhibit an idea? Put it this way, it's like staring at a row of ashtrays full of the butts of cigarettes Sartre smoked, and trying to work out what his books were about without having read them. It is also deeply saddening to stand with a bag on my shoulder that's full of twenty-year-old, yellowing and much-thumbed pamphlets, staring at the very same publications encased in perspex on an exhibition stand. How about that for 'appropriation'? 'Toujours le spectacle.' The Situationist International was 'will-o'-the-wisp', deliberately so. The organisers have scraped together just about everything they can, and laid it out simply and clearly, but inevitably it looks like leftovers from a party. I wondered what anyone coming to it cold and ignorant of the movement would make of it. There, in a cycle rack, are five white bicycles, in memory of the free bicycles of the Provos of Amsterdam. They flooded the city with thousands of them in the early seventies, for people to use free, finding one, then leaving it. A great idea, typically Situationist. People got very hot under the collar about this breathtaking, and rather simple, idea. Now here five of them stand, authentic, period Provo bikes, in the Pompidou Centre. Will the security guards stop them being ridden away? You bet. I went back the next day and tried it. They were onto me before I even got the bike's front wheel out of the rack. And that's why the exhibition is an impossibility. It also has a strange feel of involving very few people: it is like a conspiracy of friends.

Surprisingly in a way, the 'art' in the show looks very good indeed. I'd heard of Pinot Gallizo's work. Yes yes, I'd thought, from photographs, second-rate action paintings. But no, he has a glorious installation, a 'dérivist' piece, 'The Cave of Anti-Matter', which is hard to take. Not because it's aggressive, on the contrary it is a smiling and beautiful idea, but because it stinks. Then you realise the smell is lavender, crushing in the gloom under your feet. And Jamie Reid's monster collage mural, 'For the Sex Pistols', looks tremendous and far from being dead art. 'Painting is dead. It might as well be killed off. Long live painting,' reads a slogan, with blithe incoherence. The Situationists had an internal battle about art's revolutionary potential, which the artists lost. Pinot Gallizo resigned from the International in 1960 along with others, as the theorists around Guy Debord, the group's brilliant ideologue, moved closer to the ideas of the neo-Marxist sociologist Henri Lefebvre. (That is, if the documentary material that goes with the show is to be trusted. There is a strong, playful element of piss-taking going on behind everything about the Situationists. It would not be unlike them to have constructed a wholly fictional 'cultural history' of their movement.) The best 'art' in the show (to be a reviewer) is a neon-lit maze, which is a bizarre experience. It didn't seem to be attributed to anyone. You walk into harsh light to a kind of upside-down room at the maze's heart, where you meet the only other person able to get there, a stranger who said 'Enchanté' to me, both of us caught out. We laughed. 'C'était une situation.' It was the one thing in the show that tried to demonstrate a point, rather than show it. I didn't know what to make of the work of the Dutch Situationist architect, Constant. The models of his work, chipped and a bit battered, are of imaginary buildings, ethereal, light, dreams of democratic spaces in a free city. They would give Prince Charles a heart attack. But I had a nagging suspicion that if they had been constructed, they would now be hell-holes, rotting away with other sixties buildings. The hacienda for a free life remains unbuilt.

Throughout this article, I've written about the Situationists as if they are dead. Some really are, like the painter Asker Jorn, whose iconoclastic paintings are on display, snarling with brilliant colours and slashed-about paint. But the movement died by its own hand. The Situationist International disbanded itself in 1972, fearing co-option into 'cultural history', that is, exhibitions such as this. But the spirit re-emerges here and there. It was in 'The Great Rock 'n' Roll Swindle', the Sex Pistols, that wonderful and awful band of 1976, which, in fine Situationist style, auto-destructed immediately it appeared, disrupting the corner of 'the spectacle' called 'the Music Industry'. I wonder how Jamie Reid feels about his 1983 'For the Sex Pistols' mural gracing a huge wall of the Pompidou Centre? This may be bad news for him . . . but it looks like a very good bit of art, that could see off a lot of the post-war junk up on the Pompidou's third floor in the Musée d'Art Moderne.

And there is Guy Debord's book, *The Society of the Spectacle*. Re-reading it, I still find its powerful vision of the way the century works true. Like many powerful ideas it has its dark side. When the May '68 dream of mass revolt, of a popular, celebratory transformation of Society proved to be merely that, a dream, it decayed into the nightmare of handfuls of 'urban terrorists', the Angry Brigade and the Red Army Faction. A perverted reading of

Debord's book inspired them and they destroyed themselves, turning many away from the sunlit, great, democratic idea behind the May '68 revolt. But . . . the spaceman still wanders the tower blocks. 'The conquest of everyday life' has yet to be attempted. As the Situationist slogan says:

PLEASE WASH YOUR HANDS.
YOU ARE LEAVING
THE TWENTIETH CENTURY.

6. Democratic Laughter

David Hare and I had an agreement about our play Pravda: *we'd write one article each, mine at the beginning of the run, his at the end. This was mine.*

I sat in the middle of the packed Olivier Theatre watching the first preview of *Pravda*. David Hare and I had written the play together, driving each other on, often shouting and screaming lines out loud, only to lose confidence in jokes in Indian restaurants at night. (We holed up in Brighton for three weeks to write the first draft. Halcyon days: the nylon carpet of the rented flat became more and more electrically charged as we paced up and down.)

We were committed to laughter from the audience or dreadful failure, no half measures. We had never before attempted, as dramatists, either together or singly, to go over the top – in the First World War phrase the theatre uses so tastelessly for outright commitment to one thing in a show. Collaborative writing means that you speak, often shout, each line out. Or scribble, then try it out on your fellow writer, who at once grins or grimaces. We wanted to go on the attack against the sort of writing Fleet Street passes off on its readers, so we decided from the start to make the play, if we could, a monstrously funny comic monument, set up on the most prominent stage in the country.

Whether we have achieved anything near that, only time will tell. Nevertheless, at the first preview, waves of laughter crashed down onto the stage. The valiant actors, who for two months had trained in the gymnasium to be surfers, were splashing about excitedly in the noise, falling off then getting back on their surf boards, learning how to hit and ride the real water (rehearsal room laughter, especially from authors, is notoriously untrustworthy for actors).

I had a flashing moment of golden glee and confidence in our craft. 'Glee' is not a common experience for a playwright. You usually find yourself depressed, unsatisfied, knowing that you have not got a play right. But with a comedy, it must be funny; if it is not, you should be sued under the Trades Descriptions Act. A few seconds before the lights went down on the first preview I had a nightmarish thought: 'Oh my God. This lasts three hours. What if only David and I find these scenes, lines and foibles of human behaviour funny? And there is not a single laugh between now and curtain call?' I have never felt so naked, alone and absurd in a theatre. Writing comedy is a grim business; good humour and cheery laughter are hard won, which is why Joan Littlewood said the theatre should be 'fun and hard work'.

The comic tradition goes very deep in the English theatre. Even the grimmest of our tragedies are, at root, comic. H.R.H. Lear is foolish, only a twist and he is a fool, a little spin on the writing and Shakespeare would have penned a comedy about a stupid king's farcical reign. David and I are slap in the middle of the tradition. I wanted to call my savage and gloomy play *The Churchill Play*, *The Churchill Comedy*. Richard Eyre, its first director, dissuaded me, rightly, with the argument 'Call it a play. Those who find it funny, will. Those who don't, or who are shocked – there's a chance they'll sit through it.'

In 1980 I co-authored a satire on the then new Thatcher government, *A Short Sharp Shock*, with the brilliant agit-prop specialist, Tony Howard. The show was generously received by its audiences and broke the box-office record at the Theatre Royal, Stratford East. It was, predictably, slaughtered by the critics, and the then Minister for the Arts, Norman St John Stevas, apologised to the House of Commons for the show being presented in a sub-sidised theatre (he had not, of course, seen it). All this was good knockabout fun; Tony and I played up to it, giving TV interviews saying we 'wrote the play to bring the government down', trying to keep a straight face. But I thought the audience were more than kind to our efforts; largely local with a leaven of Labour and union activists bussed into the theatre, they so wanted a belly laugh after the General Election defeat a year before that they pretended *A Short Sharp Shock* was better, and funnier, than it was.

No harm in that, why not encourage the troops? And I've been to so many West End 'runaway successes', to sit in an audience that is working heroically to overcome its disappointment at the drab, flat-lined fare being mouthed by beloved stars. We can all pretend that an entertainment is better than it is, because of the hope we've invested in the occasion; we ache for something to be wonderful. Proust describes this, with the adolescent Marcel turning himself inside out to convince himself that the great actress of his dreams upon the stage before him is not a hopeless, booming ham.

But I was uneasy about *A Short Sharp Shock*'s reception: by force of will, audiences turned a dodgy play into a great night out. I think that the fault with the play was a classic playwriting mistake. It was a light, satiric comedy, but cast in the hardest of epic forms, an A-B-A-B twinning of two separate and sharply contrasting plots, to illuminate each other by the contrasts between them: playwrights are always trying to break the unbreakable nature of theatre, that one thing has to happen after another, you want to crumple the action into a ball, or stretch it, have two, three, four things played at once – all impossible (artists are always at war with art, yeah yeah). I wrote an A-B-A-B form in *Weapons Of Happiness*, Hare did in *A Map of the World*; but they were straight plays, not outright comedies. In *A Short Sharp Shock* the two plots were a farcical, cartoonish, extreme knockabout presentation of Thatcher's government, set against a gentler, affectionate presentation of a bizarre Left-wing family, a red Galsworthy saga with the family going through every conceivable Left-wing split and difficulty. The mistake was that the scabrous, belly-laugh farce of the cabinet scenes so worked the audience up that the quieter, more loving humour of the family was swamped. Crude farce blasted ironic humour off the stage. We should have written one or the other.

With *Pravda* David and I set out to write about a newspaper tycoon who would win everything. At least in that the play was to be true to life. To have Lambert Le Roux defeated, or in any way successfully opposed, would have been sentimental and false. Who can deny, except those in their pay, that the breed of authoritarian, powerful proprietors now rampant in Fleet Street brook no opposition and have their heart's desire with the papers that they own?

We had two seeds, the first things written. One was Le Roux's enigmatic phrase: 'The great melancholy of business'. The other was the exchange between Le Roux and the young editor he encourages then destroys, Andrew May:

LE ROUX: To everyone I pose a question. I am the question.
ANDREW: And what is the answer?
LE ROUX: People like you.

From them we grew the play.

The kind of comedy we tried to write is one, we hope, of democratic laughter. The audience are invited to dissociate themselves from the tiny clique of the ruling class paraded across the stage. In the behind-the-scenes deals we dramatised and in the frightening and trivial values of Le Roux's mind, our intention was to say to our audiences, 'Why do we put up with all this?' As a joke between ourselves, to keep our spirits up during the writing, we said 'We're writing this play to stop people reading newspapers.'

Neither of us is good at 'funny stories'. We enjoy them but can never remember them. There are a few in the play. One of the best we stole from Christopher Hampton (Le Roux's bizarre Weybridge swimming pool). We are both fond of aphorisms and fancy we can, on occasions, turn them. They flip the familiar upside down. But Le Roux's dismissal of the snobbish, hopeless Elliot Fruit-Norton – 'He's a fool, a joke, Mickey Mouse wears an Elliot Fruit-Norton watch' – was told us by the Political Editor of the *Mirror*, Joe Haynes: he said it, with heat, of a Right-wing trade union leader. We do, of course, claim the few borrowings in the play as our own. It's useless having some funny remarks in a notebook, the art is to hear them in a character's voice and place them properly in the text. David and I are shameless jackdaws: be careful what you say to us, you'll end up in one of our plays. By instinct, we're 'maximalists', not 'minimalists': we want to get everything into a play, however glancingly, rather than get everything out.

The predominant humour is that of the blatantly typical remark or action; it's a 'comedy of types'. (I suppose that Jonson represents the only English tradition of such a comedy, but David and I didn't think much about him, the tagging of character attributes to animals or humours is tedious in Jonson. Russian theatre has a great tradition of 'comedy of types': for example, Gogol's *The Government Inspector* and Nikolai Erdman's *The Suicide*.) There's some deliberately low-level stuff in *Pravda* (and why not?): a camp waiter, a funny bishop, a ludicrous suicide attempt. But the basic comedy of the writing has few gags. What makes us laugh the most is a line, a speech or an action, that subsumes a character, that is exquisitely, or surprisingly, typical of them, confirming something about their nature. Anthony Hopkins, with the unfailingly accurate instinct of a great actor, decided early in the rehearsal to play Lambert Le Roux with utter seriousness, and fell to studying Hitler, Stalin and P.W. Botha. His approach was a touchstone. With his director's hat on, David's line throughout the production was to let the play find its nature, disciplined by his rigorous sense of good taste. The most bizarre scene, Le Roux 'relaxing' in private, he rehearsed as a straight piece of writing; he insisted that if there were never a laugh won, it must still hold the stage. Comedy is not about pulling gags, having a funny entrance as a bishop or an England cricket captain, or having a plumb funny one-liner, a delight though these are, froth from a lovely cheap yeast in a show. But to go through ten scenes of an epic play for three hours and really be funny, you must anchor yourself in basic theatrical truths, the old saws: 'Play the action, not the moment'; 'Every character in a play, however vile, thinks they are good'; 'The wilder, the more outrageous a comic scene, the more deadly serious it must be played.'

True belly-laughing comedy, 'human comedy', is often dismissed as cheap, only a 'good entertainment'. I've come to the conclusion that it's the hardest and highest form of playwriting. It's the theatrical equivalent of being able to draw the human body well, warts and all.

7. For Mickery, with Love

When I've finished the proofs of this book, I'm going to visit the Polish theatre company,Gardzienice, to see if we can make a show together. It's bracing to go abroad, take the culture clashes, and experiment: my first adventure was with the Mickery Theatre in Holland, when I'd just begun to write. This piece was meant to promote a play I'd written for the Mickery in 1990, but it turned into a love letter.

How would you dramatise someone for whom history is dying? How could you put on the stage a figure living increasingly in the present, with any sense of the past decaying, day to day, hour by hour, eventually second by second?

Ritsaert ten Cate put this to me as an exercise while I was writing a play for the Mickery Theatre in Amsterdam, of which he is artistic director – the flamboyant, strange, elusive Mickery Theatre, which for twenty-five years has been a European nerve centre for experiment in the arts.

I replied with a story, off the top of my head. A young warehouseman is the only worker in a vast, computerised refrigeration unit, somewhere in the new European nowhere, a Strasbourg industrial estate or a suburb of Antwerp. The building's great roof, lit day and night, curves above endless galleries, full of . . . packs of frozen butter.

Yup! It's the EEC butter mountain. The young warehouseman's lonely vigil guarding this meaningless wealth drives him mad. He sets out to eat the mountain. As he gorges himself his memory deteriorates, any sense of history and then language itself disappearing. His body becomes the butter.

He is a true 'new European', living an ersatz peace in an eternal present.

Ritsaert's response to this crazy little parable was to speculate gleefully on the problems of a stage set made entirely of hundreds of kilos of butter turning rancid under theatrical lights . . .

WELSH COLLEGE OF
LIBRARY
MUSIC & DRAMA

None of this got into our play *H.I.D.* (*Hess Is Dead*), except, I suppose, for one sarcastic line – 'I will show you European culture in a mountain of surplus butter'.

But this way of 'working out', wild sessions of free association from which something may or may not appear, is typical of the Mickery's playfulness with serious themes.

To a British writer, locked in an increasingly backward political and artistic culture, the Mickery is like a window to a different world. It was founded as, and remains, a theatre with an international vision. The early Mickery looked to the American alternative scene but is now, as I understand it, engaged on a massive project, of which my play is just an episode, to explore the new European peace; hence Ritsaert ten Cate's impish challenge to dramatise someone for whom history is dying.

I eventually came up with the character of Charity Luber in *Hess Is Dead*, whom I imagined as a refugee from Thomas Mann's magic mountain, trying to slough off her European past. She became horribly real to me and walked away from the show . . . There are imaginative, as well as national, frontiers to break holes through. The Mickery is at the forefront, chisel in hand; the elusive, boundlessly innovative Mickery Theatre, always on the move, plotting bizarre shows and spectacles sometimes for years before they bear fruit . . .

*

I've a print hanging on my wall by the Belgian artist, Jan Fabre. He made it to celebrate the Mickery's twentieth birthday in 1985. It is a strange 'now you see it, now you don't' image. Someone is escaping from a group of menacing figures; a car windscreen has been smashed in a road accident or, perhaps, a shoot out. A caption on the print reads: 'Mickery with a pair of handcuffs and a police identity card he used bearing a photograph of himself. One of the many mysteries surrounding Mickery was how he obtained several police and Ministry of Justice passes.'

Like Fabre I often think of 'Mickery' as a person, a persecuted private detective who is out there in the urban jungle upon a quixotic quest . . .

The Mickery is little known in Britain but famous in Europe. It has astounded and inspired audiences all over the continent. It has nourished a huge number of theatre companies, actors, writers, dancers, film makers, singers, designers, painters, puppeteers, fire-eaters, buskers etc. etc.

Like Philip Marlowe, Ritsaert ten Cate, the Mickery's artistic director, is eccentric and wildly catholic in the 'cases' he chooses to take on – from wild video freaks to 'straight' playwrights like me. The Mickery does, for some, have an awesome reputation.

Mickery, with only his private badge of 'commitment' for identification, is not loved by the cultural police. For even in Holland, where they are used to 'experimental theatre', the mention of the Mickery can make 'conventional theatre' folk chew the carpet with rage. The noise of someone sounding off in the Dutch press against the latest Mickery venture is as common as bells ringing in Amsterdam.

Mickery loves us but he is remorseless. People don't like that. He wields his antiquated revolver with great speed. His critics and enemies get tired of him shooting them in the head again and again and again . . . with new idea after new idea after new idea.

But there is nothing directly intimidating about the Mickery's shows. I went to one of them last year in Rotterdam. At the door of a large hangar-like building my ticket was torn and I pushed through a curtain. An usher with a torch showed me to my seat. So far, so usual. I found myself on comfortable, raked seating in a room with forty or so other people. The room had a ceiling but the wall before us was missing. We faced another room of forty or so people. There was a hissing noise and we began to slide away from each other. Giggles . . . We were on hovercraft!

There were four of these 'modules'. For an hour and a half they glided slowly about the building in elegant movements, sometimes parked, sometimes swinging away from a series of scenes and events, some of which were live, some on film or tape. The contributions were from theatre troupes – the Need to Know company amongst them – and artists from all over the world. What you saw depended on which 'module' you were in.

This was great fun. As you sailed from one event to catch a glimpse of another, or heard the music from something out of eyeshot, the experience was vivid, immaculately presented and frequently funny. Now and then you would pass a New York drag artist, going crazy in this environment. A lecturer attempted, futilely, to engage the attention of a ballerina dancing before him. The weirdest 'act' my voyaging section of audience encountered was a superbly constructed model of a dinosaur, half sculpture and half puppet, which turned its sad eyes to us and began to soliloquise in L.A. American about a troubled love life and what a nice day it was going to be.

There were no shock tactics, no assaults, it was a quiet, peaceful and eerily beautiful show.

Then it hit you. Everything you had seen was about extinction. There was nothing explicitly 'green' or political about the fragments of performance and video or film, but together, in whatever 'hover-craft' you travelled, the scenes made an overpowering and moving elegy.

An elegy for our contemporary culture, no less. The Mickery are not afraid to tackle the big themes. They do so with stealth, an odd precision for bizarre details and a kind of mischievousness, which is a hallmark of much of their work. Behind the often loose, 'layer on layer' and 'far out' forms their productions take, there is a rigorous critical instinct. The Mickery is a very generous outfit to work for, and very loyal to those they take on board. They are also very hard and demanding.

I agonised and delayed delivering H.I.D. (Hess Is Dead) for two years, an eternity in British theatre terms, where the ability to 'do it and bang it on' is seen as a proof of creativity. 'Take five years, ten if you must,' Ritsaert ten Cate said to me. 'But when you give me the text you must be able to look me in the eyes and tell me it is wonderful.' A shrug, a smile, an unlit cigarette tipped up to his nose . . . 'I'll have no choice but to believe you. Will I.' That, of course, made me write and write, slowly and more carefully than I have for many years, burning more midnight oil than my body fat could spare . . .

Mickery, scuffing round the mean and the rich streets of European cities, fists in his raincoat, has a long-term plan. Every client he takes on, gets to work for it.

My debt to the Mickery Theatre began in the late sixties and early seventies when I was a raw young writer in what we called the underground, or alternative, theatre. Then, as now, there were a lot of young writers and performers with a rage to put on shows and a passionate but hazy notion of how those shows could be achieved, artistically or practically.

At that time Mickery was operating out of a farmhouse in the Dutch countryside in the village of Loenersloot, an hour on the bus from Amsterdam.

It was a wonderful hide-out. There was a barn, converted to a theatre. There were lofts and outhouses surrounded, dangerously for the ecstatic and the stoned who soon flocked there, by canals. Ritsaert ten Cate had opened the doors of this unlikely and idyllic venue in 1965, as an art gallery. He began to invite performers in, then to stage plays. Quickly the Loenersloot Mickery became a Mecca for the exploding international alternative theatre. The lofts and outhouses became dormitories for the groups passing through, Americans, Argentineans, Japanese, Germans . . . and we Brits. There was hardly a British alternative company which did not play at the Loenersloot Mickery. Ten Cate had quickly set up a touring circuit in Holland and Scandinavia. 'Doing the Mickery tour' was arduous, but without it the 'second wave' of British theatre, now written about in serious drama books, PhD theses, and the subject of 'A' level exam questions, would not have got off the ground. The early Mickery gave us a spiritual home, and a tour with some cash and many stages. It gave the British what our theatrical estab-lishment did not: something even more important than money, *excitement* and the warmth of knowing that we weren't crazy (you'd see some South American or San Francisco show on before yours and think, 'Jesus, and back in London they call *us* wild?').

It was an extraordinary achievement to run such a place. We just staggered into it, like arty lager louts, and used the set-up. Now I am amazed at the planning, the determination and the personal cost it must have taken to launch the Loenersloot Mickery. And the vision.

I have a memory of Loenersloot. Early in the morning I walked from the buildings into the fields. There was a grey sky. Fat cows sat on the rich, dull green grass, expecting rain. And there, in the middle distance . . . was a huge ship, a freighter, festooned with cranes. It was moving through the fields as if they were the sea.

Actually the ship was on the Rhine canal, 400 metres from the theatre. The EEC ship of state, sailing through the buttery grass . . .

Ritsaert got out a map and explained the mighty canal system to me.

I first worked at the Mickery with the Portable Theatre, who were doing a play of mine in 1970, which I stage-managed on the Mickery tour. While we were in Eindhoven, I saw some children playing on a bombsite; above them there shone the neon sign of the giant Philips Corporation. I told Ritsaert of this. 'Grow it into a play,' he said.

A year later I was back, trying to do just that, living and living it up in the lofts and outhouses with a company that Max Stafford-Clark ran, the Traverse Theatre Workshop.

A laboratory theatre . . . Over the years Mickery has set up many of these dubious stills, which sometimes produce the real thing, 100 per cent proof, and sometimes something undrinkable.

The result of our stay was a play called *Hitler Dances*, which the company opened in Edinburgh and London and then took back, with pride, to the Mickery. The play continues to get productions.

From the mid seventies, for ten years or more, I lost touch with the Mickery. I ploughed on with a long series of plays, flogging them down my own mean streets of the London theatre scene.

Meanwhile Ritsaert concluded the Loenersloot Mickery was becoming a kind of 'avant-garde' Glyndebourne. He hated that, so he closed Loenersloot down and opened a new Mickery on the Rozengracht, in the centre of Amsterdam. It went through good times and bad times.

I'd hear rumours of the work. But it is terrible how ten, twelve years can, when you're engaged in something as obsessional as playwriting, go in a flash. And then . . . there was Ritsaert ten Cate again, sitting in front of me in London, screwing up his nose, teasing me, saying, 'Mr. Brenton Sir, what have you been doing, what have I been doing for ten years, because you don't know . . . I don't know. Let's find out. Write Mickery a show': an offer I could not refuse.

Ritsaert and I had a series of exploratory and, for me, explodingly exciting discussions in the autumn of 1987 and the spring of 1988.

Mickery, trying to crack a case, invents many ways of not looking at the evidence. He goes roundabout, round and round, looking at everything under the sun. Until there's the evidence, staring him in the face. This can drive his clients mad.

Ritsaert has for some time wanted to set up . . . how to describe them? 'Theatrical discourses.' He very nearly got Richard Nixon to agree to take part in one. Nixon withdrew, wisely. Tricky Dicky would have found himself standing on a rather strange stage set . . .

The discussions that finally turned up the simple idea behind *H.I.D.* went all over the place. They began with a long argument about the 'Glorious Revolution' of 1688. (How a play about Rudolf Hess began as a play about William and Mary is, even for its author, impossible to recall. Mickery has the files, though.)

We'd talk for ten hours at a go, pulling out books and videos from the huge Mickery library to illustrate a point, scribbling notes and drawings, with people dropping in and out of the sessions.

If you want to do something serious, be silly about it, for as long as it takes to get it right . . . says Mickery.

At times I thought we'd never get anything together at all. Then, there it was, the 'smoking gun', a great idea for a play. All I had to do was go away and write it (which was another story).

The Mickery I first knew has expanded into an extraordinary organisation: more a 'country of the mind' than a theatre.

They are a kind of 'imaginative zone'. But they are also ferociously practical. They have launched a magazine, *Two and Two*. They make and market videos of their work, which are beautifully done (get hold of *Rembrandt, Hitler or Me*, shot by Mike Figgis). They have turned their Rozengracht theatre into a strange kind of theatre club, called 'Frau Holle', which they want to be a safe haven for rehearsal and experiment. Now they aim to present shows in 'found' spaces, which fit the theme. They have a sideline as a production company: they were behind an extraordinary production of *Iranian Nights,* the squib Tariq Ali and I wrote about Islamic fundamentalism, which was full of the best of Dutch 'avant-garde' flamboyance. The Mickery is becoming a subversive, benign cultural conspiracy . . . conspiring to make things happen, all over the place.

What is Mickery's quest? What is the grand plan on his mind, as he puts his feet up on the desk late at night in his office in the Herenmarkt in Amsterdam, reaching for some way-out video in the desk drawer?

I suspect he wants us to be free. That is a dangerous caper, and Ritsaert ten Cate put him up to it.

*

The Mickery, very imaginatively, licensed the RSC to perform *H.I.D. (Hess Is Dead)* at the Almeida Theatre in the autumn of 1989, so I could hear it rehearsed and see it performed in my language, and pick up any rewrites. Their Dutch production followed in January 1990, presented, bizarrely, in a seventeenth-century dissecting room, where the bodies of hanged men were cut open for enlightenment.

Then in 1991, Ritsaert closed down the Mickery Theatre for good; it was the twenty-fifth anniversary of the founding of the theatre, he had, he said, done everything they set out to do and could think to do.

Suddenly it's terrible to have an artistic past. I think of shows I could have written, in those ten years we were out of touch, if I was on another line of serendipity through my writing life. But there's no time travel, the arts have their own second law of thermodynamics.

And I don't really believe Mickery's not there anymore. He's a mole, out there somewhere, burrowing away. I hope he pops up in my life again.

8. The Unbearable Heaviness of Being English

This is a much shortened version of the Cheltenham Lecture, 1990, published in the New Statesman.

Why did Oscar Wilde fall?

It was not that he was particularly arrogant. Arrogance is thought to be as common amongst writers as obesity amongst barmen: but, usually, as with Oscar, it is not arrogance, but enthusiasm. People find enthusiasm very irritating in this country.

Nor did Wilde come to grief because he sought to make enemies. As Richard Ellmann points out in his magnificent biography, amongst all Wilde's aphorisms there is not a gratuitously malicious remark to be found. His most famous rude remark may be apocryphal, but even that is graceful. The story goes that when given a bouquet of rotten vegetables by his tormentor the Marquess of Queensberry, Oscar took them with a bow. 'Thank you', he said. 'I will treasure these forever. They will remind me of you.'

Nor was he ruined because he was homosexual. It was not unknown for nineteenth-century gentlemen to have homosexual affairs; it seems to have gone with the way they were taught Latin and Greek, and a love of horse-racing. Lord Byron is very revealing on this, Greek boys astride a steaming animal's flanks etc.

Oscar Wilde's 'fault', or 'virtue' depending on your point of view, was that he thought he was ahead of the mores of his day. He thought he could change the world. He thought he had English culture on the run.

He did not of course. His innocence had made him over-confident. He got cut down. In Reading gaol the chaplain would come into Oscar's cell every morning to sniff the air for the smell of semen upon the blankets. If the cleric detected the tell-tale aroma, the prisoner's rations would be cut by half that day. That was the fate of the great Irish libertarian, the scourge of hypocrisy, the paradoxical radical, the upper-class individualist who nevertheless wrote one of the great, eccentric texts of the Left, *The Soul of Man under Socialism*. Oscar Wilde was destroyed at the moment he was making the change from being joker to joker sage – a critic of society, an enemy of the status quo.

In English culture there is a wall between the aesthetic and the political. English writers who seek to breach that wall can have no end of trouble. They either get crucified upon it – as Oscar did – or bash their heads against its bricks and go mad, or just give up and become drunks – or high Anglicans – or both.

I say 'English' culture; they do not seem to have this problem in Scotland, nor do they in Eastern Europe, or the Mediterranean countries, or in South America.

Octavio Paz, the Mexican poet, was awarded the Nobel Prize for Literature last week, an occasion for celebration. For Paz there is no 'cultural wall'. Private love and the public horrors of history, the beauty of dawns and the dereliction of Mexico City intertwine effortlessly in his work. Paz wrote:

Poetry is one of the means by which modern man can say NO
to all those powers which, not content with disposing of our
lives, also want to rule our consciences. But this negation
carries within it a YES which is greater than itself.

No one in the Spanish world would dream of saying to Paz, 'Go back to writing love songs, don't meddle in politics and issues . . . ' Which is often said to writers in England. 'Stop meddling . . . just entertain . . . ' is written upon one of the bricks of our cultural wall.

Why did D.H. Lawrence, the author of *Sons and Lovers*, *The Rainbow* and the early short stories, who should have gone on to write the great, poetic, social novels of the early part of the century, leave us for endless, unhappy journeys in Italy, Australia and Mexico? And, tragically for us, why did Lawrence's work deteriorate so catastrophically into the slapdash, quasi-Fascism of *Kangaroo* and the tangled, risible mysticism of *The Plumed Serpent*?

He ran headlong into the English cultural wall. He married a German woman in time of war. He was working-class and hostile to the London cultural scene of his day, the Bloomsbury mafia. And he made an observation of life on earth, which is not unreasonable: that the matter of love and sex between men and women is at the centre of our experience. As he put it in his *Essay on Thomas Hardy:*

> In life . . . no new thing has ever arisen, or can arise, save out of the impulse of the male upon the female, the female upon the male. The interaction of the male and female spirit begat the wheel, the plough, and the first utterance that was made upon the earth.

Not unreasonable.

But . . . oh but . . . There is a whole section of bricks in our cultural wall, with glass sticking out to lacerate any who try to remove them (let me try to pull off this metaphor!) . . . bricks of mud baked hard by sexual repression. Lawrence got cut to pieces on this bit of the wall and lost his way. He was aware of his fate and tried to explain what it was about England that was destroying him, in his essay 'An Introduction to these Paintings'. You sense the hurt and anger, tipping a great and generous mind over into nonsense. He wrote:

> The English . . . are paralysed by fear. That is what thwarts and distorts the Anglo-Saxon existence. It thwarts life, it distorts vision, and it strangles impulse, this overmastering fear . . . It is an old fear which seemed to dig in to the English soul at the time of the Renaissance. Nothing could be more lovely and fearless than Chaucer. But already Shakespeare is morbid with fear, fear of consequences. That is the strange phenomenon of the English Renaissance: this mystic terror of the consequences, the consequences of action. What appeared to take full grip of the northern consciousness at the end of the sixteenth century was a terror, almost a horror of sexual life.

So . . . D.H. Lawrence felt, unlike Heineken lager (to get this argument back into the everyday . . .), that he was denied reaching parts that Chaucer could reach without any trouble.

Lawrence's explanation of this 'English Puritanism', this mind-body split, was bizarre. It was because syphilis ravaged Elizabethan and Jacobean society, distorting Anglo-Saxon culture forever.

For myself, I find this quite mad. Indeed, tragically mad. But this was Lawrence at the cultural wall; he was trying to pass through it, from being a storyteller to being a moralist . . . and was slandered. He didn't make it. A noble mind went to pieces, under the pressure of, if you like, the unbearable heaviness of being English.

Was Lawrence the great novelist of the twentieth century we did not really have . . . or have enough of? I think so. And . . . what happened to W.H. Auden?

I saw Sir Kingsley Amis on a television programme not so long ago, accusing W.H. Auden of cowardice, of running away from this country to America in 1939, because he thought Hitler was going to win. From then on, Amis maintained, he only wrote rubbish.

A bit rum of Sir Kingsley, I thought. Surely, it was in the first years of his American exile – or coward's retreat, if that was what it was – that Auden wrote some of the great poems of the language: *The Dark Years* and the two magnificent elegies, *In Memory of W.B. Yeats* and *In Memory of Sigmund Freud*, which together are the twentieth century's equivalent of Milton's *Lycidas*.

But . . . yes, it is true that after the early forties, Auden's public manner becomes windy. The pressure has gone, he becomes like the late Wordsworth, drifting on grey clouds of a soporific religiosity.

Unlike Wilde, Auden leapt onto the literary scene as a fully fledged social critic, loved and loathed at once. It was as if he was first heard on the top of our 'cultural wall', shouting his head off.

What happened?

Auden tried to tell us. There is a long poem, *New Year Letter*, written in 1940. It is a poem of anguish and confusion, both public and private, convoluted, even evasive. It is about being unable to be English any more, at, of all times, England's time 'of greatest peril'.

> The New Year brings an earth afraid,
> Democracy a ready-made
> And noisy tradesman's slogan, and
> The poor betrayed into the hand
> Of lackeys with ideas, and truth
> Whipped by their elders out of youth,
> The peaceful fainting in their tracks
> With martyrs' tombstones on their backs,
> And culture on all fours to greet
> A butch and criminal *élite*,
> While in the vale of silly sheep
> Rheumatic old patricians weep.

It was a terrible time for a great poet to despair. His epitaph could be 'England unmade me'.

Meanwhile in my neck of the woods, the English theatre, the casualty wards are not a pretty sight. The whole first generation of Royal Court lions seems to have given up.

Most writers, after the first exuberant flush of excitement in finding that they can entertain on the stage, or story-tell, or rhyme and scan and hold a public, undergo a shift, a sea-change.

But sooner or later, a crisis comes; what are the new jokes, the new scenes, to *be about*? And you fall to the bedrock of what being a writer means. To write well is no longer enough. The joker becomes a joker sage, the entertainer becomes a social critic, the pen – becomes – a – sword.

So W.B. Yeats, not by nature a political soul, starts as an 'art for art's sake', 'Georgian' lyric poet, and by middle life finds himself writing *Easter 1916*, undoubtedly a great poem and undoubtedly political, a revolutionary republican hymn that can still raise English hackles.

This transition is natural. But why, in England, do so many writers encounter an hysterical opprobrium when they make it? Why is the English cultural wall there?

I don't think Lawrence's psycho-sexual explanation works; it has to be read autobiographically, as about his own anger and frustration.

I suggest historical reasons. We had our revolution early, in the seventeenth century, and we do not acknowledge it. We pretend that the Commonwealth failed, whereas everything it stood for came to pass. We have an absurd myth that modern 'England' was founded by the Elizabethans, when actually it was founded by Cromwell. This gives us a haziness about our nation, a smugness that 'all's right with the world' – and they who say that, demonstrably, all is not right, are said to be 'unpatriotic', to have a chip on their shoulder.

Also, the European Romantic enlightenment, which saw writers and poets as 'the unacknowledged legislators of mankind', is not in our tradition. Rousseau and Goethe are not part of our mental landscape. For decades, the wars with Revolutionary France made it almost treasonable to read Rousseau. Goethe happens to be very difficult to translate – you read the doggerel of the Penguin edition, or even of Louis MacNeice's version, and you just cannot see why this is the great mind of the enlightenment. And the one poet who could have become our Goethe, or even a nineteenth-century English Dante, Shelley, stupidly got himself killed while messing about with boats. Chance . . . Shelley died and we got Tennyson instead, poetry as highbrow muzak. (Cultural traditions, like historical events, are not inevitable; they are made, they need not necessarily have been so.)

Culture should be, in Howard Barker's majestic phrase, 'that good between us'. Instead we have a mass of philistine assumptions that have 'grown between us'. We should be careful. A culture can turn nasty on us all, it can become censorious and anti-democratic, and viciously proscriptive: 'not this kind of book, not this kind of play'; then audiences and readers cannot find their way to their writers and performers. The wall between the aesthetic and the political, against which so many English writers have been wrecked, is such a proscription.

What to do? Well . . . a wall has come down in Europe. Surely we can dismantle a wall that is really only in our heads.

9. The Best We Have, Alas: Bertolt Brecht

The original version of this essay was published in an American theatre magazine, hence the remarks about Americans and Brecht. It was also written before the fax machine speeded up re-writing film scripts.

1

In 1980, I wrote an English version of Brecht's *Life of Galileo* for a production at the National Theatre. It was directed by John Dexter, with Michael Gambon as Galileo; it was a wonderful show, with Gambon, until then thought of as a 'light' actor because of his success in comedy, delivering a performance of superb gravitas, monumental yet swift with Brechtian irony and grace. It was one of the greatest performances I've ever seen.

I was in awe of Dexter, and there was a generation gap between us: his Royal Court was George Devine's, mine was Max Stafford-Clark's, two different planets given to occasional interstellar nuclear warfare. On the other hand John, I learnt later when we got to know each other, told me that for most of the rehearsals he was convinced I was going off each evening to a committee of 'comrades in leather jackets', from whom I received my orders for what I would say in next day's rehearsal. (The energy of paranoia in the theatre always amazes me, not that I'm ever really free of it myself.)

But the production was, in the end, a cleansing experience. Like many contemporary playwrights, I've felt Brecht on my back, a weight, an inhibition. I used to say something fatuous like 'I'm a Left anti-Brechtian', to avoid having to think about his influence. With others, I was trying to write an epic theatre which was contemporary, not parable-like, which was hot with the moment of its production and varied each scene with wild changes of style.

Brecht's example was clean not 'dirty', cool not 'hot'; and, what's more, tedious beyond belief because of the dead-mouthed official translations the Brecht Estate insisted upon. Brecht was an iron collar that Left-wing theatre didn't need around its neck . . . I thought. But happily, thanks to watching Dexter and Gambon and an excellent cast rehearse and perform my Galileo version, I sorted my mind out about Bert Brecht, the great playwright of our century, yes, the greatest, the best we have, alas.

2

Recently I was talking to a British friend who had just finished writing a screenplay. He rehearsed a Byzantine struggle between the British and American producers; the latter, of course, had the money. The problem was that my friend had written a quest story: the journey of a woman to find her lost child. The Americans, in their demands for re-writes, were trying to turn the film into a struggle between good and evil: the mother 'good', the abductor 'evil'.

The culture clash my friend fought across the Atlantic, the weapons pink re-write sheets by express airmail, illustrates the difficulty of explaining Brecht's work to America. (I assume for the purposes of this article that the readers of this magazine do not dismiss Brecht out of hand for being the convinced Communist he unquestionably was.)

Brecht is a writer of quests. He has none of the Christian moralism which is at the root of American sensibility; in a way he did not believe in absolute evil or absolute good at all. His heroes and heroines are a mixed bag of what many would call 'morally ambiguous' figures. Azdak, Galileo, Courage, even the Mother are, in themselves, unremarkable. They are not 'great persons'. They do not embody great virtues, or even flawed virtues, as American heroes always do, from Willy Loman to Rambo. What makes them remarkable, even great, is the journey they go on, what experience does to them and what they do to the people around them. It is a Marxist morality: you are what you do, 'by their acts ye shall know them', or 'by the consequences of their acts ye shall know them'.

For example, in the last scene of *The Life of Galileo* a book is smuggled across the Italian border. The leading actor is not present nor is the name of the character he plays mentioned. The book is the 'Discorsi', a culmination of Galileo's life's work and a cornerstone of rational science, a cornerstone, that is, of the modern world. It is a very Brechtian irony. The audience sits through three and a half hours of Galileo in triumph, torment, treachery and defeat, but all the magnificent raging scenes are there so that in the last moments of the play we watch a book cross the stage and see it as the birth of our era. The scene is often cut – it does not help that Brecht left it in draft form. Without the last scene the play ends with Galileo under house arrest talking to his daughter.

GALILEO: . . . What's the night like?
VIRGINIA (*at the window*): Clear.

The play is reduced to the study of an individual's private predicament. But with the last scene retained, the play goes beyond the personal and becomes a social epic about modern science, humanity's dangerous but exhilarating intervention in nature.

Brecht's massive output, his exploration of a form, epic theatre, to express a socialist vision of human nature, his brilliance as a director, the theoretical essays which have inspired – as well as confused – post-war generations of theatre workers, the range of his styles from the anarchy of his youth to the simple, Olympian grandeur of his last epics – surely, only a twentieth-century Euripides could have achieved all this. Or so many believe.

For me, much of Brecht's dramatic writing is thin. The irony is strained, the love and hate in it are unconvincing. At his worst he wrote schematically, like a crossword compiler – a symmetrical pattern of black and white. Because of what he gave witness to, it is impossible to see him as anything other than the greatest playwright of the first half of this century. But, in the end, I find myself saying 'Yes. The best we have, alas'.

For example *Puntila* and *Man is Man* should be great plays; on a quick reading they seem like great plays. But on the stage they weary and bore an audience because the dialectic is expressed in banal and obvious parables. Things are said, not dramatised. One gag, Puntila's sober then drunk behaviour, or Galy-Gay's innocence, is driven into the ground by repetition. It is as if his drama is a simulacrum, a sketch for what a great playwright of our time would produce, but not the real thing. When you get up close to it, when you try to make it work, it is frequently in stage terms 'colourless'. Brecht was a superb constructor of texts and productions, but as a writer he has a fatal stage blindness. He did not 'see' his characters. I am not making the absurd criticism so often bandied about, that Brecht 'lacked emotion'. His work is always passionate. No, I suspect there was a fault in his imagination. He did not 'see' or imagine the reality of his scenes strongly enough. I think that is why what he thought was clarity and fierce presentation of humanity in action often plays as a dehumanised and static pageant. The point of a long evening is grasped by everyone in the first couple of scenes.

The two masterpieces, *The Mother* and *The Life of Galileo*, are exceptions. With the first, he had the powerful humanism of Maxim Gorky's novel driving the writing. With *The Life of Galileo*, he found himself working on its three versions throughout the war years, with history itself horrifically confirming the play's awesome theme when the atomic bomb was dropped on Hiroshima. I am also convinced that the play is so rich because, as he wrote it, he changed his mind. Brecht the poet wrote frequently about 'dialectical doubt', a way of thinking Brecht the playwright rarely applied to his dramatic craft. But with *The Life of Galileo* you sense in the text that he set out to write a straightforward presentation of a Renaissance hero as a socialist hero. Brecht was attracted to Galileo's populism, to the fact that he wrote in the vernacular not in Latin, that he challenged the church, the state within a state, which, rightly, feared him. Galileo was a founder of our secular age. It is not surprising that Brecht set out to claim him for the Left.

But as Brecht wrote the play, he could not handle the ambiguity of Galileo's character; the recantation and the years of secret work under luxurious 'house arrest' made it impossible to stage Galileo as in any way a precise socialist exemplar. Ambiguity dragged at Brecht as the play twisted through its wartime drafts, finally yielding its great insight of the flaw at the heart of our European enlightenment.

This is the only time he achieved dialectical tension in a character's progression through a play. Because Brecht himself, as he wrote the play, had to find out what he thought, the play lives.

And yet . . .

3

And yet . . . to write orotund critical phrases in a magazine is easy. To write plays in exile from your country, in a dark Europe and an alien America, was not. In a safer environment, not threatened by arrest or deportation, even Bernard Shaw lost his grip upon reality before the bulldozing success of Fascism in Italy then Germany, and fell to writing nonsense.

Brecht was of sterner stuff. He always kept his nerve. He did not crack and abandon his convictions, as so many left-wing writers of the 1930s did. I wonder how my generation would fare, under the pressures of Brecht's life. Compare later W.H. Auden, say *About the House*, to Brecht's *Buckow Elegies*. Auden has lost all radical edge and wallows in flabbily versified, vague religious feelings and a mindless domesticity. The late Brecht persists: his beautifully simple poems of hard-won insight speak directly to us and for now.

He put down markers that many of us in today's theatre have, sneakily, slipped into our pockets. He gave us a way of busting wide open the decayed Ibsenite drama of closed rooms and closed minds. He reinstated direct, broad popular storytelling as the basic art of playwriting. His stagecraft, Max Reinhardt's stagecraft with blazing light, showed how to sweep the stage of pictorial clutter and put the actor at its centre.

Perhaps he was an 'overreacher', an exemplar, as Christopher Marlowe was for the Elizabethan and Jacobean stage, and that is why in the last twenty-five years his heirs have written so many good plays.

4

FOCO NOVO AND CONVERSATIONS IN EXILE

Roland Rees, as artistic director of Foco Novo theatre company, often dreamt up a show . . . 'wouldn't it be great if . . . ', then commissioned it. He is a benign, left-wing Sam Spiegel of the British alternative theatre. In 1983 he wanted to present a new play by the black writer Alfred Fagon, *Four Hundred Pounds*. The play is a comic and moving account of two British pool players, would-be professionals, living off the bets they lay on their games. It was set around a pool table and lasted an hour. Roland needed another two-hander for black actors to make a double-bill. Suddenly he realised that the predicament of Fagon's characters reminded him of Kalle and Tiffel in Brecht's *Conversations in Exile*. The pieces echoed each other in that they were about 'daily genius': the cunning and human skill the poor, and the exiled, need just to get through a day more or less intact. Both plays were about 'Einsteins of ordinary life'. So he said, 'Let black actors play the German exiles. If anyone asks why, reply why not? . . . ' Foco Novo has a long record of putting on the work of black playwrights. 'And,' continues Roland Rees in Spiegelian form, 'since in the first play pool is not played, in the Brecht there will be a full, properly played game . . . and I'll hire Howard Brenton to make an adaptation of the script.'

Conversations in Exile was written while Brecht was in Finland in 1937, himself an exile from Nazi Germany. It has the low-key, sly, twisty and topsy-turvy thought of his poetry. It feels like a way of making long, empty afternoons in a country you do not like much bearable. A short poem of Brecht's describes his state of mind:

Changing the Wheel

I sit by the roadside.
The driver changes the wheel.
I do not like the place I have come from.
I do not like the place I am going to.
Why with impatience do I
Watch him changing the wheel?

In its full form the play is three and a half, even four hours long: if it were ever played, that is, for it is not really a play. It is a philosophical dialogue between two aspects of Brecht's personality – the professional middle-class man who wants to do well, to 'belong' and see the best in things (Tiffel) and the working-class alienated, foxy rebel, whose doubt and cynicism are weapons of creativity (Kalle). Interestingly, at times they swap characteristics, melding into each other. It is as if they are not characters, but two tones of the same voice. The theme is survival in dark times. Brecht turns the characters this way and that, holding ideas up to the light for inspection: it's like a playwright's doodle which spreads into extraordinary and revealing shapes. The piece has a wisp of plot: they come to trust each other and on the last page decide to do something. But the episodes could be played in any order. It is a suspended meeting, in an historical limbo, between two men whose names are certainly not the names they give each other and who may be lying through their teeth.

They are ordinary men, in the process of being forced to become extra-ordinary. From that comes the piece's optimism, its devil-may-care quality. Human transformation is in the air.

10. How Can We Do It, Vsevolod?

This article was written for an argument in The Independent *for and against political theatre. Meyerhold came to mind because I'd just been working on a huge play about Gorbachev, written with Tariq Ali for the RSC.*

On 14 March 1936, fighting for his theatre and for his life, the revolutionary Russian theatre director, Vsevolod Meyerhold, made a ferociously uncompromising and complex speech at the Soviet Writers' Union attacking 'socialist realism'.

He was defending himself against the Stalinist crime of 'formalism'. His argument is an immemorial one that would have been recognised by Euripides: 'the artist becomes a true master by endless observation, reflection and study, by consolidating form and content.' He attacked what he called 'Meyerholditis', the use of what looked like the political theatre he had invented but which was drained of any sense of what people were really thinking and doing, of any real dialectic – bravely, he was trying to turn the tables on his tormentors, accusing the hacks of a dead 'formalism'. He spoke for a protean theatre that is experimental, in which form is never fixed but capable of infinite invention to serve its content, in a way a theatre without an aesthetic at all – but which is on the side of the ruled and not the rulers, and plugged directly into reality. He compounded the offence by going on to defend Shostakovich's recently banned opera 'The Lady Macbeth of the Mtsensk District'.

The speech cost him both his theatre and his life. Because of 'Glasnost' we now know how he died; he was murdered by the NKVD in the Lubianka prison on 2 February 1940, after his fingers had been broken one by one and urine had been poured over his head.

When I was in Moscow last summer I visited the one shrine there is to Meyerhold's mighty work. In a little theatre museum in a quiet, tree-lined street, I was ushered into a room crammed with just about every memento of a great career that the secret police did not smash. I was the only visitor. As a guide droned on, I stopped listening, for the dilapidated set models for shows that once entertained thousands, the yellowed posters, the typescripts of texts scribbled with pencilled notes, had begun to pulsate with life.

Meyerhold's output was of great variety. He could bash out a thumping, militant, pro-revolutionary extravaganza, then turn to a subtle reworking of a Russian classic, with the text untouched. He premiered new plays, most famously by Nikolai Erdman and Vladimir Mayakovsky, satires against Moscow gangsters and party timeservers. The four strands of work ran side by side – outright political extravaganzas, renewal of the classics, new plays by living playwrights, and 'issue plays'. And all the work was shot through with a kind of madness: he had a barmy theory of acting, 'bio-mechanics', which was a reaction to the Stanislavsky school, and he was endlessly drawing up plans for a huge, fantastical and probably unworkable auditorium. His wonderfully attractive, mercurial craziness came from a sense of showmanship, of flair and a love of the new.

Like most Russian theatre directors, the man was also a fear-some martinet. But he sensed that to do something really profound in the theatre, you should not take the theatre itself too seriously. He was a relentless perfectionist whose work was informed by a contempt for orthodoxies, including his own, and always on the side of the ruled, not the rulers. Staring at the detritus of his career in that dusty Moscow museum, I began to see how a political theatre can be a living drama about changing our lives – not a sermon, but an event.

I write about Meyerhold because it's important to remind ourselves that the Left too has its twentieth-century martyrs. It is insulting to the memory of a great artist to suggest that 'the theatre should not engage in political themes'. That is exactly what Meyerhold did, tren-chantly, and with such success that the predecessors of those now called 'conservatives' in the the Soviet Union had him murdered.

*

Tony Harrison, who translated Aeschylus' *Oresteia* for the National Theatre, told me that the *Eumenides*, with its famous Aeschylean moral, 'the doer shall suffer', was probably very near the bone for its first audiences. There was violence in Athens between immigrants and the longer established communities, exasperated by a religious clash. The play dramatises a settlement. We assume the meaning of the play is so lofty as to be almost beyond human comprehension – actually it was written straight out of contemporary troubles, for life and about life, tackling a hot contemporary subject (would a pro-Rushdie Aeschylus please come to the stage).

I remember watching the National's production with mounting panic. Aeschylus is credited with inventing 'the play' as we know it. He seemed, what's more, to have made up every playwright's trick in the book, in one go – think of a dramatic device, oh . . . realism, humour mixed with tragedy, chorus, disguise, revelation, 'high and low' on the stage, the powerful off-stage character . . . and it's there embedded in *Oresteia*. The theatre is a profoundly archaic art. Meyerhold demonstrated that, paradoxically, that's why it can be such a vibrant modern form: since everything has been done before, you can find a way of putting *anything* on a stage.

But what you cannot do, is write generally, or, sin of sins, to write 'for posterity' – our contemporary theatre is littered with the corpses of plays that took themselves too lightly or far too seriously, but above all too vaguely. As Meyerhold proved, the theatre is capable of endless renewal, if it rolls up its sleeves and gets stuck into what really matters in its day, what is really going on, and fights a real fight. There is an infinite variety of ways of making theatre, but only one theme which, inevitably, Aeschylus was on to – it's simply 'how can we live justly?' Recall a great play or a great comic's act that you have enjoyed, *The Three Sisters* or Jacques Tati, and at root that will be the brazenly political theme.

11. A Cheery Day
Margaret Thatcher's Resignation

Oppositional fire blazed in the arts through the 1980s. This article was written the day Thatcher fell, for the Guardian, *as a small celebration . . . before we all got stuck in again.*

If there is one insight that comes from the most noted novels, television drama series and plays of the 1980s, it is that during the decade we were overtaken by something malevolent. It may seem exaggerated, but it was as if some kind of evil was abroad in our society, a palpable degradation of the spirit.

On 'enlightenment Thursday', when Thatcher resigned, it was to many of us in the arts as if the curse had been lifted, if only for a day. Parties broke out, the phone never stopped ringing. An eminent theatre director – a very level-headed man – rang me laughing with joy. 'I've just been down to Downing Street,' he said, 'to see her off the premises. It seemed the only place to be.' That afternoon, crossing a South London high street, I was hailed by a painter who has worked for years in obscurity hardly selling anything and who could be, for all I know, our Van Gogh. 'The bastards thought I'd be dead by now,' he cried, sheets of hardboard under his arm for new works, 'but I'm still here!' Roland Rees, whose gallant little touring company Foco Novo was axed by the Arts Council in the mid-eighties, rang to say, 'Perhaps now we can all get back to normal.'

It was the talk of excited survivors who experienced the eighties as a philistine hurricane against the idea of culture itself. Theatre workers felt, on that Thursday morning: 'Well! Not all of our theatres may be left standing, but we still are.'

For these have been very tacky years. There has been a sense of ill-being abroad, which Clare McIntyre memorably characterised as 'low level panic'. Recently a much overworked social worker, the kind of person who should be honoured as the salt of the earth in our society but whose profession has been calumnied in the past ten years, described her experience of the eighties to me as 'feeling inauthentic, feeling that there is nothing you can do because there is nothing for you in the country'.

Writers have tried to describe this eighties 'state of the soul'. I think the record is surprisingly impressive, more so than it seemed at the time, when it was fashionable to say the arts were impotent.

Television gave us Alan Bleasdale's *Boys from the Blackstuff*, about the loss of the dignity of work, and Troy Kennedy Martin's *Edge of Darkness*, about our loss of the trust of mother nature. They are two very different works, but they were both shot through with a profound anxiety, which, typically of eighties' writing, the authors could not quite articulate. None of us could: human evil, unlike the glamorous religious evil of Milton's Satan, is banal, grotty and everyday.

For me, two novels brilliantly caught the ethos of the Thatcher years. Martin Amis's *Money*, with its ultimate yuppy hero, John Self, duped by the brave new world he so lasciviously embraced, is a modern *Vanity Fair*. Because of the murderous religious hatred it has attracted, it seems to have been forgotten that Salman Rushdie's unruly *The Satanic Verses* is actually an attack on contemporary manifestations of human evil, and a 1980s' classic. It should be re-read, even actually read, and extensively reviewed again.

In the theatre, Caryl Churchill's *Serious Money* and, perhaps, *Pravda* by myself and David Hare, dramatised a 'black hole' of amorality in the public world of the day, into which traditional liberal values were sucked away without trace. The most successful dramatist of the past decade, Alan Ayckbourn, is in some ways the poet of the lower-middle classes, whose values have, in effect, been in power throughout it. But since 1985, his boulevard comedies have begun to take dark turns as if he smells something putrid behind the privet hedges and net curtains of Thatcher's natural constituency.

Looking at these successes by writers – and there were many more, Clare McIntyre's plays, Hanif Kureishi's movie scripts, a constant mortar fire of dangerous novels from Fay Weldon – it strikes me that nearly all of them, despite radically different sensibilities, are comic, almost at times to the point of hysteria, and they are wildly inventive, manipulating genres. Writers felt driven to extremes as they tried to describe the banal desolation of what happened in our country in the eighties. Also, all this work has within it a sense of mourning, of grief for lost opportunities, that something loved between us was being strangled – our culture.

Thatcherism, like all authoritarian dogmas, was brightly coloured. Writers were trying to get at the darkness, the social cruelty and suffering behind the numbingly neon-bright phrases – 'the right to choose', 'freedom under the law', 'rolling back the state'. It was as if a hyperactive demon was flitting about amongst us, seeking with its touch to turn everything into a banal conformity, a single-value culture with one creed – 'by their sales returns ye shall know them'.

Trying to define culture has defeated far subtler minds than mine. But as I see it, the arts are only part of 'culture', which could be defined as 'what we do to each other'. Malcolm Muggeridge (not a hero of mine, but on this he was interesting) once described culture as a national café of the mind, in which we are all the clientèle; a meeting place which can be raucous at times, both political assembly and place of entertainment, dance floor and theatre, with all kinds of rooms off it. (Muggeridge, in cynical mood, went on to say he was sick of it and leaving. Me, I love to hang out there.) When the café's working, we all take part; the rows, the jokes, the outbursts of singing, the meals we eat together, give us our sense of identity. This was the thinking behind Joan Little-wood's great, but now forgotten, idea for a 'fun palace'. But the café is vulnerable, it can be taken over and become a Bierkeller, with louts thumping out one song over and over again, while the rest of us sit silent and miserable in the corners.

There was bound to be grief when Thatcherite free-market prin-ciples met the arts and cultural activity. Theatrical producers and movie people talk of 'product', but we all know that actually the arts are simultaneously worthless and priceless. As a market the arts are hopeless, because although the stall-holders like money as much as anyone else, their instinct is to give their wares away free, and to go on making them against all financial odds, even if people don't want them. Indeed, all true artists, when they find they can do something that people like, discontinue the line at once, and risk something new. This is the economics of the madhouse of the imagination.

The clash was surreal. The Arts Council, a socialist idea albeit a mild one, was founded out of a sense of national pride, to make modest investments of public money in the arts, to encourage the arts to grow and delight wider audiences: that is, to liven up the floorshow in the national café. Under the Thatcher government the Arts Council, became, de facto, a politically censorious production agency. Getting any support from them became a nightmare. An Orwellian 'artspeak' developed: theatre companies had to deliver 'assessments of achievement of financial performance targets' and attend brain-melting seminars on subjects such as 'the development of a donor constituency'. I remember a heated meeting with an Arts Council officer. We pleaded for support for a fringe company which produced new plays. The official said, with a cautious tone, 'It is Council policy that there is room for idiosyncratic self-expression.' We didn't get the money.

It is extraordinary how deeply the Thatcherites' simplistic, Gradgrindish economic rule of thumb cut into our culture, and did such damage. It has just about killed off the British cinema industry. It has all but wrecked the British theatre: reps can no longer perform Shakespeare, unless they cut the sub-plots to reduce the cast. If something is not done quickly by the new government, television will be atomised, Skyward. Publishing books, that slow and kindly activity, became a murderous occupation in which publishing houses behaved as if they were the House of Borgia. Cuts in music schools, as Sir Yehudi Menuhin protested, are threatening the training of classical musicans – we can no longer make motorbikes or helicopters, soon we may not even be able to make music. The 'Legoland', 'dinky' architecture of the period, with its uniform, formula porches and 'let's pretend we're in a village' roofs, even though we're in the middle of Birmingham, is a visual expression of conformity. This wave of building was meant to be 'post-modernist', but, I suspect, it will quickly become known as the 'Thatcher style' and be found to be as rotten within as the tower blocks of a previous 'new spirit'.

But culture is, as I've argued, partly about the mental architecture of our shared perceptions and attitudes. Something nasty has happened to British apathy. It used to be commonly assumed in Britain that politics have little or no effect on everyday life, let alone personal happiness and the arts. Now good old British apathy, with its loathing of the pretentious, seems in retrospect to have been a positively healthy attitude. Thatcherism did something very unBritish to Britain: it managed, in a baleful way, to politicise everything. Apathy became militantly philistine: Norman Tebbit's recent attack on Salman Rushdie was a classic expression of it, full of an unreasoned ire at the unquantifiable imagination (and accurately shot down by Hanif Kureishi).

I think it is not too exaggerated to say that when the crash came in '87, and in '88 when the beggars appeared on the streets after Lawson's tax-cutting budget, a curious peeling away from reality set in. What people in public life said on television about the country seemed finally to lose any relation at all to what it was like to live in it, or to walk down the street. Again and again Thatcher and her ministers claimed success, in torrents of figures. Everything was better and 'up by 11 per cent'. This unreality reached a surreal apogee in Thatcher's farewell speech in the House of Commons. She seemed to think her premiership had established a Utopia that we had been living in for the past eleven and a half years: surprising news. It was a most fantastical speech.

This characteristic unreality of the late Thatcher years has been countered culturally by flourishing and wildly diverse music scenes. It's unexpected that a really effective 'counter culture' in the late eighties should begin in music, from opera to the new Manchester rock bands. David Pountney, the ENO director, tells me the resurgence of interest in opera is not, in his view, merely 'a yuppy thing'; it comes from a desire in the audience to escape from materialism, to be hit in the guts. It is as if the ENO's public has turned to this old-fashioned, almost impossible art form, which works by delivering an emotional pounding, as a reaction against the 'banal unreality' of everyday life.

My sixteen-year-old son has introduced me to the Manchester bands, Stone Roses, Inspiral Carpets, Happy Mondays, and their fellow bands, Ride, from 'the wrong side of Oxford', and the Charlatans from Northwich ('We're really proud of the Charlatans', said a middle-aged man in the street on a TV pop programme. 'We never thought anything could come from Northwich' – a voice from the cultural desert). Rock 'n' roll, despite the filthy music industry's chewing up of young musicians, seems to be able to regenerate itself endlessly. The Manchester sound is strong stuff, from a flourishing club circuit, true 'garage bands' playing home-made, survival-kit music.

There has, of course, been a lot of schlock in the past ten years, and, for historians, it is the schlock that speaks of a period as much as the true work. In the novel, Victorian pastiche, the literary equivalent of that 'dinky' architecture, has been all the rage. Much of television's film output has become minimal domestic anecdote, often set in the fifties by the seaside, reflecting Thatcher's infamous dictum, 'there is no such thing as society, only individuals and their families'. Right-wing theatre has found its voice not in new work but in a particular style of reviving Shakespeare's plays, draining their social content and sentimental-ising their pyschology. And there has been a markedly new virulence in newspaper criticism; discourse in the arts has become something of a brawl in the last ten years. Even the *Independent*, which claims to be as gently balanced as a seesaw in the park, has taken to knee-capping any of the children at play showing Leftish tendencies in their games.

But schlock is always with us, and newspaper attacks are part of the hurly-burly. What matters is that we, the artists, are still here and the desire for the 'good between us' is still with our audiences. The country needs a Jack Lang who sees no difference between a sense of fun and the public good, a rock 'n' roll fan who is not afraid of Samuel Beckett, who knows that a good school gym with decent gym mats is as culturally important as an opera house, and who would close down the Arts Council and build a national café, with a programme for the delight of all. We won't get such a figure with the new Tory government. No doubt there is misery ahead, that miserable dereliction and weary, sneery contempt for artists so typical of our present establishment. Nevertheless, we have learnt, keeping our feet in Thatcherism's philistine hurricane, that there is the possibility of making a new counter-culture, which may, fingers crossed and hope in heart, help toward making a new Britain. The fun palace may yet be built.

12. Shakespeare: Playing in the Ruins

I read about the Elizabethan theatre in some detail in 1993, researching for a television series about the life of Christopher Marlowe. The series collapsed before I wrote it; but the research turned up things about Shakespeare and his theatre which surprised me. Then I was asked to write an article for an excellent, raucous, iconoclastic theatre company, 'The Sturdy Beggars', who were performing a very bold and inventive new version of Measure for Measure. *The article was an opportunity to sort out my thoughts about our classical theatre.*

Measure for Measure was performed on 26 December 1604, at the Court of King James I. It was probably first given a showing at the Globe in the autumn of that year, to attract an offer from the Court: six plays were performed at Court every Christmas, and it was financially important for a theatre to get at least one of its plays accepted. In one glorious year for Shakespeare's income, all six plays at Court were by him and his company.

Shakespeare, as his career advanced, pushed his business relentlessly upmarket. That his theatre was a rough 'n' ready, devil-may-care outfit is a 'Merrie England' myth. Contrary to the modern romancing about the Globe – which was probably a bit of a barn of a theatre, not as playable as the more intimate Rose nearby – prices were not cheap. Money equivalents are tricky, but it was roughly two pounds fifty to stand and between twenty and thirty pounds to sit down in the Globe: its galleries were as expensive as the RSC's stalls at the Barbican Theatre today. When he could afford to pay for the conversion of the hall of an old monastery north of the river, Shakespeare moved out of the old-fashioned Globe into the indoor Blackfriars Theatre, which became a very posh venue indeed, where no 'groundling' ventured. It mustn't be forgotten that Shakespeare fired his greatest clown, Will Kemp, for lewd improvisation; and that he cut the gigue, the lavish dance by the actors at the end of a performance which you could pay to see separately, as it was proving more popular than the plays. No, 'our Bill' was never, for all our modern fantasising, a 'people's theatre' man. For a third of his career he wore a uniform as one of 'The King's Men', like a footman whose job was to entertain his master. Shakespeare was, alas, something of an Establishment creep. That is, he was a man who could be trusted to have a safe pair of hands when it came to politics dramatised on the stage. 'Safe hands' were, it must be said at once, necessary if you were to remain breathing at the Elizabethan and Jacobean courts. James I, after all, gave the nod for the execution of his mother (Mary Stuart), thus clearing the way to his eventual accession to the English throne. This was the man Shakespeare wrote *Macbeth* for, presenting it to the Court at Christmas in 1606: flattery was in the job description. (Banquo is hinted to be the first of the Stuart line. And at Oxford earlier that year, James had said that he preferred 'short plays'. Surprise! *Macbeth* is Shakespeare's shortest play.)

We rightly sense that Shakespeare's plays are what we would call 'conservative', but we do not grasp how brazenly, blazingly political they were in their own day. Today it's usually assumed that a 'political' play will, by definition, be oppositional, attacking someone in authority or a ruling philosophy. But there was no possibility whatsoever in the 1590s and the 1600s that a play could be in any way oppositional. Thomas Kyd was torn apart on the rack, accused of writing an anti-government poster about Dutch immigration – and his torturers almost certainly knew he was innocent. Thomas Nashe and Ben Jonson were sentenced to gaol for six months for writing *The Isle of Dogs*, which criticised the Mayor of London for corruption: no copy of the play survives. Christopher Marlowe's *Doctor Faustus* was ruined by the censor, and Marlowe, who flirted with atheism, magic, buggery and Catholicism – an oppositional, 'try anything' writer by nature – ended up knifed in the eye in Deptford before his writing career had truly begun. And there was one sickening moment when Shakespeare could have gone down to 'Little Ease', the racking dungeon in the Marshalsea prison: in 1601 a revival of *Richard II* was taken to support the rebellious Earl of Essex and, frighteningly for the author, was quoted at the Earl's trial. We can assume the play left the repertoire sharpish.

The Privy Council ran England, a small, energetic, chaotic country, with the social problems which some Third World countries suffer today, on a very tight rein. Elizabethan England was an authoritarian regime, which appeared to be monolithic, but which was actually made up of personal fiefdoms; it was a 'divide and rule' structure, with all kinds of corruptions, deals, favouritism, and spiteful vendettas going on out of sight. A writer, living by his wits, would seek to attach himself to one of the great loose cannons on the state's deck – Northumberland, Leicester, Essex, Lord Strange – for protection as much as for payment. Elizabeth let the great of the land vie for power and agonise about their status 'in her affections', while her omnipresent security network of 'intelligencers' and moles watched them all.

So in that world, yes, a good play was expected to be brazenly, blazingly political – but *on the side of the status quo.*

Measure for Measure is an attack on the Puritans. It's a political dystopia; it imagines the state's enemies coming to power. This was very hot stuff in 1604. James's reign was dominated by the growth of Puritanism, a movement which in the century to come was to execute a king, give rise to parliamentary sovereignty, and establish the notion of personal liberty as a democratic right – a concept Shakespeare would not have understood. The Puritans were the revolutionaries of their day, and *Measure for Measure* is a blistering, unscrupulous attack upon them. It's also a comedy, with all put to rights at the end: the king-figure in the play restores the old regime, legitimacy and true religion. It must have been music to the king's ear: he got what he paid for.

In one way the modern English theatre is blessed by having the Shakespeare plays as our 'classical theatre', but in another way it is cursed. French playwrights have the corsets of Racine and Corneille strangling their stagecraft – three actors in a triangle intoning about their lives; it even got to the self-taught Jean Genet. German playwrights these days try to pretend there was no Bertolt Brecht. But English writers have a tradition of messy Shakespeare: of 'high' and 'low' writing, scruffy prose and refined verse, organically within one text; of a theatre that's situated next to restaurants, bath-houses, brothels and gardens, not next to church and town hall (as in nineteenth-century German towns); and a theatre that is broad in its social perspective, fifteen actors being able to describe 'the theatre of the world'.

The curse of Shakespearean drama is that these plays which in plot are so social, have lost all their political meaning. For Shakespeare was not, of course, merely an Elizabethan and Jacobean propagandist. Like artists under twentieth-century authoritarian regimes – Shostakovich is an example – his work has hidden meanings that lie deep in the work, in codes. Some of the hidden meanings are pointed, for those in the know, in the same way as newspapers today make allusions about political scandals – Shakespeare probably was a supporter of 'sweet Robyn', the Earl of Essex – but other things are lost upon us, like the religious meanings in *Measure for Measure*.

With their codes lost, their political radioactivity decayed away, the plays are called 'universal': they are all things to anyone, to the point of meaninglessness. Directors pretend that *Hamlet* is about life in Romania, or that *Coriolanus* is an anti-fascist play, or *As You Like It* is a feminist play, or even that *The Merchant of Venice* is pro-Jewish drama, but what comes over is a feeble, generalised moralising. A mass cultural self-hypnotism sets in; audiences, prepared for the hypnotic Shakespearean trance by rituals of paying through the nose, and by the very name of the author, glaze over their boredom and fool themselves that they are seeing something profound. The plays, which really are shattered, brilliant fragments mixed with dross, which we will never put back together again, are used for a kind of divination. This makes them very safe, very good official theatre for our day, which is poisonous for the growth of new work.

If, then, the Shakespeare plays are ruins, it may be fun to walk away with the stones and construct new buildings. What if there is a *Measure for Measure* in which Angelo wins, and the Duke fails to reinstate the *ancien régime*? Angelo's secret police could hold him under house arrest, in an old folk's home . . . Would that not be truer, more real? We could make an alternative to quasi-official, 'hypno' productions of Shakespeare and reconstruct, yes REWRITE the old plays, to see what is in them for us, when we are wide awake.

13. Hooks and Eyes and Plays and a Poem

This is about my Berlin play, Berlin Bertie, *performed at the Royal Court in 1992, and a poem, Douglas Oliver's mighty satirical epic,* Penniless Politics, *which has since been published by Bloodaxe Books.*

I was told the story that, after many transformations, became the plot of my play *Berlin Bertie*, while I was visiting East Berlin in February of 1990. It was a brief anecdote. But I knew, even as my informant was speaking, that it was the seed from which a play would grow and that I was about to 'steal' a life because it was a good story. But, in defence of the sometimes unscrupulous behaviour of members of my craft, what we steal we change so much that our sources rarely realise they have been robbed.

Back in London, I told the story to Max Stafford-Clark at the Royal Court Theatre. He offered a commission, but what I wanted was help. Already the anecdote was changing in my mind and I had the idea of a London episode, set on the coming Easter weekend. Detail seemed important: I thought that a play about people going through extreme changes should be 'rooted', imagined to have happened on a specific three days. So, with Max's blessing, I got together a monitoring team of people who were working at the Royal Court. Wrapped in bin-liners in my loft are all the newspapers of 13 to 15 April, 1990; ten video tapes of all channels, and all the ITV, BBC and Sky newscasts; three tape cassettes of radio material; and scrapbook diaries, kept by my helpful monitors, cutting out what caught the eye.

Four and a half years on, I've been looking at this archive we made.

It is odd, and a little disturbing, to see how unreality has begun to tarnish what seemed real only four years ago. What is the odd, false edge of insincerity in the recorded voices? Do accents shift, even in fifty or so months? Mrs Thatcher was meeting President

Bush in the Bahamas. In an interview she seems weirdly dated, frivolous, almost camp. When you see some politicians on film and now on video, it seems inconceivable that they ever had power; it's the Neville Chamberlain effect.

The big news, that Easter, was the 'Iraqi supergun'. Experts appear talking of 'high milling standards', most of them certain that the tubes were *not* for a gun. Madonna launched her 'tin woman/cream corset' look at a Basque concert. Gorbachev was meeting General Jaruzelski of Poland (remember him? Sunglasses, and an ironing board down the back of his uniform, and probably a very good man). The West Indies were destroying the England cricket team in the Caribbean. The Arsenal manager acquired an American girlfriend – 'MUM LEAVES BABY FOR SOCCER BOSS' (headline of the *Sunday Mirror*). The Soviet government, still, just, in power, acknowledged responsibility for the Katyn massacre of Polish partisans. The *Sun* had a front-page exclusive on Easter Saturday, with a religious theme: 'NAUGHTY HABITS OF MY NUNS'; and Nelson Mandela addressed a packed Wembley Stadium at a concert celebrating his release from prison, two months previously. To a tumultuous, almost all-white audience, who are singing, 'You'll never walk alone' ('What is that?' Mandela asks a helper; 'A football song' comes the reply, at which he looks puzzled), he says, 'Thank you for choosing to care', a remark that will not erode into insincerity.

I finally got to write *Berlin Bertie* in the summer of 1991. All of the play, but for a flashback of memory, came to be set in London, not in Berlin. I didn't really use much of the hours of tape and the bale of newsprint we collected (though it did hail on that Easter Sunday afternoon in South London, as one of the characters complains). Coleridge described the imagination as a well, into which stories, experiences, half-heard phrases are thrown; they stick to each other, like the hooks and eyes of burrs, and change; then when you draw them up to the light, memories have formed themselves into something else . . . Mmm. Yes, it is like that.

For I remember how, in February 1990, a few months after the Wall had opened, and when for a moment there was a strange interim government in the fading GDR, I caught a tram in East

Berlin to keep an appointment in the suburbs; it wandered, rattling along its old rails set in the cobbles, at one time stopping for a lazy ten minutes, for no apparent reason. No one seemed to mind. Everyone on the tram was very . . . quiet, sunk in their thoughts, eye-contact an impossibility. The sense of dislocation was overpowering: it was as if the bones had been wrenched from their sockets in that place, but no one was screaming, no one was saying anything at all. Then, at my destination, sitting in a brown and dowdy room, glimpsing through the window the pale blue sky of a hard, cold Berlin winter's day above a dark church, someone leaned forward over a cup of coffee and said: 'One night in Berlin, last October . . . '. I was being given the play.

Two years later, while *Berlin Bertie* was in production at the Royal Court Theatre, I was asked to write an article about the play for the *Guardian*. I came across an extraordinary long poem, which focused something I'd seen hazily in Berlin, and had tried to express in the play. This is the article.

PENNILESS POLITICS

What was the shock like, reading T.S. Eliot's 'The Waste Land' when it was published in 1922? I think I know. I've just read Douglas Oliver's epoch-making long poem, 'Penniless Politics'. I never thought I would ever read anything like it in the 1990s. 'Penniless Politics' speaks for a new era and sets the literary agenda for the next twenty years.

Douglas Oliver is, from what 'the poet' says of himself in the text, white and an 'Anglo-Scot' living as an outsider in a wrecked district of Manhattan, where the poem is set. He is wonderfully bloody-minded; his great poem is at the moment only available in a curious samizdat edition, set from the original typescript.

As with Eliot's masterpiece, Oliver's poem will divide friends. I had a furious argument with an old Lefty about it: 'How can you think *this* is poetry? What's all this about voodoo? It's repugnant! Pseudo art, pseudo politics . . . You'll be a laughing-stock if you praise this garbage . . . '. I fear Douglas Oliver is going to need a heavyweight champion, as did Eliot; no doubt his F.R. Leavis will appear, but, meanwhile, let's try to read his poem without losing our tempers.

Bizarrely, the poem's plot resembles the old British film, *Passport to Pimlico*, though Ealing comedy this ain't. A poor district of Manhattan declares 'UDI', reinventing politics from the ground, indeed from the groin, upwards – the sex in the poem is terrific.

'To begin with everything missing . . . ', says the second stanza. And from a heady brew of voodoo notions of spirit, curious visitations of communal inspirations, democratic seances, a melt-down of old politics, grassroots scams and 'buy-ups' of neighbourhoods, a political movement stirs amongst the poor of New York and 'District A1' is born, a truly free zone. It thrives, then in a second disappears, its 'spirit' aged. For how are politics possible in the Utopian dreams of a poem? This is a diamond-hard mind talking to us:

> . . . What did you expect? You, hypocrite reader, et cetera?
> You want some opiate, a poetic abracadabra so your ordinary
> responsibility for our ordinary political failure can be
> charmed away?

The poem is, formally, a satire, a 'criticism in verse of folly and vice'. But its attack on late-twentieth-century America is startlingly original. Rather than attempting to ridicule things as they are, as *Bonfire of the Vanities* failed to do, since no fictional New York folly can exceed the outrage of the real thing, Oliver turns the negativity of satire on its head. He does so by describing his imaginary, alternative America with a blazing optimism. A crazed but certain faith that human invention could transform the New York urban nightmare surges through the poem's three hundred or more eight-lined, elaborately rhymed and rhythmed stanzas, white-hot with linguistic energy, coining new poetic devices with abandon. The poem even includes a new U.S. constitution.

And there is the authentic beauty of Oliver's city writing. Try this description of a market:

> As cabbage leaves drift on the sidewalk, and cherries, squashed, bleep
> their stones, ice sparkles under broccoli, the washed beans seep

water through slats of wood out at Hunt's Point, and it's only 6.30,
the wholesale market already almost done, the rest of the city
barely waking as the dawn gleams on unsold boxes of onions,
the trucks in circles like cowboy wagons . . . '

In *Berlin Bertie*, each of its five characters at some point suddenly
speaks an aside to the audience. These 'asides', in the midst of a
very realistic play, are in verse, and, artistically, very disruptive.
They have always been in the text through its various drafts, and
I've had the devil of a time in rehearsals explaining what these
outbursts mean. Then I read 'Penniless Politics' and saw the theme
I'd stumbled upon identified: *desire*, a ferocious, overwhelming
desire for the human spirit to change. The 'asides' are in character
and some of the desires they express are off the wall; what goes on
in Bertie's mind is, to say the least, suspect. And my play is a world
away from Oliver's poem; he is obsessively 'politically correct', my
play takes a sledgehammer to the 'right on' clichés that have debili-
tated recent radical theatre in Britain (enter working-class black
lesbian in Islamic dress to speak meaning of play etc). But as great
writing will, 'Penniless Politics' identifies a new era's themes that
we all sense to be there, just beyond language, waiting for their
first expression.

And it is gloriously *unofficial*. It is way beyond the pale of what
is, at the moment, acceptable as literature.

I find this exemplary. When I began writing *Berlin Bertie*, which
is psychological, character-driven, quite unlike anything else I've
tried to do, I knew I was kicking over the traces. The 'British epic'
theatre with its 'issue plays' that my generation of playwrights
invented and wrote through the seventies and eighties with some
success (*Plenty*, *Comedians*, Howard Barker's *Victory*, *Maydays*,
Pravda, *Serious Money*, etc.), has died on us. Ways of writing that
David Hare and I had to fight tooth and nail to get anywhere near
a stage when we were young are now the official wisdom for every
other new play at the Court, National or the RSC. This is normal
artistic life; what was once white-hot invention becomes dead
convention, mere theatricality. We must get back in love with reality. We need new ways of dramatising what people are thinking

and feeling out there. Ironically, we could become rebels against the official orthodoxy we ourselves helped to make. The first line of 'Penniless Politics' is:

All politics the same crux: to define humankind richly.

Great stuff. Let's get on with it.

Part II

Diaries

On Tour

In 1982 Michael Bogdanov, the director of my play The Romans in Britain, which had been premiered at the National's Olivier Theatre in 1980, was charged under a section of the Sexual Offences Act in a private prosecution brought by a 'moral campaigner', Mrs Mary Whitehouse. She objected to a scene in Act One of the play, an attempted rape of a male Celt by a Roman soldier.

The case was a bizarre affair that dragged on for well over a year, through three hearings in a magistrates' court before we ended up in the Old Bailey. Though it was Michael who was going on trial, one of the most wretched aspects was that it was my play that had put him there.

I wanted to do something and decided to go on a one-man tour, reading the play, to raise money for the Theatre Defence Fund, which had been set up to raise money for what we feared was going to be a hefty legal bill.

In the first act of the play, Julius Caesar encounters a small settlement of Celts north of the Thames. In the second act, set partly in our time, a British Intelligence Officer, Lt. Chichester, loses his mind in a field in Northern Ireland.

On 16 February 1982, three weeks before the trial was due to begin at the Old Bailey, I set off.

TUESDAY 16TH FEBRUARY

Breakfast in Newcastle. Last night I read *The Romans in Britain* for the first time in public at the Newcastle Playhouse.

I don't understand this hotel. It's huge and rambling, tatty, lots of rooms, lounges with fat, plastic chairs in phalanxes. Some kind of hard-drinking scene goes on at night between a handful of men around a pool table. I think they're locals. Suddenly this morning I thought 'What's wrong here?' What's wrong is the place is empty. Upstairs thirty rooms are silent beneath their peeling polystyrene ceiling tiles. In the breakfast room I was alone but for a young couple, clearly on an adventure. He was discovering she liked scrambled eggs.

*

Last Sunday, I was in Oxford speaking at a 'forum' with my fellow playwright Stephen Poliakoff, chaired by Melvyn Bragg. The forum was in two parts, part one for novelists, Salman Rushdie, Michael Frayn and Malcolm Bradbury, the second with Stephen and me. We interrupted each other's turn when we felt like it. These 'forums' or 'workshops' used to be called 'talks'. They can go badly wrong. The writers can fall to squabbling, their minds wandering to the beer afterwards, you can get trapped into non-discussions (e.g. 'form v content'). But this was an exception and highly enjoyable. I think it was because we were all frightened by the occasion. I'd expected a dozen or so in a small room. Instead we walked into the huge New College Hall and a packed audience of four hundred students on low benches, jammed between the dark wood panels and paintings of bishops, dead academics, and generals.

The echo was horrific. No chance for squabbling with reactionary brother writers on 'the panel'. You had to choose a few words and belt them out. Fear hit me, good practice for the reading.

*

Monday morning I left Oxford for Newcastle, a six-hour journey.

From Oxford to London I read George Orwell's *Homage to Catalonia*. Outside Paddington Station an anarchist slogan – 'I am an angry and passionate soul alone I scream at the mediocrity around me.' Anarchy. Orwell writing about the CNT, the Catalan anarchist party, two million strong at the beginning of the Spanish Civil War. A working-class movement. Anarchy in Britain means a few students who go off their heads, good middle-class children with their minds burst. It's difficult to understand what Spanish anarchy was and, indeed, still is.

Crossed London. Flying Scotsman. The return fare, Oxford to Newcastle, cost me sixty-one pounds and forty pence. (I have to return to Oxford tomorrow to read the play.) The cost is impossible. I'll have to play the cheap fares or go by coach. With the price of travel going like this, soon only the rich will be able to move from city to city.

*

The Newcastle Playhouse. I met John Blackmore, the artistic director. He was recovering from one of those exhaustion diseases theatre workers are prone to, a viral pneumonia. Roger Spence, his assistant, looked after me. Five people had booked for the reading. The evening ahead had that tomb-like echo in the skull I remember from when I began writing plays for the touring Portable Theatre – the fear that the show doesn't exist!

I went to the hotel, washed, controlled my nervousness by being unaccustomedly neat: toothpaste, shaving brush, TCP and jar of honey (a present from my wife for the expected reader's sore throat) all in a row on the glass shelf over the hotel basin. I even hung my clothes up in the cupboard.

I dressed for the reading. The idea of the presentation, which Bogdanov has helped me with, is to get the audience to relax. The only hope in hell you have of doing that is to relax yourself. So, wear clothes and shoes you're comfortable in. A light blue shirt, not white, as that would dazzle in the lights, a dark sleeveless pullover, so the audience can see your face clearly and, above all, see your eyes. Blue cords, casual shoes. The setting – a chair with arms that you can sit up straight in, as well as sprawl or contort, if that's how the reading takes you. Beside the chair, a small table, a jug of iced water and a glass. John Blackmore suggested a pint of Guinness, traditional actor's throat medicine. This I did, it's good advice (though Guinness makes you spit: this morning I find the text has little brown spots over its pages). Lighting: houselights on half so the audience can see each other and anyone getting brain damage can feel relaxed about leaving and so I can see them, essential in a reading. The chair as close as possible to the edge of the stage and the stage lit around and behind the chair, so that the audience don't get strained by having to watch a talking head in the dark. Also to make the chair lonely on the stage is to my advantage, it says, 'This really is it, a man sitting in a chair.' The lighting should be warm with all the pink gels going – you are the beast from the swamp who wrote this notorious play, so turn up looking as human as possible and maybe you've got a chance.

*

I went to the theatre at four o'clock and did a radio interview for a local radio station. Then I worked out on the stage for an hour and a half, trying to get the stiffness out of my shoulders. The 'lie down think your way through your body' exercise (dangerous stuff, do it right and you fall asleep). Then voice, hitting consonants, breathing, pulling your rib-cage up, back and front. I sat and read aloud to the empty auditorium then quoted some favourite Dylan Thomas from memory. It's a tricky four-hundred seater, a big stage with the seats in a single, slightly curving bank before you. Roger Spence came in and did a hearing check for me. A lot of dead spots. I did the beginning and ends of the fifteen scenes, then walked about speaking Chichester's opening soliloquy. I ended by singing, clapping and stamping, 'Rose, rose, rose red', falsetto, tenor and bass.

The work-out calmed me down and warmed me. I went to the foyer and chatted with John Blackmore. Then to the dressing room, alone amongst the actors' places before the line of mirrors, the make-up trays and personal props (fangs and bones – the Playhouse is doing yet one more *Dracula*). The stage manager called me. I walked through the maze of tat and dusty drapes most stages have in their wings – waited in the prompt corner while the stage manager rang the bells and got clearance, then walked on – before a house that was still, to first glance, as empty as that to which I'd sung 'Rose red' an hour before. Eighteen people. Ah well.

*

I was delighted with the way it went.

I have written the play out as a narrative. The basis of it is simply saying 'he said, she said' rather than driving an audience mad by saying the name of a character before each speech. I try to describe the landscape, the look of the people, the physical presences. So it is a piece of story-telling. I've 'barded' the play. This is how it begins:

> The edge of a forest at night. Against the night sky the forest looks like a black cliff.
>
> Silence.
>
> Then, in the distance, dogs bark. It is just past midnight on the 27th of August, 54 BC. We are fifty miles north of the River Thames.
>
> In the trees, someone stifles a cry.
>
> Then, out of the trees, come two figures. One is a big man, with big head and big hands, the other a small man, quick and ferret-like. They are in rags. Their skin is weathered and filthy. The small man clutches a large, leather bag. He looks about him, then speaks.
>
> 'Where the fuck are we?'

*

There is an actor's joke, first told me by John Nettles when he was in a play of mine at the RSC.

A: Ask me 'What is the secret of acting?'

B: 'What is the secret of a – '

A: (*Interrupting.*) Timing.

*

What have I learnt from the first reading?

It takes far longer than the dry runs I did to the wallpaper in my workroom. Part One took an hour and a half, Part Two fifty-five minutes. With interval, that's two and three-quarter hours.

I have a barmy machismo-like pride in having spoken such a monster of an evening and not having lost one of the eighteen souls before me.

But that will pass. There's a lot of work to do.

I did the first scene too fast. The big, complex passage, the second scene, with the killing of one of the Irish fugitives, the rejection of the Casivellaun envoys and the mother telling her young husband what's what went well, though the village debate was a pain in the neck (as it was in the rehearsals at the National). The rape scene didn't give me and didn't seem to give them any trouble at all. I got the would-be rapist, the 'Third Soldier', very well. That helped. I think they *saw* that man.

I lost Julius Caesar. I couldn't see him. I tried to mimic Michael Bryant's magnificent performance in the National production; a stupid thing to try, I couldn't get anywhere near it. In desperation I read him as myself. I felt my voice going up and 'young' on me. I was fumbling to get the lightness I felt in Caesar's personality when I wrote him, a light, deadly mind. It's in Yeats's poem:

> Our master Caesar is in the tent
> Where the maps are spread,
> His eyes fixed upon nothing,
> A hand under his head.
> Like a long-legged fly upon the stream
> His mind moves upon silence.

I got nowhere near it. A pity, it's a passage that should be brought off well in a reading.

The sudden description of 'a stage' in the last moments of Part One felt good. It's the only time in the descriptions that I mention the theatre, the rest is all straight figures in the landscape. The idea is to smash the imagined landscape into the imagined theatre at the moment the British Army appears, metamorphosed from the Roman legions.

I was high and over-confident in the interval. Stupidly I felt: 'Great. Now it's relaxed, comic reading here on in. I've cracked it.' I've not. The second part (really a second play) is the more difficult to read. Part One is far from easy but its landscape is clear, you're a guide leading your tour party round slabs of scenes, a storyteller's Stonehenge.

But Part Two is quirky, with comic characters. It's about a human *slyness* which I love. These cooks and runaways are our ancestors. We have the genes of survivors not heroes in us: the heroes got killed. The cowards were our fore-fathers and fore-mothers.

But, as I expected, I don't have an actor's timing: the eye-catching and taking, being wrong-footed, 'balancing off-balance', double-taking, the athletics of making fun. Mind you, it would be fiendish enough for a gifted actor reading alone. How do you double-take on yourself? I'm going to have to, somehow.

Concentration!

I have to make a decision. As I read, out there, *what am I seeing?* The National Theatre production or the play imagined in the open, in the real landscape? When you write a play you see both, landscape and stagescape, people living their lives and actors performing them. But at times I 'bleached out', lost contact and was frightened to find myself just with words on a printed page before me. I then had to fight to get the vision back, and it always took a long time.

Concentration.

I felt tremendously well after the reading. Roger and Judy took me for a smashing Indian meal. Tandoori chicken and adrenalin. They were very kind. They were at the end of their day, I was at the height of mine.

*

Judy is a dancer with the Scottish Ballet. She was very interesting about dancers. Some have to work a lot, some don't. Some starve themselves. She woofed down a huge Indian meal, nearly all meat. Health blazed out of her like heat. As there is a cast of mind so there is a cast of body. She said those who force it, diet and have to punish themselves, break down. 'It's something you do or you don't,' she said. There was a flattering 'I dance, you write' attitude. To each our natural athleticism, dancing or writing. (Hugely flattering. 'Yeeees,' I said, feeling my shoulders and spine set in my concrete 'writer's neck'.) Didn't Artaud call actors 'athletes of the heart'?

Aie aie, if flowery conversations can't flower late at night when can they? We parted in a Newcastle car park at one in the morning and in great good humour. Very kindly they've offered me their Glasgow flat to stay in when I read at the Citizens Theatre.

*

Today I'm walking about Newcastle. I've just been to see the Civic Centre, built at the height of Labour Party funny money and optimism in the 1960s, the famous 'Dan's Castle'. T. Dan Smith's monument. It looked so naive, so childish. A lighthouse, over a round council chamber, a pumpkin on legs. It's really a town hall. They did a lot of damage, Smith and Poulson, yes. But looking at their earthly, civic remains I thought – you can sympathise. After the dreary, Tory 1950s they came to power, money was flooding in the veins, and they thought, 'Right! It's our turn.' And built. When you look at 'Dan's Castle' you think, 'How the hell did they ever think they were going to get away with that?' It was a fantasy. And beside the real crimes of money – Nestlés in the Third World, the United Fruit Company, the Vodka-Cola nexus, American 'aid' to El Salvador – 'Dan's Castle' looks pathetic, even quaint. It's almost a pity they can't be forgiven. They can't be because of the misery they brought to so many in the high-rise flats they built.

WEDNESDAY 17TH FEBRUARY

On the train, Newcastle-to-London-to-Oxford, writing this.

My wife had disturbing news on the phone last night; the time at the Oxford Playhouse has been changed from seven to nine-thirty. This is going to be fun. The reading won't end until 12.15 am. What to do? Won't cut or skip.

I rang Andrew Leigh, who set the tour up for me. He was mortified, the good soul, at there only being eighteen in the audience. 'Oh no, oh no, oh no,' he moaned, 'I'm so sorry, oh no.' I tried to reassure him I was in good heart. But, as I said to him, the point of this jaunt is to raise money for the Theatre Defence Fund, not to bankrupt it by zinging me around the country getting a free education in how to read aloud. I think, by me scrimping a bit, the first leg of Newcastle to Oxford won't lose us money. I got fifteen pounds of donations for the Fund from the Newcastle audience. We may just be in the black. I asked Andrew to phone the Oxford Playhouse to make sure their staff agree to having the studio (it's called 'The Burton Room') open late. When I get to Kings Cross, two hours from now, I'll phone him again.

Clearly, 'on the road' you've got to live in a bubble of personal calm. Arrangements can crinkle. You mustn't rely on anything ahead, just make sure you've got your text, your TCP, honey and toothbrush and – turn up, ready to make the most of it.

England through the train window, hereabouts, wherever that may be, is brown and flat. Grey cloud and mist drift past the train window. A Bunny Club hostess in dazzling make-up, black dress and gold jewellery eats a bacon sandwich opposite me, leaning forward over the British Rail paper plate, licking finely painted scarlet fingernails. We chat a little. She's a croupier. (Isn't the

Bunny Club going bust? I don't bring that up. The Bunny Club emblem, tiny in gold, glitters on her neck chain.) She sleeps. On the other side of the carriage a Japanese couple, in fine clothes with red leather baggage, looking like airline passengers, sleep. I've finished *Homage to Catalonia*. I open a folder with the twenty-three pages I've written for my new stage play. I stare at them. In my bubble.

*

A memory of the Newcastle reading. A blind gentleman sat a few feet from me in the middle of the front row. I didn't, during the reading, realise he was sightless for he looked straight at me throughout, smiling with blue eyes, reacting to the play all the time but for a passage at the beginning of Part Two, when he had his eyes closed. I thought he was asleep. But maybe he was not, just listening. Nevertheless I was hoping against hope to wake him up for those fifteen minutes (the Cai, Corda and Morgana scene). I was immensely glad of his presence, his blue eyes radiated encouragement. I was amazed when Roger Spence told me he'd helped him into and out of the theatre. He wasn't a regular.

There, outside Paddington Station, is the Anarchist slogan, 'I am . . .' And I am on this train.

On Paddington I rang Andrew. The Oxford Playhouse are relaxed about the reading ending at a quarter-past midnight. He's having trouble finding me a bed, the students aren't helpful. (They're shy. I saw that at the forum over the weekend, a crippling shyness amongst these privileged children. I had it when I was a student; at bad times it comes back with a vengeance.) Andrew is trying mates in the area, if that falls through he'll book a hotel room. 'Oh oh,' I hummed and hawed, into one of the absurdly opulent digital public telephones they've just installed at Paddington. Standing there with the row of the station behind me, talking about money and the Defence Fund, I was haunted by the image of a thirty-foot high, sixty-pound rail ticket floating over eighteen faces in a four hundred seat theatre.

*

Food becomes a different matter on tour. I had a big breakfast in the Newcastle hotel this morning, sausage, egg, bacon the lot, will have no lunch and won't eat again until after I've read the play tonight. You can go either way on a caper like this, very fat or very thin.

*

When am I going to have my first rowdy audience? Tonight, undergraduate wags with eight pints in 'em? No idea.

*

It's an epic play. The first scene of an epic is crucial, the first story. If you don't get it home for them, you're in trouble. You don't have ten minutes fooling around with drawing curtains, pouring tea while the late-comers settle and attention swivels to the stage and the evening ahead, like in the 'Ibsenite' theatre. An epic play has to go off bang, at once.

Deep into the reading in Newcastle I found the confidence to improvise, in a minor way, with the descriptions. Don't get over-ambitious with that tonight, but take it if it comes.

LATER: 12.40 AM

I did it! I did it again! Fifty there. I lost four. From the laughs they were still awake at twelve-fifteen this morning. Notes tomorrow. We had to get out of the building at once. Nowhere to go. So, got a hamburger and a hot dog and a can of Coca-Cola from a hot dog van, a lonely pulpit of onion smells at the bus station outside this hotel. Now I'm sitting up in bed with sweater and dressing gown on. It's cold. Sleety snow was falling when I went over to the theatre. I'm raging with adrenalin, intolerably lonely and intolerably happy. Never mind, I did it, I did it again and held them and was a lot better than last night. Chew on it tomorrow. My sister was there, with a friend, which was a delight.

*

THURSDAY 18TH FEBRUARY

The reading yesterday.

When I arrived, a few, forlorn pink balloons were bobbing above the door to the Burton Room, which turned out to be a nondescript, small, square room with a low ceiling. The balloons were there because the students are doing Orton's *The Erpingham Camp*. I chose a chair from a store room and decided to sit on a rostrum, to be seen, and did the lighting.

Then I went to the hotel, rooms over a pub called 'The Welsh Pony'. Dirt cheap for these times, eight pounds a night with breakfast. Musty, chipped, a frighteningly senile Alsatian dog at the foot of the stairs. I liked the place. There was a communal bathroom with a big, old-fashioned bath with splayed lions' feet and huge taps that let fall a Niagara of hot water. I bathed, dozed for an hour and a half, worked out in the hotel room, cutting my hand on the electric light's pink plastic shade and went to the theatre through the sleety snow.

I waited in the store-room which doubles as a dressing room, a mess of broken chairs and tables, the clothes of the student actors performing in the studio above strewn over the up-ended chair legs. A Beckett premiere was opening late night in the Playhouse, a prose splinter done as a twenty-minute play after the main show. I caressed my nerves in the company of a professional actor who was similarly preoccupied. His opinion of the Beckett piece was as minimal as the stuff he was about to perform. 'Come on, come on,' I mumbled, pacing up and down, 'let's do it, let's do it.' He laughed. I was glad of his sardonic company.

*

I mustn't be over-confident, this was a student audience. They laughed readily, in a fizzy, light-headed way. And the two officers, Chichester and Maitland, whose conversation greatly amused the audience, were of their class: it was laughter of recognition.

Never sneer at an audience that finds your funny lines funny, but watch it or you'll drown with them. Hearing the laughter, I hit

Chichester's death hard. An audience identifying like that 'goes into' a play and often laughs at each tree but is lost in the wood. They then tire quickly – first-night audiences in London are often lost to a play that way. It's up to the actors to get an audience out of it sooner or later so that they can see the whole story.

The voice is OK. The strangest sounds come out across a range that surprises me. The archaic theories of acting, that you're 'taken over' and that you 'become' a character may be baloney, but they are a description of part of the experience of performing. As, indeed, with writing: you may not believe in a muse, a goddess or demon whispering in your ear, but the experience is often like that. You come on song, in a few days you write what you've struggled over for months, as if it were being dictated to you.

*

10 am. To the Oxford Playhouse where I met Guy Hibbert, playwright, and Victor Glyn, director, who are planning to stage a reading of the trial's transcript, day by day. They are going to get on the train to Oxford after the day at the Old Bailey, work on the transcript, get off the train, photocopy it and go straight into rehearsal and perform it at 10 pm. Lawyers swarm about their heads like wasps. It's a wonderful project. Brave, too, of the actors who will not know what is coming into their hands each evening. It struck me that the most difficult days will be when there are legal submissions that can't be reported. That could knock out the first couple of days when the interest in the show will be at its height. Guy and Victor suggested readings from the play, but I said 'no' because I don't want extracts, the so-called 'juicy bits', being done alone. They discussed other ideas – a history of censorship or a dramatisation of the Sexual Offences Act 1956. They had the quiet manner and wild light in the eye of theatre people with a good show firmly held by the throat.

*

Tony Bicât came and found me talking to Guy and Victor in the Playhouse coffee bar. He'd come to talk about my television play

Desert of Lies [finally transmitted in 1983]. Mike Wearing, the BBC producer, is in blood up to his armpits trying to get the money, film days and studio time it needs. Tony will direct it if it all comes right.

We went to a pub. 'I want something to eat,' said Tony and went off for a sandwich. He came back with an earthenware bowl, in it mushroom in garlic, parsley and croutons. 'It's all they had,' he said, staring at the concoction. Oxford University. The riches of the earth, eh? Provençal dishes over a pub bar. I flushed Puritan. I saw the University dripping with butter and garlic, the ancient façades smeared with it, the bluey-pale cheeks of the students sweating garlic, a fantasy land of butteriness, the breath of privilege hot with its strange smell.

I'd had enough of it. A rail strike day so I got a coach back to London.

FRIDAY 19TH FEBRUARY

I went to the National Theatre to discuss my version of *Danton's Death* with Peter Gill, who plans a production of the play later in the year. Whether he will use my version, based on Jane's translation – deadline, 1st April – I don't know. [He did.] While I was there I bumped into Michael Bogdanov. We went for a cup of tea in the canteen. He's back from a week's tour in the Far East, setting up shows and tours. He was jet-lagged by thirty-six hours and unmarked, came straight from Heathrow to meetings at the theatre. He was appalled at the Newcastle house. He'll be on the phone complaining to John Blackmore, an old mate of his. I tried to restrain him: no use. 'Were there collecting boxes in the foyer?' he said. 'No,' I said. He scowled. Michael wants a celebratory, campaigning, generous, bright-bannered theatre. There is a Will Kemp in him. The theatrical institutions are tired. The last thing Michael Bogdanov is, is tired. It drives him into a fury that the profession will not take things seriously and will not get up and dance.

*

Then I went down under the grey underpasses of the South Bank
to the Old Vic to visit Andrew Leigh. He sat at the board room
table in the theatre with a mosaic of papers before him on the
black velvet tablecloth (velvet with a tired and dusty look, of
settled cigarette smoke and the bad breath of many desperate
meetings over the last few years). Gave him receipts, he gave me
times of the performances ahead, train times and telephone numbers. 'I'm sorry to be sordid with an artiste like you,' he said and
laughed. 'But you're your own company manager now. Go to Euston Station tomorrow, buy an Inter City ticket to Glasgow . . . ' etc.
We had a drink of whisky and parted outside the Old Vic. He is
greatly pleased that I go to the Glasgow Citizens Theatre tomorrow. He was the administrator there for five years, before the
present management. 'You can whisper, whisper on that stage and
be heard.' Andrew is one of the hard men of the theatre, the
administrators. You do meet administrators in the theatre who are
dead between the eyes, fantasising that they are businessmen,
talking about plays as 'product'. But Andrew has the essential madness. He sees himself as much as an entertainer as actors on a stage
he administrates. Which is how it should be but is not: all of the
staff of a theatre are entertainers.

SATURDAY 20TH FEBRUARY

Euston Railway Station, 8 am. Travellers' tales. I needed a shit.
Blew my only two pence piece on a cubicle in the gents with no
lavatory paper. Approached by a man at the wash-basins. A drunk,
gone already, that porridge smell about him of someone who lives
out on the street. Gave him a ten-pence piece. Rushed out to a
coffee bar. British Rail policy: no giving of change. 'Give us a cup
of coffee then,' I said. It cost twenty-nine pence. One p change!
I sweet-talked the woman serving coffee into contravening the
regulations of the station authorities.

In the buffet on the station a young woman with a Scots accent,
probably a student, tried to find out the price of a round of toast
from a kitchen worker who was putting sandwiches out into the

self-service shelves. He didn't know. I saw a list on the wall. '16p,' I said. Her face fell. She bought no toast.

*

The Bristol Little Theatre and the Actors Workshop, Brighton, asked for me to read, their interest provoked by an article in this week's *Stage*. Bristol then back-tracked, almost at once: 'board trouble'. I'd like to do the Actors Workshop, they did my *Christie in Love* last year despite a local councillor getting at them in the local press, but I don't have the time.

The only theatre that said 'no' outright to my reading was the Cambridge Arts Theatre. The grapevine has it there was a row at a board meeting. I can only say 'huh' to the pinprick of the insult. But that's how it can go, so easily, with theatre managements – a lowly fear of the law will freeze the theatre into an ice-age of self-censorship if we lose at the Old Bailey. (An old Situationist saying that I've ripped off several times in my plays comes to mind: 'the policeman in the head'.) Bernard Williams, the philosopher, sent Andrew a message saying he was outraged at the decision, which was good of him.

*

On the train to Glasgow. We stopped at Watford. There was discomfort and tension as mothers with their children got onto the packed train. The carriages are full of families, the women without their husbands, Scots accents, a lot of luggage, the look about them of a major journey. What is this migration? It's not school half-term, it's not a public holiday. The to- and fro-ing took half an hour to settle down. Opposite me, a cheerful grandfather, in league with his daughter's rampant two young children. Next to him a young woman with the headphones of a cassette recorder about her ears.

*

England is grey and green beyond the train window. Ever since

I began working on *The Romans in Britain,* every stretch of ground I look at in the countryside heaves and seethes like an ocean in a slow, centuries-long swell, barrows, medieval fields, dew ponds, strip cultivation, hill forts, banks, ditches riding under the grass. The landscape is riven by human work.

*

Crewe, at the heart of England, where politicians and lovers change trains. There is a story, no doubt apocryphal, that, during the Poulson scandal in the Labour Party ten years ago, Harold Wilson had a ten-minute meeting with T. Dan Smith in a waiting room on one of these platforms.

*

Where are we? Twenty miles north of Crewe? Just then, suddenly, out of the window, I saw a river bank, a stretch of meadow, rising gently for a hundred yards to a wall of trees. Just like Act One, Scene Three, the 'rape scene'. Eerie. When I read that scene tomorrow night that stretch of water, grass and tall trees, there and gone from the moving train, will be with me.

*

Now right up north, crossing over the border. A blue, slate-like sky over the rolling hills. The little dark brick back-to-backs on the outskirts of Carlisle.

The Citizens have invited me to see their production of Genet's *The Balcony* tonight. It'll be a joy to see the great play again. In interviews when I'm asked 'what are your favourite modern playwrights?' I tell them, Strindberg, Wilde and Genet, but they don't hear and assume I've said Ibsen, Shaw and Brecht. What's a red playwright got to like about Oscar Wilde and Jean Genet? 'Kulchur' comes in little, easy-tear sachets, like the instant milk powder on the carriage table by my hand as I write this. Not from bleeding udders of real cows, blood, grass and infections in the cream, eh?

I'm enjoying this journey. It wears and warms. Now there are empty spaces, sleepers, plastic cups, paper plates and napkins from the buffet all over the place. Stationary in Carlisle as I write, an hour and twenty minutes from Glasgow. The sun blazes across the platform through the massed wire and tubular steel of station trolleys.

*

Into the brown grandeur of the Scots lowlands, in sunshine and distant blue mist. Now and then a dry-stone wall goes in a long, wavering line up a hillside to the skyline. Electricity pylons lope hand in hand over the turf. The train sails along a high embankment beside a fast, shallow river that glitters on a stony bed. Desolate hills, but sodden with rain, and the valley wet.

*

In Glasgow I must buy a bottle of TCP, a bottle of shampoo and find out the times of trains to Liverpool.

SUNDAY 21ST FEBRUARY

Late at night. Just back to the flat I'm staying in from reading the play at the Citizens.

It was sweet, sweet, sweet. A marvellous theatre. On its stage you feel like a knife. You can carve any word on any part of the auditorium. For half an hour I felt myself overworking, a mess, sweating and straining, knowing that all I had to do was – do it.

You could let the book levitate out of your hand and make the play up on the spot.

I'm high, I must calm down.

The northern audience laughed at the southern dialects, the Legate and Tom Chichester. British audiences have perfect pitch when it comes to regional speech and class.

I did feel tonight I was performing the play. Really I'm only sitting there for two and three-quarter hours, reading it. But by some kind of sleight of hand, or mutual agreement, it's a performance. Odd.

Someone said to me afterwards, 'How the hell did they stage it?' Good.

In the dressing room I remembered an acting exercise to fix on characters by thinking of them as animals. A crude but fierce 'talisman' of a character. I did that and it helped. I remember the director, Barry Kyle, after eight weeks' work with Ray Westwell in the RSC rehearsals of *The Churchill Play*, saying one word to Ray, about to play my Churchill on the opening night: 'Bulldog.'

The Citizens have every show watched by the assistant director, Kim Dambaek, so notes are given every evening. My reading was no exception. A good system: the National have it, the RSC don't. Kim said I could syncopate more, go further with throwing my voice about. He also soothed my paranoia about the reading being boring. It is not boring. (Why the hell isn't it? It should be the most boring thing on earth, someone reading a play at enormous length. Perhaps the expectation is so low that you start on the floor, so everything and anything you can do for the audience, is a plus. I certainly sense the apprehension at the beginning of the reading: 'Oh my God he's going to read it – all of it.' Then ten minutes on, 'Oh. A woman with a strange hair-do and six dogs at her heels. Oh. I see.' And you're away.)

Now, food! Bath! The white wine the Citizens staff gave me to take to my lonely bed.

MONDAY 22ND FEBRUARY.

The Citizens Theatre stands in a levelled area, the Gorbals. The desolation and civic ugliness makes anger clutch at your throat. But it's not a desert, people are living there. The high-rise blocks of flats are lit at night by powerful lights on the edges of their roofs. They must burn all night into the windows of the flats. 'For aircraft?' I asked. No one knew. Perhaps they are put there to torment the tenants in their bedrooms. Amid this, the roads that were once the streets to the doors of the slum tenements go through a wasteland of stretches of gravel and asphalt, laid down for no discernible reason except perhaps to stop grass growing. And along one, in isolation, like a lighthouse on a dried-up sea-bed, stands the Citizens Theatre.

I saw *The Balcony* on Saturday night. The theatre is in wonderful nick, vividly painted inside, greens, purples, yellows, blues picking out the stucco excess of the Victorian horseshoe circles and boxes, beneath a huge chandelier. Backstage everything is pristine and well-ordered. No muck and musty black drapes and weights to stub the reader's toe here. The staff are relaxed, friendly and funny. In short – the theatre smells of success. What a joy to be, for once, in a theatre where you smell that. They charge 90 pence for each seat, anywhere in the auditorium, 60 pence for students. It's free for the unemployed. Robert David MacDonald explained that the price of a seat is pegged to the cost of a packet of cigarettes. The house was full for *The Balcony,* eight hundred people.

The Citizens is famous for its style of production, which is wildly imaginative, flamboyant, 'decadent', a 'high' form of theatre, deliberately beyond the pale of Royal Court or RSC worthiness. I'd not seen it before. You're told it's camp. But camp means 'not serious', which this is. What I didn't expect was the thumping, no-holds barred coarseness of the acting and delivery within the fabulous, bizarre staging. The boxes either side of the stage were adorned with brothel-Titian paintings, red-shaded lights and strange bunches of black satin to make dripping, sculptured, brothel-walls of fantasy. These walls were then, in perfect detail, recreated three times at odd angles on the stage so the theatre, as if by mirrors, became the setting for Genet's play. The Carmen actress performed all the whores. Economy, but sense was made of it. The Chief of Police was in SS uniform, Hitler moustache, jack-boots and Nazi salute with swastika armband. Wham bang. Roger the revolutionary was black. Robert David MacDonald had cut a lot. When I saw the play in an RSC production, it was three hours and twenty minutes; at the Citizens they'd lost an hour of that . . .

But the play wasn't harmed. Genet's writing is half in, half out of the theatre: he writes for a theatre that doesn't exist, to drum up a theatre that will never be wholly performable, as if there's something about his work that's twisted into some fifth, sixth or seventh dimension of dreams and poetry. He's a visionary and a cheating trickster, all in one. You look and it's crude stuff, you look again and it's brilliant dramatic writing; difficult, pretentious, la-de-da, high-flown, poetical rubbish then whoosh, it jells and anyone can understand it. What price craven 'populism' if a huge public can twig Jean Genet?

Afterwards Giles Havergal and Robert David MacDonald took me out for a drink. We talked nineteen-to-the dozen about Genet, the Citizens. They wanted to know all about the trial. Two huge hawks, swooping on anecdotes, stories, gossip, ideas, jokes. They were very kind and encouraging. I think their view is that the theatre is disreputable and pretends at its cost to be anything else.

*

Cold Glasgow. The cold is in the stones of the buildings and the pavements. Children are everywhere in the streets, in groups of five or more, most of them under ten years old. You hear them in the early morning and late at night. I couldn't understand a word they said. Giles and David drove me late at night to see 'the bridge', an abandoned one hundred and fifty yards of motorway in the middle of the city, up on stilts, going from the window of one third storey of an old building to another. When the money went in the early seventies, this 'inner ring road' or whatever was just stopped. It is a local monument and joke. I'm a tourist. What are we doing, thought the tourist, smashing the surface of the planet and smashing lives up with the human artefact we call Glasgow? Who was and is to blame? Who deserves a bullet in the back of the neck for that lot and then who will put it right? Beautiful Glasgow, though. I'd be very happy to live there, despite the mythologically 'dangerous streets'. Which are dangerous.

*

Billy Connolly sent a very funny letter to the theatre complaining about my reading in high Calvinist tones.

How slandered the play's been! It's just coming home to me. I see it in people's faces after the show. They can't believe that they find it simply a story, a play with a story. What on earth can their preconceptions be, built from the attacks on the piece and the scandal? A pit of snakes? And what do they expect the author to be? Some horrific, bald, red-eyed creature with a mack on and sores around his mouth, crouched in a chair mumbling obscenities at his knees?

*

Today's journey: leave Glasgow at 11.15 am, change at Preston and arrive in Liverpool at 3.23 pm. Read the play this evening at the Liverpool Playhouse Studio. Stay the night I know not where. Then tomorrow's journey to Banbury via Birmingham, and a few days out.

I can't wait for the reading tonight. Tiredness is the only problem. At the end of the Citizens' reading I felt every cell in my body was leaking steam. A wonderful feeling, but it's called 'exhaustion' and is not an addiction to be trifled with.

TUESDAY 23RD FEBRUARY

I woke up this morning to a lovely Liverpool morning of mist and sunshine. I stayed with Bill Morrison and his wife Val. We were up carousing and talking, theatre gossip, of cats and of ancestors, until 3 am. Great Irish hospitality.

11.45 am, writing this on a train, Liverpool to Banbury. We speed, rattle and bump through thick fog, beneath it the hoar frost glittering white on the long grass of the embankments.

*

The corridors of the Liverpool Playhouse were a gloomy maze of red fire doors and chipped, thick paint. The theatre's staff were at full stretch with a musical version of *The Erpingham Camp* in its technical. The strain was on everyone's face, that fuzziness from being hot and in need of a sleep and bath.

*

I arrived at the theatre at 3.30 pm. and at once gave two interviews, one press, the *Daily Post*, and one for a Merseyside radio station. The radio interviewer was a comrade, the newspaper man a pro. This morning he wrote up the interview fairly, and next to it there was a rave review of the reading!

I stood in the buffet of Liverpool Lime Street Station fizzing with joy. A good review? I beamed. I circled round the self-service rabbit-run for a cup of coffee, went right through without buying anything and came back to my table and picked up the *Daily Post* again. The review was still in it, and it was still a rave! This is appalling behaviour! I am still radiating pleasure. I have six copies in my bag. So this is what a good notice does to a performer. Enough of this. I'll post it to Andrew in London, and he can circulate it to the dates ahead. Fizz! Come on what is this, you hard playwright, who has weathered the worst critical battering since Edward Bond without a scratch, rolled over by unexpected praise? Yuck. Yippee.

*

On the outskirts of Wolverhampton the train bumps on beside a green, slime-watered canal with a vast, burnt embankment.

*

In Liverpool they've just closed a school to give the pupils two weeks' breathing space to calm down. A primary school, children eight and nine years old. They were smashing the classrooms and the teachers' cars and beating teachers up. The children, I am told, are disturbed throughout the city. This is not one incident. Parents are finding their children gone mad. It's like Hitchcock's *The Birds*. As in the early scenes of the film people look up and say, 'What's the matter with the birds?' so in Liverpool they are looking up and saying, 'What's wrong with the kids?'

The city is dying. The docks are losing trade. The black economy is rife. Families are leaving the system and living as best they can doing fly-by-night building jobs, roofing and pointing, plastering in the middle-class districts, the second-hand car market, theft, moonlighting. The Liverpool Council is in the grip of a fantasy about a ring road. But the traffic load is decreasing. Liverpool is being passed by. It's the recession, the unemployment, the dereliction. 'How is it ever going to be put to rights?' I asked. 'It's not. Ever,' was one reply. The clubs are packed with drinkers on black economy money. Children move house, leaving a drunken father or mother, moving in with a friend's parents: a kind of improvised fostering has begun.

I was hearing about something terrible, 'the ruin of Britain' in slow motion. The black economy means gangsterism, some doing well if they've got the wit, the flyness and the evil, while others go to the wall. People are living outside any welfare, democracy or social justice. Life becomes more and more vicious and precarious; Rolls Royces and flash hotels for a few who do well, the gangsters and the local 'impresarios', poverty and worry for most.

SUNDAY 28TH FEBRUARY

I'm staying with friends, Paul and Grace Merchant, in Leamington Spa, before reading at Warwick University Students' Union. Paul teaches in the English Department. Paul gave me a wonderful present three years ago while I was writing *The Romans in Britain*: three objects, a stone-age hand axe, and two fragments of pottery picked up in a field that was once Chesterton Roman Camp, straddling the Fosse Way. One bit of pottery is Roman, picked up at what was the centre of the camp; the other is Celtic, picked up just outside. You imagine huts of the locals who worked inside the camp but lived outside it. When my wife and I took our children to the site we walked through the ploughed field and one of our young sons picked up a piece of Roman floor tile. While I wrote the play I'd often have these bits and pieces on the table by my typewriter. They were like a map of the play, or a mantra, a key: I'd stare at them when I was stuck.

*

My sister drove me to Leamington from where she lives. Our families have had the week together. On the way we drove to Edge Hill, the site of the first battle of the Civil War. There's a pub which was a folly built in the eighteenth century on the spot where Charles I set his standard on the long ridge overlooking the battlefield. From the pub's garden you look down the steep slope through the trees at fields, still buckled with traces of strip farming, where the two armies fought to a bloody stalemate on 23 October 1642. On another visit we found 'the red road', which runs from the village of Kineton, four miles away, to the heart of the battlefield. The wounded came down it all that long afternoon. It's disused now and ends in a wire fence with a Ministry of Defence notice telling you not to trespass. From the ridge to your right, amongst the hedgerows and small woods, you can see concrete bunkers, low and greyish white in a regular pattern over a huge area. This is a combined Arms Dump where they store nuclear warheads for the three services. Driving around the minor roads in the area it suddenly strikes you that there are telephone wires everywhere, radio masts, single-line rail tracks coming out of the woods, unmade roads of apparent insignificance blocked off by red warning signs. A baleful atmosphere hangs over the fields and copses. The English Midlands are pretty: you look again and the English Midlands are an armed military camp. American servicemen are everywhere, but discreetly, they have their own pubs from which the locals are discouraged, their own schools, shops and housing estates on their bases. This peaceful, green landscape is a terrible place. Where the first battle for a republican England was fought they now store atom bombs. When they laid the foundations of the concrete bunkers did they dig a few bones of Levellers who fought in the battle that bit deeper? The defeat of republican England goes on and on and on, eh?

At my sister's I did some work on *Danton's Death*. My brother-in-law is a local teacher and a Punch and Judy man, who has a busy summer season taking the sausages and the crocodile around Northamptonshire and Oxfordshire garden fêtes and fairs. He's also an amateur magician. He showed me Houdini's beheading trick, transposed head and all, in an odd and rather rare book. What an extreme routine! Bizarre, elaborate – Peter Gill wants the guillotine in the National production of *Danton*. If he does the Houdini method, that's eight weeks' rehearsal plus hospital bills.

*

The last few days I've been talking with Andrew on the phone about the dates ahead. Also the reading by the actors at the Old Vic. Because I'm on the road we asked Charles Hanson to cast it. He was the assistant director on the National production. But Michael's lawyers have asked him to have nothing to do with it because he's going to be a witness. They also said I shouldn't be involved. Their concern is that a judge may freak if he finds that key witnesses have been waving red rags at the public in the days just before the trial. I understand about not having Peter Sproule or Greg Hicks take part, they'll have enough rubbish to put up with in the witness box, we must spare them the possibility of the judge fulminating against them as well. But I can't *not* be involved with the Old Vic reading. I'm learning too much reading it solo – I must have a whole day with the company and stage it as I want. And I'm eager to read my new stage directions with them. No, I'm going to do it. The lawyers phrase is 'keeping the witnesses clean'. But my hands are dirty. I'm on this tour, I wrote the play. No.

MONDAY 1ST MARCH

Now I'm at Warwick University, a guest of the Student Union. It's raining. The concrete of the campus is sodden, and the windows are steamed up. I'm sitting in the Arts Centre coffee bar. It's typical of the 'Arts Centres' built in the sixties on university campuses. It's a white elephant, a car-drive away from any public and ignored by most of the students. It has an ugly main house but a good studio theatre.

I spent a happy and turbulent year here, 1978 to 1979, as 'Resident Writer'. I got some free teaching. A maths teacher gave me an idea for my new play *The Genius* [premiered at the Royal Court in 1983]. I ran a weekly workshop, wrote in the student newspaper, did a farewell improvised play and wrote most of *The Romans*, sitting in a sun-trap, concrete-walled, little garden at the back of my campus flat. It was an idyll. Rolf Lass, one of the teachers in the English Department and an old mentor from my Cambridge days, even got me reading Anglo-Saxon poetry for the first time.

Sadly all the students I knew in 1979 have left. The generations pass in a university, three years on and nothing of the young people I knew, what they did or thought, is left. There's no transmission of memory amongst 'the student body'. They have tradition, but no memory.

I've lost my tobacco. The rain's drenched my trousers. There's no advertising for the reading. Everything's grey and smelling of rotting grass. And I have a premonition: they've got the day wrong!

Right. To the gents to clean up, to the University bookshop to cheer up, then I'll go and find Dave Chumbley, organiser of this gig.

*

I just rang Andrew – care of a free phone in the Union office – about the arrangements for the final reading with the cast at the Old Vic. The lawyers are saying 'no publicity'. Equity have mentioned it in a newsletter – but what actors read that? – we'll have to drum up the audience by word of mouth. Then Andrew says the penultimate reading, at the Nottingham Playhouse, is set for 10.30 at night! I panic. I won't be through until 1.30 am. Who will come, who will stay? Should I edit? 'Don't,' says Andrew.

*

Back to reality at Warwick University. I'll be reading in 'The Elephants Nest', a room at the top of the seventies' Union building, all arty odd angles with pillars. I'm warned there'll be a disco down below. Could be a tough gig. I think I'll be in the room and chat with anyone who turns up, so if it's Paul, Grace and a couple of homophobic beer-swillers (every University has 'em!) *some* decency will be preserved.

*

11.10 pm. It was packed and went wonderfully well. They kept on coming, I zapped around the room, arranging chairs for them. Some sat on the floor, others stood – for the whole reading – at the back.

When I arrived, the room was filthy. Fag ends, beer mugs, full ashtrays.

*

Performance notes. I got a jolt, I couldn't concentrate on the introduction, I didn't tell them the date (27 August 54BC). Shocked, I clenched all the concentration I could summon. The audience were laughy. I tried to make the reading quicker and lighter, dropping 'he said, they said' bridges, confident that I was syncopating the voices distinctly.

It was very sweet to do the reading again. I've missed it. But now I'm going to have the next problem with a show – decay. It can 'go off' in two ways: proficiency, I could glaze an audience by being efficient – 'All those voices he does . . . listen to him' – rather than getting them to hear the voices, see the bodies they come from; secondly, mannerism, I could relish throwing my voice around for the sake of it. So, again and again, take John Barton's advice, 'coin it!' Every line spoken as if it's for the first time.

WEDNESDAY 3RD MARCH

In London for the day. At lunchtime I went to the National to see

Michael Bogdanov. He was in good heart. Michael's found out about the judge. He is Christopher Staughton QC. It will be his first case as a judge. He's forty-nine, was educated at Eton and Cambridge, an ex-army officer in the 11th Hussars and is an expert in shipping cases. He plays bridge and grows dahlias. I scan the text desperately – Caesar's ships are mentioned, but there are no dahlias.

Michael said he wants the jury to see a performance. If we can't bring that off, I offered to read the play to the jury and asked Michael to see what he thinks when he hears the reading at Leicester.

We go through our arguments about the attempted rape scene. He and Andrew are going to the Old Bailey on Friday to case the gig. From what I remember, sitting in the public gallery at the Old Bailey a few years ago to see what went on, the difficult thing is that the pace of the proceedings is odd. They write everything down. Words hobble in a law court.

We discussed whether Michael can keep out of the cells or not – he may have to sleep there. We talked of 'evidence as performance', how all the rules of performance apply: keep a clear head, if you make a mistake go on, speak up, concentrate, instate your timing not theirs.

The 'proof' of my evidence was waiting for me. I amended a few things, but it's fine, a credit to the National's solicitor, Richard Butcher, who's worked hard on this.

The feeling of the lawyers is that we will lose. We have no illusions about the ugliness of this matter. They want to destroy our theatre using the law of Olde England, and they can.

THURSDAY 4TH MARCH

On the train. At Birmingham International station, the 'National Exhibition Centre', a dozen lads, sixteen or seventeen years old, with 'official visitor' badges on their jackets, sway onto the train chanting 'Oggi oggi oggi'. The English know no songs, only football chants. 'Oggi oggi oggi' is a folk-song.

Birmingham to Wolverhampton. The occasional 'For sale' notice up before a factory in the jumbled-up, crumpled industrial landscape of black shed roofs, red brick, glass, chimneys, derelict sites red with the brick debris of levelled buildings, canals, walls and the old houses, terraces of tiny windows beneath tiny roofs and the new estates being grimed and run down into slums. In the distance, beneath an apocalyptically deep grey sky, motorways on stilts curve amongst blocks of working-class flats.

I'm met at the station by Philip Tilstone, a nice man, enthusiastic and putting himself out to help. He drives me to a live interview with a local radio station, Beacon Radio, in between the pop music. It's great to sound off out of earshot of London lawyers. Then, in the Wolverhampton rain, Phil drives me to the Poly-technic, a rambling warren of an agglomeration of buildings, cor-ridors, and dead-end walkways. It's an ugly studio with a brown, parquet floor, jet black drapes, seats in a bank. After a local press interview – hostile, Daily Mailish – I sit in Phil's office till 5.30, feeling very tired. The office has marks of institutional poverty about it, even in the odd assortment of drawing pins on the notice board. 'Scrape, save, fear the cuts!'

*

I wasn't happy with the reading. Phil's anticipated full-house didn't materialise: twelve came. There'd been a student sit-in against the cuts, and they'd packed it in and all gone home. The twelve were very tense, I couldn't get humour going for them. They must have thought it was all very odd. I began to do too much, then Caesar became a ghost to me and I couldn't present him at all. Chichester was good. But I was fighting against myself all the time. The journey, the ugly office, the interviews had spent something, and I couldn't get it back. An 'extra long' British Rail sausage-roll lay in my stomach. So that's what acting is like on a really bad night: the feeling of doing something utterly pointless is overwhelming! I had to dredge reserves to talk about the play, the case etc. to students afterwards with every cell screaming, 'Out! Out! Out of Wolver-hampton.'

Then came the best event of the day: I met Chrissie Poulter and her man, Tom, who were waiting in the station car-park to drive me to Birmingham.

Within five minutes I felt I'd known them for years. We fell into a Birmingham Indian restaurant, ordered a huge meal and rapped until one o'clock in the morning.

Back in the street, the three of us witnessed a full-scale gangster-like chase between two Ford Cortinas, suspensions tilted, the screeches of tyres echoing in the sodium-lit, concrete landscape. Ah, celebrate England's second city, the gangsters, the clubs, the bodies of murdered accountants entombed in the flyovers! Actually, it's a dreary, recession-gripped city, all semblance of a human scale torn apart by the planners. The middle classes, and no doubt the gangsters, do all they can to get out and live in Kidderminster.

*

Morning: an interview on the phone with a DJ on a Derby radio station. I lay on the bed, a scarf round my neck, trying to nurse my consonants. 'Recording now, Howard. Here's Terry.' ''Ello 'Oward, Terry 'ere,' said a cockney voice. 'Hello Terry,' I said, hitting the T. I began to feel potty. Good questions, though: he knew the play was England in Ireland. Because I'm challenged directly, I can speak directly, a relief after the 'you wrote this play 'cos you're bent, didn't you' subtext of some journalists' questions.

*

The Allardyce Nicoll Studio is in the basement of a tower block in the Arts Faculty, on Birmingham University campus. The theatre's a good space, but the block was built by Charles Poulson and it's horrible: you look for the plasticine in the cracks. The most frightening thing in the building is the kind of lift England's most famous architect installed: human dumbwaiters, one going up the other going down, in perpetual movement. You judge your moment and jump on. Try doing it with a cup of coffee.

SATURDAY 6TH MARCH

Notes. Two hours before I do it.

1.) Cut down the actor's exercises.
2.) Be ready at the half, sit in the dressing room.
3.) Relax and relax them.
4.) Go through the landscapes of the play, the colours, the look, the weather of the play.
5.) No eating. A spoonful of honey. Maybe foolhardy, but you've got to light up in the reading chair, get sinew, expression, syncopation, all the rhythms vivid again.
6.) Wake up! Wake them up! If it's just a man and a dog in the audience? OK man, OK dog, get this!

*

1.40 am. My my. The best so far. I'm bewildered. I did nothing, far less than before. It's frightening: I don't know why it worked.

*

The 3.50 to Derby. A new high-speed train, 'The Devonian', pristine and empty but for middle-aged men in padded anoraks and with camping packs, in charge of nine-year-old children, similarly equipped. They must be going to Devon, to walk on the moors. The kids run along the carriage to find the buffet, giggling about hamburgers.

*

Derby Station, into a taxi: 'Friary Hotel please'. 'Fawlty Towers, the snooker players call it,' the driver says.

A foyer of fake, dark wood and two real coal fires, a moose's head over the bar. The chairs are of worn green velvet with sagging tassels. A sign reads 'Under new management. P. Donovan.' 'Just a minute,' said the man at the reception desk, 'it's chaos. The book's here somewhere.' He ducked down under the desk, rummaging papers. I looked down; the book was in front of me on the desk.

Now on his knees, his head popped up, level with the book. 'Oh, there it is.' The taxi driver was right, it's just like Fawlty Towers. Even the moose is there.

*

I'm not reading tonight, and, feeling like a spaceman, I wander out on this Saturday afternoon. We Martians are perspex, people look right through us. The shopping precincts and the shops are deserted. From within a brightly-lit shop full of hi-fi equipment, a tubby young salesman stares out of the window, his right leg twitching to a private tune. At 4.30 on a Saturday afternoon Peckham is packed. On this tour I've seen northern towns empty of customers on late afternoons, perpetual 'Sale' notices in the windows of shoe, clothes, hi-fi and furniture shops.

The streets of Derby seem to have been spared the planners' blast; they have a tatty, red-brick look. I like the town. On a bus I hear the beautiful, soft, sardonic dialect. I've heard so many voices of my country on this tour; the greatest, in bloom and power of expression, was Geordie.

SUNDAY 7TH MARCH

Last night there was a disco in the hotel and I went down to have a look at it. The men in sharp suits, some with velvet lapels, their hair shaped and finely cut; the women in high heels and short skirts, elaborate hair-dos, silky calves, gold belts, painted toe-nails. I was looking in on a complete, self-sufficient world. There are kids, too. I go to the reception. 'Do you think you could ask them to turn the disco down a bit?' The man (P. Donovan?) stares at me. 'That's Terry Griffith's disco. You seriously want me to go and ask Terry Griffiths to turn his disco down?'

Terry Griffiths, the great snooker player . . . The professional circus is in town for the Yamaha Organ Trophy.

*

10.50 pm. Back at the hotel. Did it. Not bad. Well within myself, a bit . . . glacial. I find that I now know whole tracts of the play by heart. A warning: you're not jolted as you once were, when the 'visuals in your head' go. The rule, 'see it as you speak, then they will see it' still applies.

A magnificent scene in this hotel. The snooker players are of two groups. There are the older hands, a little shabby in their cardigans, a chalk-on-the-knuckles aspect to them, and there's the new generation of players, princes and swashbucklers with known-on-TV faces, in elaborate shirts and fine suits, accompanied by beautiful young women in high-heeled shoes. They all seemed a nice bunch, some with families and children, relaxed, friendly to the punters around them and their groupies, extras and local players flattered to be drinking with them. I have a drink at a table with some of the older guys. 'Terry, he's lovely,' says one. 'Looks after us,' says another. What I think happens is that the older players, from the pre-TV days, still take part but are knocked out in early rounds which the viewer never sees; this way the fathers of the modern game are looked after by its flashy, and rich, sons. And they all spend their time together, moving like a circus, or modern sports court of monarchs of the green baize, from town to town. It's an interesting world; could theatre move like this, a festival of shows, big and large, from town to town for a season?

MONDAY 8TH MARCH

A busy day, whizzing around the Midlands. I was picked up at the Friary Hotel by James Beresford, Press Officer for the Nottingham Playhouse. Interviews. One with a bright young woman then one with an old bogey, Frank Higgins, who sometimes gave Richard Eyre's management at the Playhouse a hard time. Frank and I chaffed each other: it's all blood under the bridge. Then a live interview at the local radio station with the board sitting upstairs and a lawyer in the corner of the studio. A good professional did the programme. There are journalists 'out in the sticks' who are much better at their jobs than some of the fat cats down on the London, national papers.

After the lawyer-scrutinised radio interview I was picked up by Vicky Allen of East Midlands Arts. She drove me to the Phoenix Theatre, Leicester, for an interview with a Leicester radio station. The Phoenix looks gungy, that is shabby and alive. Then Vicky drove me to Northampton and I booked into a big, bland hotel, 'The Grand': muzak of lonely pianos, fish in a big tank, bubbly cream wallpaper everywhere and acre after acre of glaring vermilion carpet.

For the first time exhaustion's a problem. I've given four interviews and been in four different towns in six hours. I have an hour and, deciding against a cat-nap, I throw my aching, early-middle-aged body into a thorough work-out in the steamy hotel bathroom.

*

The Arts Centre at the Northampton College of Education: the place is full of chaotic evidence of constant use; posters are impacted on the walls. The students are at ease in the place; they're dressy, too, post punk. I improvised a dressing room for myself in a paint shop and gargled amongst paint pots and brushes. Working out in the studio, I fell through a rostrum! A basic nightmare while being on tour: that the stage collapses under you. No harm done.

The audience was young, with twenty members of the public and a party of fifteen-year-old school children. The work-out in the hotel and the challenge of an audience who didn't know me from Adam, and who were in danger of collapsing in giggles at the material, woke me up. Two of the school children giggled and whispered to each other right through the first half. I worked and worked to keep their attention. What did they talk of? They were using as many words as I was, up front! I really got them with the app-earance of the British Army, though.

After the reading Vicky took me to an opulent Italian restaurant. 'The only one open past eleven in this town.' How many times have I heard that said about these towns on tour? I begin to think my country's hardly open for anything.

Phew, what a day. Vicky and I woofed the chianti down; she was much relieved. I think she had feared there would be 'an incident'.

TUESDAY 9TH MARCH

At lunchtime I went back to the Arts Centre and talked to the students who were at the reading last night. They were sparky and sharp. Their questions and their attention made me break the ground rules of the tour and put the matter of the coming trial to them, in confidence and humorously. It was good to joke about the prosecution, its baleful seriousness and ludicrous pretension. It may have been 'indiscreet' to speak my mind about the attacks on my work and the branding of Michael Bogdanov as a pimp, because he directed my play. As a guest I didn't want to compromise the excellent Martin Banks, who runs the Arts Centre, but we mustn't shut up. The mechanisms to make us shut up turn a deadly clockwork, everywhere.

*

After the talk, I get some of the politics of Colleges of Further Education from Martin and a couple of his colleagues. These places are being flooded with school leavers under the Government's various schemes to keep them off the unemployment register. The college bulges with a surplus of the young unemployed. Northampton makes shoes, local unemployment is at twelve and a half per cent: it's higher in other places but this, traditionally, is the fattest of Midland towns. In the thirties it escaped the ravages of the first depression, but it is getting hit badly by the second in the early eighties.

The teachers are divided about the new education reforms. It means more rapid promotion and the teachers' unions don't oppose the policy. But clearly it's immoral. For students who need and want the facilities of the College, suddenly it's crowded, there's discomfort and lack of materials to go round. For the unemployed it's a pain in the neck being stuffed back into classrooms. When I passed through Leicester, the Phoenix Theatre was packed with an audience of young people who are unemployed. They were enjoying a free afternoon film show paid for by Leicester Council. It was a rock 'n' roll-cum-gangster film of the mid-sixties.

Dump the young, that's the policy. Dump them in Colleges of Further Education or in improvised cinemas, anywhere, but dump them. If you can fiddle their heads off the count of the unemployment register by listing them as students, all the better. Let local education budgets take the strain, particularly in Labour towns.

*

In the Station Hotel, outside Wellingborough's tiny, rural-like railway station, waiting for the Nottingham train, I sat alone in the bar listening to an Abbey National insurance man plying his trade over the beer nozzles to the landlady of the pub. She let slip personal details of a lifetime's hard work in a difficult trade, of family illness. In the conversation over the salesman's tables and pocket calculator there was a kind of longing for green pastures and a world without cares. Though what happens when people retire? Ill health, depression, suddenly, after a life's work you're flooded with a spiritual meaninglessness? No sweet fields, I fear. Present sweat is happiness.

*

5.15 pm. I was collected in the foyer of a grandly bland hotel by two guys and driven to the Open University in Milton Keynes.

Confident people met me, glad that I'd come. A difficult gig: I read in a common room. Modernish, nowhere architecture; the room had a softish, nylon carpet, curtains. I tried the room three ways, but I couldn't find a way of hearing myself off a back wall.

The room was full and the reading went well, but I found not hearing myself disturbing. I worried about wrenching my voice; keeping concentration was hard. The carpet soaked everything up.

THURSDAY 11TH MARCH

Nottingham. At 11 am I meet Joan Bakewell and do an interview with her for BBC 2's 'Newsnight' programme. Joan and I walk up and down outside the Playhouse, pretending to chat without a care in the world, while a few feet in front of us the director and the camera crew walk backwards. We repeat this several times, including, I suppose for reasons of art, a shot of our feet. Whether interview and feet will get through the BBC lawyers is dodgy. Joan will do what she can.

An evening meal with good friends, Pat and Bill Silburn. Trevor Griffiths turned up with Jill, passing through. Trevor and I spar for a while, as playwrights do.

THURSDAY 11TH MARCH

Sleep on the tour has become fractured and full of dreams. This afternoon, napping before going to the theatre, I dreamt that hundreds of us were in a huge cathedral, quarantined because we had 'a contagious mental disease' (!). Outside the cathedral there was the English countryside and 'the barrier'. There followed a sumptuous pageant of a dream in which there grew new societies, split into tribes, who invented new sciences, clothes, behaviour, fought wars, made entertainments amongst the gothic pillars, arches and sunlit stained-glass windows. We partitioned the cathedral off, hanging up banners and tapestries. There was one telephone to the outside world, in a side chapel. We never used it. We began to speed up, centuries of history were condensed into weeks, days, then minutes. In one episode I went outside to look at 'the barrier'. It was a hedgerow in a field, nothing unusual about it. But on the slope beyond there were thousands of cars, film cameras, army vehicles, all the lenses and windscreens pointing up at the huge edifice of the cathedral behind me. It was a comic and pleasurable dream, like a vast novel.

*

At the Nottingham Playhouse I was in dressing room 'C', Paul

Dawkins' old dressing room. Paul played Alfred Bagley in *Brass-neck*, the comedy David Hare and I wrote together to open Richard Eyre's season at this theatre, and he played Churchill in *The Churchill Play*. Sadly, Paul died a few years back. In 1974 I sat in that dressing room with Paul, discussing Oscar Wilde with him. Paul was a declared bankrupt, unable to have a bank account; all his worldly possessions were in a large, old-fashioned trunk. He delved into it and gave me a script he'd written about Oscar. There was something graceful and elegant about Paul, despite what I fear was a difficult life: it was as if there was a dancer hidden in his shambolic body. A terrible sadness overcame me.

*

There actually were people there, a hundred and twenty-seven of them. Geoffrey Strachan came from Methuen, it was great to see him. I missed Caesar and just read it technically, seeing nothing. I didn't begin to read the second half until 12.20 am! It was strange being on the main stage in a big space again, after the studios of the last few readings. I was eager to be bright and positive because of the late hour. Two policemen were there, spottable through the light haze, in civvies, looking shabby and lonely. One applauded at the end of Part One the other did not, neither stayed for Part Two. Otherwise I lost four. Not bad.

FRIDAY 12TH MARCH

The last reading at Michael Bogdanov's old theatre, the Leicester Phoenix. My wife, Andrew Leigh and Michael were there. I was fighting exhaustion. A stupid little thing bothered me: when I came to wash my hair around four o'clock before going to the Phoenix, I found I'd left my shampoo in the Nottingham hotel. I washed my hair in plain hot water. It became greasy and plastered to my head. In the dressing room at the Phoenix I combed it again and again. I walked out on the stage feeling a freak, not at all relaxed. This sounds so prissy, so poncy! I was tired and easily upset and overcome by wanting to do well in front of Michael, Jane, Andrew and a fair-sized audience.

But going crazy about my hair . . . it did show me, in a risible way, how essential self-confidence is in a performance. The jokes about an actor's vanity before a dressing room mirror are wrong – it's not about vanity, it's about self-control.

I felt the audience were serious and a bit stuffy, I couldn't get the humour going for them. With 'Caesar' I woke up and I heard and saw him clearly: a reversion to the pattern of bad nights at the National when audiences didn't settle until the redoubtable Michael Bryant hit Caesar and the static, 'well-written' speeches reassured them. I kicked myself in the interval, concentrated and did Part Two as well as I've ever done it.

Afterwards the evening was drunken and serious by turns. We laughed with Michael's old friends in the bar. Then Grahame Watkins took Michael, Andrew, my wife and me to a restaurant in the fat suburbs of Leicester. Huge buildings: the money that was once in that town . . . ! (And probably still is, for there to be a restaurant like that.) We rapped about the trial, we ate, we drank.

SATURDAY 13TH MARCH

Michael, Andrew, Jane and I met on the 10.25 am train back to London. We had a great morning's journey, the four of us sitting in the buffet, the fields through the window in brilliant sunlight.

Michael's lawyers are worried about the interview with Joan going out on Monday night, because I'll be in the box giving evidence the following day. He agrees with their argument, which is, 'Don't get on the wrong side of the judge, keep Howard "clean".' Privately, though, this pisses me off. I don't like being shut up, I don't like suppressing anything, our only hope is to get to the public; and I said nothing in the interview that I've not said many times before. But I defer to Michael. The aim next week is to win and bury the new Right, Puritan England; or, more modestly, at least to put a spade in the turf to begin the grave. If the interview won't help us win, stop it: the Stalinist in me understands.

SUNDAY 14TH MARCH

The day of the reading with the whole cast at the Old Vic, with the author doing the stage directions. In the morning, the actors assembled in the Old Vic's rehearsal room. Coffee. 'Don't look at the kettle while it's boiling,' said Andrew: a new superstition to me! We cast the reading: Michael Bryant as Chichester as well as Caesar, Melvyn Bedford as the raping soldier and Peter Harding as Marban, Joss Buckley as the Steward in the Dark Age scenes, Jane Evans as Adona. I was very grateful to Melvyn and Peter for taking the 'contentious' roles. Apart from these, the cast was the same as at the National. We bashed through it and were done by twenty-five past one. Then, 'Newsnight' arrived with a film crew; the news about Michael's lawyers wanting to stop the coverage hadn't reached the director. Despicably, I decided not to tell him, the lawyers may yet agree. Geoffrey Robertson told me on the phone that he's keen on the Newsnight extract going ahead as well as the other contentious item: Nick Kent's dramatised reading of the trial, day by day as it happens, at the Oxford Playhouse (Patrick Allen and Hugh MacDiarmid are taking part).

But I was worried that the lawyers hadn't got to the BBC. Lawyers are fitful; they're calm, then suddenly they're waving their arms in the air. It's very public school: they're afraid of judges in the way that prefects are afraid of a headmaster, trying to read his likely opinions and moods.

They finished filming extracts from the reading at half-past three, then we ran the reading. We finished at six-fifteen. I hid in Andrew's office, went round the dressing rooms giving a few notes.

It was wonderful to sit on the Old Vic's stage with a company of top actors as they zinged the lines around that beautiful theatre.

Michael had crept into the stage door just before and had gone round the dressing rooms. His lawyers had told him not to hear the reading. At the end he was waiting down in the wine bar, sitting in front of a tank of tropical fish, grinning: we all flooded in and swept him up in our arms.

POSTSCRIPT (14th AUGUST 1994)

After four days, the prosecution of *The Romans in Britain* collapsed. The trial was abandoned by the reading of a 'nolle prosequi'; in effect by the Queen coming down to her court and saying, 'I stop this nonsense.' This was caused by Mary Whitehouse's lawyer going to the judge to tell him he no longer had confidence in the case against the play. My comrade, friend and fellow innocent, Michael Bogdanov, was set free from a court of Olde England, acquitted of being a pimp because he told actors to act. Michael went on to direct wonderful Shakespeare productions with a troupe he founded, the English Stage Company.

Twelve years later, getting this diary out of my loft and typing it up for this book, I have a sense of anguish for the people I met: for the actors who did the final reading with me at the Old Vic, for that shop assistant in Derby, that woman publican in Wellingborough, the Morrisons in Liverpool, the militant Midlands Arts officials, my riff-raff audiences in the small gigs, the snooker players, the drinkers on trains; Roger, Judy, Pat, Bill, Jill, Tony, Vicky, Rolf, Paul, Grace, Tony, Chrissie, Tom, Vicky, Grahame; John Goodwin and Nicky Moody in the National Theatre's Press Office, whom I rang daily and who counselled me endlessly; Peter Hall whom I remember wandering about the National's offices on the first day of the trial with a bag of dirty laundry, muttering 'first things first', making us all laugh; and for all the good souls who had the bottle to come up and just talk to me, during those nasty weeks.

The anguish is that we were in a nowhere time: the first recession of the Thatcher years. We all spent a lot of energy on an agenda that we didn't set: the defence of my play. If anybody who helped 'The Romans crew' is reading this, all these years later, thank you.

The tour didn't raise much money, about six thousand pounds. But we didn't have to pay any lawyers and Mary Whitehouse didn't get to waste a penny of precious theatre funds. The money is held in a trust for anyone in the theatre who gets into censorship difficulties.

For myself, I drew great strength from the experience of reading the play twelve times in three weeks. I had to behave like, think like and try to be an actor. It gave a playwright a hard lesson.

To Hayden Griffin and Fiona Williams

Troppo*
Rural Rides in North Queensland

This diary was written on a journey through 'FNQ', Far North Queensland, Australia, between the 17th and 19th parallels in the Tropic of Capricorn.

Returning to temperate England, where everything is subtly grey and dirty blue and bright red looks like dull vermilion, I doubt whether these jottings communicate the ferocity of the outer and inner landscapes of the tropics.

Ten hours back, jet-lagged, I stood staring at the River Thames with David Hare, who knows Australia. 'Does everything in England look as if it's under a tea cosy?' he said.

It did.

*

I was in FNQ in 1986 researching a story for a film. I went with Hayden Griffin, the theatre and film designer, my visual collaborator and the father of the idea for the project, and with Fiona Williams, whom the producers of the film employed as our business manager.

The three of us had a hell of a time, in the two senses of that phrase — difficult, also wonderful.

Of course, everyone knew whom I met. A stranger could not have moved about that landscape without it being known, all the time, but I've tried to keep to my undertaking 'to protect my sources'. People were universally friendly and talked to me freely. They seemed to find the sudden appearance of 'that pommy wanker' in the district rather funny.

I've no idea what the area is like now, nine years later. I hope I wasn't recording a way of life that was dying.

* Troppo: tropical madness. Also Italian for 'too much'.

A FACT OF LIFE

Once the cane is burnt, it must be in the mill within 24 hours, 36 at the outside.

A POLITICAL POINT

The order of burning is fixed by the Awards Board of the Cane Growers' Association. There is an advantageous time to burn, when the cane is at its sweetest. The farmers take it in turns – you burnt at the best time this year, next year your allotted time to burn will not be so good.

But, but . . .

The visitor, struggling to understand even the simplest facts about a farmer's year, is told contrary things about growing, burning and crushing sugar cane. In FNQ even basic information contains an 'imaginative', often totally imaginary, content.

VENDETTA

It has been known for someone to burn an enemy's fields, when the enemy's turn at the mill is not due – thus ruining him.

WASH DOWN

If you have a hillside of rain forest at the back of your cane field, you burn it off – so the soil will wash down from the hill onto your field. This is accepted practice.

JAP SHIPS

Raw sugar, the product of the mills, is driven in 55-ton trucks to the terminals at Cairns and Townsville, where it is shipped off for refinement in Japan. The refined sugar is returned to Australia for domestic consumption and export to the world markets.

CRIME STORY

On the coast, a few miles south of Port Douglas, there is a 'private motel' in a secluded bay. There are white wooden verandas from which you can step onto the beach. There are no other buildings near, no signs, and you can hardly see the 'motel' from the road. And there are no guests. It is a smuggling post for dope traffic, the visitor is told.

SOUND

In the rain forests, the noise of the screeching, drumming cicadas rises to an ear-splitting crescendo for a moment, then dies away.

DRINK

'Tinny' – a tin of beer. 'Stubby' – a bottle of beer. 'Stubby holder' – a polystyrene tube, in which a stubby is served to prevent your hand warming the beer.

PLACE

'Tassy' – Tasmania.

LOCAL HISTORY

On the top of Black Mountain, near Mossman, there is a rock 150 feet high, Black Thumb. Beside it, high above the rain-forested slopes of the mountain, there is a small clear platform, 'the Chinese garden', called so because the Chinese immigrants grew opium there and used Black Thumb rock as a look-out for their ship.

IT LOOKS . . .

The miles of flat light-green cane fields press against the steep sides of the mountains covered in dark green rain forest.

A RAIN FOREST PLANT

The Lawyer Cane – when young it has strong, thin tendrils six to eight feet long, covered with razor-sharp thorns. In this form it is called 'Wait a While'. The tendrils grow into the mighty 'Tarzan' creepers of the forests. They hang, wandering in the branches of the great trees. Eventually they get to the forest floor, and, at the end of a creeper which may be 30 to 40 metres long, they sprout into a young 'Wait a While'.

TRAINS, DISTANCES

The nearest railway terminal to Mossman is at Cairns, 70 miles to the south.

Cairns is 2,000 miles from Sydney, 2,200 miles by road. The train journey from Sydney to Cairns takes 5 days. (The drunken scenes on this journey are said to be appalling – that is legendary.)

The railways in North Queensland are a different gauge to other states. You have to change trains.

PRIDE IN DISTANCE

Local people are proud of their isolation, that the capital of Queensland, Brisbane, is 1,200 miles to the south.

TRAMWAYS

All across the landscape around Mossman the 'tramways' run. They are small-gauge railway lines, along the sides of fields, over bridges across the creeks, crossing roads and tracks suddenly out of the green banks of cane. The road signs are minimal. There are accidents.

Yellow trucks, the 'bins', take the cane to the mill. The bins are detachable. They wait on ramps beside a field. When full, they are loaded onto lorries owned by the mill and driven by 'transport drivers' to a tram terminal.

THE CRUSHING

The cane-cutting season – 'the crushing' – begins in June and ends in mid November.

THE SLACK

The rest of the year is called 'the slack season', simply 'the slack'.

THE MILL (i)

There is a local romance that the mill is full of antiquated 19th-century machinery,

Later, the visitor finds that this is merely the industry mythologising itself. The Mossman Mill is controlled through a Honeywell computer of great power. Twelve trained and trusted operators do the work that it took 120 to do, 25 years ago. A few old engines are kept running, partly as the Chief Engineer's hobby, partly to impress visitors.

But the process seems to the visitor to be old-fashioned; they have applied computerised control to an antiquated factory. Much of the machinery is relatively new, it is the thinking that is old-fashioned, but this is the tropics and thinking in the tropics is difficult.

BY-PRODUCTS

The crushing of sugar cane through the mill produces raw sugar and three by-products – begasses, the fibre of the cane plant used in the mill to fuel the furnaces; molasses, a treacly syrup (English 'golden syrup' is molasses cleaned up a bit; in America molasses is sold on 'the health food market' – where there is a mistaken impression that it is 'less harmful' than sugar); and mill mud, the dust, earth and scraps from the washed cane which is mixed with ash from the furnaces and returned to the fields as fertiliser.

WHAT SUN BIRDS DO

The sun bird builds a nest that hangs like a pendulum from the leaf of a plant.

One hung by the veranda on which the visitor began this sun bird notebook. Two sun birds watched from a tree. They are tiny, like lean sparrows, with brilliant yellow breasts and long curved beaks, a species of humming bird.

FABLED ODD ANIMAL

The duck-billed platypus lives in the banks of pools in the rain forest. The entrances to the burrows lie just below the water line. The visitor snorkelled in such a pool, along a bank where they are meant to live. Not surprisingly, they did not appear.

They are very shy. North Queenslanders you ask at once say they've seen a platypus – and hasten to add that it is unlikely that the visitor will.

MAKING A BUCK

The prices of goods in the few Mossman shops vary wildly along the main street, sometimes by 100%.

WASH AWAY

During 'The Wet', the monsoon, earth from the fields washes into the creeks, which run blood red. The sandbanks at the mouths of rivers and streams are modern creations of the cane industry, caused by the massive erosion.

TALL TALES

White North Queenslanders, rich or poor, love mystery in their conversation, whether it be spun from total ignorance or from intimate knowledge. It is not that they lie, they spin yarns. They love to shock a visitor, not to impress but to test his stupidity. Oddly, the more stupid you seem, the more they appear to like you, and the more they end up telling you.

The truth of anything in the yarns is a moveable feast, be it about a plant, an animal, a farming practice.

Yarning crosses class boundaries. It is a North Queensland national characteristic. The visitor is definitely informed about something, quite non-controversial, by a millionaire mill director on the veranda of his ancestral house, drinking tea and eating chocolate cake, only to have it totally contradicted in a cane farmer's living room a few hours later, with a pet wallaby pissing on the floor and a one-day test match on the TV.

One difficulty is that if an informant suspects you have been told something by someone they dislike, he or she will do anything to discredit it.

The visitor begins to perceive the social and psychological landscape of tropical Far North Queensland to be as luxuriant, strange, virulent and forceful as that of the natural world.

LOCAL HEAVIES

The Cane Growers' Association, referred to as 'The Cane Growers', is dominated by five families of English descent. They are the big plantation owners. There are five directors of the mill, from the five families.

MORE LOCAL HEAVIES

Italian cane farmers, whose families first penetrated the area in the 1900s, have never been allowed on the board of the Cane Growers. Italian families speak of exclusion, a private club, an English conspiracy against them.

REALLY HEAVY LOCALS

On the other hand, an informant, not Italian and not a farmer, tells the visitor that there are three Sicilian-descended Mafia families who dominate real estate in the Mossman area and that they have invested in development associated with the notorious road through the forests around Cape Tribulation (see below).

Any information about who is the local power is not necessarily true. What is true is that the above things are said.

And what is said in the closed, intimate rural community around Mossman, is, by definition, therefore true.

Ideas, rumours, prejudices, put out creepers through the small society as strong and as far-reaching as the Lawyer Cane.

UNDER TREES

A few hundred yards from the main street of Mossman, on the

road north, there are huge rain trees. Aboriginals sit under them all day long.

TWO WORLDS

Across the main street, two pubs face each other. The Exchange Hotel is largely for white drinkers, The Mossman Hotel largely for aboriginals.

The visitor and his male companion park their conspicuously bright yellow four-wheel drive vehicle and stride into the aboriginal pub. As in a scene in a third-rate spaghetti Western, people stare, eyes follow them. Huge men in the opposite white pub swivel slowly on their stools to observe.

(Mossman main street looks like a set for a Western – verandas, colonnades of spindly iron work, wooden buildings of peeling weatherboard – though the illusion is broken by the bright window of a video hire shop.)

A WORD

The aboriginal word for crocodile is 'belgimo'.

TRIBES

There are three aboriginal tribes in the area (or what is left of them). The tribe of the coast and the Mossman valley floor; a tribe from the Atherton table lands; and a tribe that is coming down into the area from the north, walking the 'new road'. The intruders are causing trouble, the visitor was told by an aboriginal – there are fights.

LANGUAGES

There is not 'the aboriginal people' – there are many nations, who do not recognise each other as the same people. The aboriginals of the Mossman area cannot understand the language of the tribe coming down the road from Cook Town.

NON-HISTORY

Whites who lived with aboriginals, in the early colonial days, were called 'wild white men'. Aboriginals thought that whites were the 'inside-out spirits' of black people. So whites, in dealings with blacks, called themselves the spirits of the dead.

WHITES SAY . . .

Whites in Mossman say that the aboriginals of the Mossman area were cannibals until 1920.

MYTHICAL HISTORY . . .

Whites also say that aboriginals used to eat the Chinese settlers – that they preferred them because the Chinese were vegetarians, and the flesh tasted the better for it. (Racism is so strong in the area that anything said by whites about blacks is to be distrusted, of course.)

THE GIN JOCKEY

A gin is an aboriginal woman. A 'gin jockey' is a white man who sleeps with an aboriginal woman.

GIN ROOTING

'Gin rooting' is slang for having sex with aboriginal women.

'I know all about it,' says a farmer's wife. 'Men go gin rooting, no worries. Like my uncle, my uncle went gin rooting, catching VD, ay? What men do, men do, but if my son wanted one in the house I'd say out.'

Another farmer's wife on the same subject – 'What I say is, black, white, love each other we do, I mean they brought me up, know what I mean? But best we have nothing to do with each other.'

ROOTING

Rooting is common slang for sexual intercourse, as in the joke –

Q. Why is a woman on a one-night stand like a koala bear? A. 'Cos she eats roots and leaves.

A TERM
'Cc content' – the sugar content of cane.

A SIGHT
When a field of cane is burnt during the crushing, eagles and hawks hover in the smoke, hunting the snakes and small animals that run from the fire.

TWO IMPRESSIVE FACTS
Sugar cane is a grass. Tea is a species of camellia.

TEA PLANTATION
Near Daintree, the visitor sees a field of tea. The bushes are a bright, luscious, privet-green and cut level across the large field. It stretches away smooth as a billiard table to a wall of rain forest.

CHERRIES
Coffee beans are called 'cherries'.

GIN BAITING
An aboriginal told the visitor of a sport they play in a bar. Two black women are sitting at either end. The men go back and forth, telling each woman that the other is 'rooting' their man. Eventually the two women rush to the centre of the bar and fight, to the entertainment of the other drinkers.

SIT-DOWN MONEY
'Sit-down money' is aboriginal for the dole money.

HEAT
The temperature is in the high 90s. The humidity is thick. You

walk through wet curtains. You wear shorts and sandals. Sweat pours from the visitor. Contrary advice is given . . . Drink a lot, don't drink a lot as 'It comes straight out of you but'.

SALT

After a few days, the visitor, not given to any self-dramatising about his health, feels faint and ill. He goes for a walk – after two hundred yards, he finds himself on his knees with a word in his brain – 'salt'. He gets back to the house where he is staying and, nauseous, forces salt and water down him. It is revolting. In half an hour he has wholly revived. From then on he equips himself with sodium tablets and . . .

STAMINADE

Everyone replaces lost potassium with 'Staminade'. It is a bottle of pale green powder which, with water, makes a bright green drink. The visitor was told to drink at least ten glasses a day. He was once given a drink of it liberally laced with Bundaberg rum.

IN THE MOSSMAN HOTEL

Six-thirty in the evening, the visitor and his companions drink in the bar of the Mossman Hotel. The black drinkers are mostly far gone. They speak pidgin to each other, a rapping mix of English and aboriginal words. They are not in a good state. After ten minutes or so of unease at our presence, introductions are made and one guy in particular talks about Mossman and his life. He is less drunk than the others – that he has approached us makes the others relaxed. He has some residual 'top man' authority amongst these poor, blasted people, perhaps.

He says that he came to cut cane ten years ago. That two years ago the farmer that he works for gave him a small .plot of land, five acres. 'And he was a white man . . . ' he says. He says that until five years ago blacks did not have equal pay with white workers, now they do during the crushing. He discusses black and white. He compares his skin to that of the visitor's, arm against arm.

WELSH COLLEGE OF
LIBRARY
MUSIC & DRAMA

As he talks, his daughter, who is standing outside the pub in a fury, makes sorties into the bar and shouts at him. 'Come home! Mother and the baby want to eat!' She is furious with him. He orders four Fosters tinnies wrapped in brown paper, and eventually leaves.

A FLAG AND A SNAKE

Gerhart Van Heisling runs a coffee plantation near Daintree. He is Austrian. He has a story of being a starving child in refugee camps, of fistfuls of American dollars with nothing to buy but women's nylons. He wears a sarong and serves coffee to visitors on the veranda of his house.

The house is built of breeze blocks – against cyclones the windows have no glass or frames ('Who needs windows?') – and is in the shape of a child's toy castle, with battlements and a tower. His family flag, a crest upon it, flies from a pole on the tower.

In the plantation's processing shed he has a carpet snake in a sack. She has eaten a chook (chicken) – not one of his, a neighbour's, which makes him laugh. The snake bulges with a large lump in its midriff. He opens the sack to show the visitor but does not want to disturb the snake, as she would regurgitate the chook ('and the smell is horrible, you know?'). The snake will rest for three days and digest everything, feathers and bones. Its excrement is white and chalky.

Gerhart – 'Geb' – sells the coffee he grows locally and to visitors, whom he charges for sampling coffee on his veranda. He doesn't want to get into big-scale, commercial marketing. He is thinking of growing vanilla. He has some in a glass jar, six-inch long strips, the smell very strong.

His coffee is wonderfully strong. After two cups, colours brighten.

His wife left him a week ago. He seems content about it. He is in his forties, happy to maintain a self-contained existence running the coffee plantation, he is well-known in the area and maintains a good life, he says. 'Who needs it?' is a phrase he uses again and again, about travel, or business expansion, or sex.

PAY

A young man who has worked as a casual labourer, cleaning in the mill, says you are paid 10 to 15 dollars a day. He says 'as long as the mill is running, you don't have to look busy!'

A QUEENSLAND PHRASE

'Easy easy.' 'Steady steady.'

WHAT THEY ALL SAY

The sugar cane industry is in recession, because of EEC sugar beet flooding the world market.

THE WET

The visitor is in the district in the weeks before 'The Wet' – the monsoon – which is daily expected. The rainy season in January lasts for two months. But 'The Wet' is the true, tropical downpour that the rain forest and the cane crop need. From Reginald Laird's records, in the last ten years The Wet has come as early as January 3rd and as late as February 10th. There can be a two-week-long, constant downpour. The huge and darkly shady rain trees are said to open their leaves just before it comes. The visitor has been amazed at the heavy showers that fall now and then, for ten minutes or half an hour – he is warned that they are not at all like 'The Wet'.

REGINALD LAIRD

Reginald Laird came from London to the Daintree River to live alone in the rain forest in 1933. A remarkable and moral man, he decided to be a willing Robinson Crusoe in the jungle because of something he did at Passchendaele in the First World War, which has haunted him all his life. When he mentions the battle, there are tears in his eyes.

In the early thirties he was working in London as an insurance man. With a certain pride he recalls he had five telephones on his desk – the five telephones are a symbol of the world he left. He went to 'the institute' – the night school of the time – to learn the skills he would need, carpentry, plumbing, brick-laying. He built his wooden and tin-roofed house from the trees he cleared. The rain forest crowds in on the small building and its garden. He has no electricity, therefore no television or telephone. He doesn't believe in it – he says 'the use of electricity is wrong', he is convinced it 'causes an imbalance in nature'.

He is small, wiry, looks twenty years younger than his great age, in baggy shorts and canvas shoes, his walnut-like stomach and chest still hard and muscular. He speaks without a trace of Australian accent or grammar – he has the voice of a First-World-War officer and gentlemen.

He decided not to get married, not to drink or smoke. He eats very little. He is convinced that vitamin pills have kept him alive and fit for so long. Most of his food is from his garden or from the rain forest, coconuts, bananas, paw-paw, nuts.

He has recorded his life in a series of notebooks and letters. He has the dates of 'The Wets' for all the years he has lived in the rain forest, the accounts of building his house, what he has grown, what he has seen. He labels every cupboard he builds in the house, every rafter, and in the garden and the forest every tree he plants.

At the back of his house there is a concrete cyclone shelter which doubles as a shower and bathroom and also has a safe in it. When a cyclone threatens he takes his papers and notebooks out to the shelter. The last cyclone to hit the Daintree area was in 1976.

He has built a dam, 100 yards into the rain forest, from which a pipe brings water to the house. He lets the sediment settle in bowls on his small veranda. He has a cistern that fills in the rainy season and which he uses to water his garden.

Recently he fell and broke his hip. It happened in the garden. He got into the house, up the two steps of the veranda, on his backside, using his hands and his 'good leg'. He lay on the floor. Then he got his whistle and blew for attention. No one heard – the track is yards away and people rarely come along it. Night came: he got into bed levering himself up the drawers of a chest. He planned to get down toward the track as far as he could in the morning and drum on an empty can with a stick. Fortunately in the morning someone called to see him. 'It was nothing,' he says, 'when you've been in the mud of Passchendaele, a thing like that is nothing.'

When he was in hospital in Cairns, he said to the doctors, 'While I'm in here you may as well fix this nerve on my wrist. And you can take out my prostate too.' And they did.

Now in his nineties his sense of mortality is unswerving and unsentimental. He is a rationalist, 'a scientific thinker'. Moving bent on a stick, he says he will have to sell up, but he clearly hopes to die on his property. He says that when he knows he is dying he will burn all his records and notes, his life's work done and his penance complete.

COCONUT WATER

In his garden, a cane farmer waves a long length of metal piping up at a coconut palm. A nut falls. With three blows of a machete, he exposes the inside and offers it to the visitor with a straw to drink the water. The layer of flesh inside is thin, soft and creamy, the 'milk' is clear refreshing water. He dismisses the coconuts sold overseas as, literally, 'rotten'.

SUN AND SHOWERS

It is an anxious time as everyone waits for 'The Wet'. The cane farmers fear it won't come. The farmers with fruit trees fear it will be too heavy and smash their orchards. In the hills, at the foot of the table land, it is blisteringly hot, over 100° F. Then the sky piles high with cloud and suddenly there is a downpour of warm rain, a curtain of glass rods from heaven to earth. It lasts five or ten minutes. The sky clears, the sun blazes. The puddles are too hot for sandalled feet. On the mountains the deep green canopy of the rain forest steams.

A SPECULATING MAN

Arnie Peterson, a land speculator and multi-millionaire, is credited with having said, 'For six days we buy, on the seventh we rest'.

THE MAN OF A SPECULATING MAN

George Quaid is estate agent for the sale of an area of rain forest, bought dead cheap just north of the ferry across the Daintree River.

'DAINTREE FREEHOLD RAIN FOREST'

Constantly on Queensland TV there are adverts designed to sell the Peterson/Quaid 'blocks' of rain forest. The visitor, after driving along the dirt track that, as yet, is all there is of this development, cut through the mighty virgin forest, thinks . . .

1. You can have a primeval rain forest.

2. You can have a housing estate.

Both are excellent growths.

3. But you can't have a housing estate in a rain forest.

If you try to build a housing estate in a rain forest, you'll end up with a housing estate in half-scrub, half-desert, with mud in the wet season, probably infested with an abnormally high population of snakes.

A MOSSMAN COCKTAIL

Mossman people enjoy a drink – it is soursop and Bundaberg rum, mixed with ganja. Some boast of drinking it for breakfast on Sunday mornings, 'before church'.

LEECHES

Leeches in the rain forest during the rainy season are in the damp, rotting leaves. They stick to your feet as you walk. It is best to go barefoot, then you see them before they can dig in.

BAD BLOOD

For mosquito bites, take vitamin B. Mosquitoes don't like the taste in your blood.

A RESPECTABLE WOMAN

Sitting on a bench outside a Mossman store, a white woman, respectably dressed with white permed hair, rests with her shopping bag. She looks middle-class and very English, she would not be out of place shopping in Guildford. She says she still dreams of living in Sydney, 'It's lovely down there'. Ten feet from her stand three aboriginals, two of them women. The women are barefooted.

A FARMER'S WIFE

At the end of a two-hour monologue by a farmer who, with his wife, had dropped into another's house for a Sunday afternoon drink, the wife said just five words. They were, 'I think we'd better go'.

THE STINGING TREE

The tree's leaves are heart-shaped, with long hairs beneath them. It is common. Contact with it can, it is said, kill because of the shock of the intense pain. The pain can last for a year. The local remedy is to repeatedly apply sticking plaster to the stung areas of skin, ripping it off again and again.

THE RAIN FOREST

The visitor, from a temperate zone and a small island cultivated, stripped, moulded and replanted for 4,000 years, finds himself standing for the first time in an intact primeval landscape. (Primeval – 'Of or pertaining to the first age of the world'. OED.)

The visitor did once walk in a desert in Northern Syria, leaving a car for a few minutes in 120° F of heat. An urban soul, he could not bear the appalling ochre and vermilion landscape. He retreated to the car (his Arab hosts laughed at him).

In a desert, there is life, but it looks as if there is nothing. In a wet tropical rain forest, there is it seems everything nature can conceive. It is dark, the word 'cathedral' comes to mind. The canopy, a hundred or more feet above, glitters with brilliant yellows and greens. Creeks, with pools full of carp, occasionally wander through the trees, huge Mountain Blue butterflies with iridescent wings flashing blue and turquoise zig-zag over the water. The activity of animals is everywhere. Scrub hens have exposed roots of trees. The visitor saw one of their strange earthen mounds, about five feet high, in which they lay and incubate their eggs (they are a kind of wild turkey). Fortunately he did not encounter one of the wild pigs, the males are said to be ferocious, and they are out of control in the rain forests, doing great damage. The parrots, high in the middle layer of the forest's vertical zones of life, call and counter-call. The noise comes and goes in waves – odd scuffling and banging noises on the forest's floor, the drumming of insects, the birds, none of which the visitor can understand. Then the forest is eerily silent. The intact morass of violent growth, cedars that go up to a hundred feet before branching, the mighty milky palms encased by their parasite strangler figs, long thin hands clutching the huge trunks . . . seems suddenly inert. Its presence is overpowering. The mad notion comes into the visitor's mind that the forest is waiting to think something, even to speak . . .

His reaction is similar to being in a desert. There is something appalling about the glory and meaninglessness of virgin nature.

His friends find him, they go back to their vehicle. He finds himself in a foul temper and that tears are streaming down his face, which he hides from his companions.

THE ROAD

North of the Daintree River, past Cape Tribulation up to the Bloomfield River, a road has been bull-dozed through the virgin rain forest. It is of earth, it is dusty, precarious and will be washed away in 'The Wet'. It is dangerous, twisting and turning at odd angles and violent cambers.

SURVEYING BY BULLDOZER

The road was built without any proper surveying, they got into their bulldozers and drove north through the wilderness of the forests. It is called locally 'surveying by bulldozer'. The visitor was driven about two-thirds north along 'the road'. 'The Wet' had not yet started, he was in a most powerful four-wheel-drive vehicle – even with that and a practised local driver, many times the car could have overturned.

GREENIES

Ecologists – 'greenies' – protested against the building of 'the road'. They climbed the trees and chained themselves to the branches, in front of the bulldozers.

The dozers went around them . . .

That is why the road zig-zags so crazily, up and down the uneven floor of the forest.

A 'greenie' whom the visitor met in Mossman's Mainstreet said that two of his friends had chained themselves to a concrete block and buried the block. They waited two days for the bulldozers to reach them. When they did, the workmen tried to cut the chains but could not. Eventually they dug the concrete block up. The protesters were gaoled for two weeks, beaten, then released with charges dropped.

The 'greenies' came from all over Australia and were detested by the local people for their long hair and pot smoking. Where 'the road' begins there is a dilapidated shack under the trees. 'Greenies' call it 'the outpost'. A sign outside reads 'Craft Centre'. A slogan is wonkily written on a board in white paint: 'The earth is our Mother, why do we want to kill her?'.

The local people who care what happens to the forest and know it intimately – Reginald Laird and David Thompson, the editor of the Mossman newspaper among them – also resented the invasion of the 'greenies' – their hippy lifestyle did not help to win the argument with the deeply conservative cane farmers and local councillors.

DIE BACK

The death of the forest beside a road or a clearing is called 'die back'. The canopy cools the ground. If the ground is hotter than 72° F, the forest cannot sustain itself. Already, though 'the road' was bulldozed under two years ago, in patches the forest is dying, and guinea grass – the weed of derelict, ruined land – is beginning to grow by the roadside.

REVENGE BY ROAD

Why was 'the road' built, when it goes through the wilderness of the rain forest in effect to nowhere, and there is another, usable, road fifty miles to the west up to Bloomfield and Cook Town?

Some say it is an act of revenge on the forest. And, indeed, it looks to a traveller like a temper tantrum by a child who has got his hands on huge earth-moving machines. Trees lie smashed and up-rooted either side. Root boles of giant milky palms stick out of crudely cut embankments. The red earth, torn up by the appalling engineering, makes it look like a bloody wound slashed through the deep green of the forest.

JOH BIELKE PETERSON

The premier of Queensland, Joh Bielke Peterson, says the road is 'progress'. The visitor sees him interviewed on Queensland TV. Of South African extraction, a vigorous seventy-year-old, he has an unctuous, silky tone. He is interviewed in the seat of his personal bulldozer, his political campaigning symbol. The respectful interviewer explains that 'Joh' has, as usual, spent the recent Christmas holiday clearing trees on his estate.

CAPE TRIBULATION

Cape Tribulation was named by Captain Cook when his ship, The Endeavour, was holed on the Great Barrier Reef.

They slung canvas under the keel and limped into the estuary of the Daintree River, where they did temporary repairs before sailing

north to what is now Cook Town. (The visitor is told this, and re-
solves to read Cook's journals, famous for their meticulous detail.)

Seen from a clearing high in the National Park area above the
Daintree estuary and the Cape, the panorama of the broad snaking
estuary, the miles of forest, the curve of the coastline beneath an
early rainy season sky, is the stuff of postcards and glossy
photographs in coffee-table books. Standing before the real thing,
you realise the impossibility of any photographic (or verbal)
imagery ever describing its beauty.

THEY SAY. . .

They say that Captain Cook had pigs on board. Some escaped – it
is their descendants that roam the forest. They are hunted for
sport. The pigs are highly successful, they can be found as far
south as Melbourne and as far north-west as Darwin.

PIGS

There is a theory that the pigs are responsible for damage to the
Great Barrier Reef through an ecological chain that begins with the
pigs eating turtles' eggs buried in the sand on the beaches, that
involves the Giant Triton (a shellfish) and ends with the Crown of
Thorns starfish proliferating and eating the live coral.

THE REEF

But there is a school of thought which says that this summer the
plague of the Crown of Thorns on the reef is abating – some tip of
the balance is decreasing their number.

REVENGE ON THE REEF

A tale of imagined revenge – to murder a board member of the
mill and bury his body under the coral, out on the reef (from an
angry cane farmer).

POLICE

North of Mossman, up to Daintree and Cape Tribulation, and beyond, there are no police posts and no patrols.

SLAVERY

The visitor is told that until 1920, in Mackay, there was slavery, under a scheme of 'assisted passage'.

CANE TOADS

Cane toads were introduced from Hawaii to eat the cane beetle. They didn't. The toads have a poisonous gland in the back of their heads. The snakes eat frogs: they eat the cane toads and die.

CANE TOAD BLOWING

A North Queensland sport. A lighted cigarette is, with some skill, lodged in the mouth of a cane toad. The smoke makes the toad swell up and, eventually, burst. Bets are laid.

There is a law in Queensland that 'no deviants, perverts, homosexuals, child-molesters or drug dealers are allowed to be served alcohol in Queensland hotels'.

JOH AGAIN

Joh Bielke Peterson, the premier of Queensland, is said to have diverted the railway from Brisbane to the Gold Coast so it ran through the suburbs owned by his then minister of police, Russ Hinze, who was much enriched thereby.

RICH MAN

There is a story of a multi-millionaire land speculator, in his lavish house, serving dinner guests with Plumrose sausages from a tin and a frozen loaf of bread, talking the meanwhile of a 5-million-dollar deal he had done that day.

THE POOR

Palm Island is an aboriginal reservation, set up after the devastation of a cyclone in the 1930s. The cyclone was an opportunity to clear aboriginals off the mainland between Cairns and Townsville. Six tribes, with their six languages, were rammed together. There is a legal limitation on the number of bottles and tins of booze that can be taken to the island, but there is rampant smuggling and alcoholism is rife.

From a boat, the visitor sees the wharf in Townsville harbour from which the supplies are taken to Palm Island. On the wharfside there is a rusty oil drum, on it are painted the words, 'Fuck you'.

RAT'S PISS ETC.

One of the main diseases of sugar cane is Weil's disease, Lepto Spira, which comes from rat's urine.

A RAT

The white-tailed rat is a rain forest rat – from time to time they have given Reginald Laird a good deal of trouble, invading his house.

A FROG

Tree frogs are common dwellers in houses. They are bright green and black-eyed – their fingers are bulbous and have pads with which they climb and stick to walls and rafters. They eat the cockroaches.

THE MIRACLE TREE

After you eat the fruit of the miracle tree, anything sour tastes sweet: you can eat a lemon and swear it is an orange.

MAN TALK

A man asking another man about a woman's sexuality, 'She a good rider?'.

SNAKE

The carpet snake, or rock python, is six to seven feet long. It is not poisonous, but its bite is fearsome, the teeth are long, thin and curved inwards like scimitars. When it bites it shakes its head, like a dog. It is, however, readily tameable.

SOLDIER CRABS

On a beach just north of Cape Tribulation, at low tide, thousands of soldier crabs march back and forth in 'armies'. They make a buzzing sound by the clanking of their mandibles. They are small, their shells an inch, an inch and a half across. They are accompanied by a scattering of 'captains', bigger soldier crabs who climb over the mass of the soldiers, guiding the columns. The visitor and his companions stand looking at the hordes before them on the sand: they stamp their feet and suddenly the crabs, en masse, disappear into the sand. The tiny deposits thrown up by their burrowings are everywhere, whole areas of the vast beach below the high-water mark look as if they have been raked over.

MANGROVE TREES

On 'soldier crab beach', there are mangrove trees below the tide mark. They stand up on their roots, looking like great insects with many legs about to run off down the beach. From the branches of the mature trees, air roots hang down to the sand.

COCONUT

To plant a coconut. Half bury it in its husk, on its side. It puts down two roots and the sapling grows from one end. They like sandy and salty soil and so grow at the back of beaches.

DEATH ON WHEELS

A 25-year-old farmer's son has seen nine of his old school classmates killed in motorcycle accidents around Mossman. Motorcycling in groups is one of the main pastimes of local young people. The 25-year-old was out with his best friend in the wild.

They split up. When he got home, the news of the death of his friend was waiting for him. He has gone overseas, swearing never to return to FNQ.

A TRANSPORT DRIVER

Harold Woolfield was a transport driver for 17 years (17 crushings), an employee of the Mossman Mill. Transport drivers load the bins at the side of the fields onto their trucks and take them to rail terminals. The mill let him go when he suffered a destroyed nerve in his shoulder, during an accident when he was trapped hitching a dog trailer to the back of his truck.

The trucks are prone to jack-knifing, and during the crushing they are driven day and night, often at 100 miles an hour.

Harold once hit a tram on one of the ill-marked crossings. He described it as slow motion. He saw the loco driver jump from his cab. He did everything by numbers, pumped the air-brakes, crashed the gears down, pulled the hand-brake. His truck hit the last two bins of the trainload. His head shattered the windscreen (no seat belt), his legs got jammed under the steering wheel. One of the bins went over the top of his truck.

Bruised and cut, his first thoughts were to get the load of cane transferred to another truck, which he did. The demands of the difficult product, that it will be useless if not in the mill in 24 hours, are remorseless.

TRANSPORT DRIVERS' LORE

It is the first rule for transport drivers to 'stay on the bitumen'. Cane fields can conceal pits, ditches; a truck that careers off the road can be done for.

GOD'S BITUMEN

It is a local saying that 'the bitumen runs to the homes that go to church'. When the bitumen runs out and the road is dirt, all the houses beyond are godless.

LOST WHEELS

A transport driver once lost the middle two nearside wheels of his tandem truck. Moving fast, they bounced into a cane field at night. The driver only realised they had gone when he got to the mill. They went back to find them and couldn't. A reward was offered. They were only found months later by the farmer of the field.

EDEN

'Like the garden of Eden, ain't it?' says a cane farmer who is diversifying into fruit farming, showing the visitor around the many kinds of fruit tree on the hillside above his farmhouse. 'Got the snakes for it and all,' he adds.

THE GLASS NOTE

Sitting at a dinner table, the fruit farmer, an expert tree-grafter, his fingers strong and thick with a soft delicate touch, quietly took a glass and ran his finger around the rim. A pure, high note rang out into the hot sultry night.

HANKERS

'Hit the hankers' – jam on the brakes of a truck.

TRAFFIC OFFICER

The Traffic Officer for the Mossman Mill has no device to plot the whereabouts of trains moving about the fields during the crushing. He is admired for carrying it all in his head.

CANE

By law, cane has to go to the mill. A farmer cannot send it elsewhere. If you don't cut it, the mill can send workers, 'even the army', to do it. 'Cane belongs to the flag.'

NOAH'S ARK

Harold Woolfield is building a boat in his backyard (i.e. garden). It dominates his small wooden and galvanised-iron house – the propeller sits head-height, three feet from the kitchen door. The boat is fibreglass, weighs nine tons, a fortress of a deep-sea vessel. In the heat, he can be found covered in fibreglass dust, as he sprays and thickens the hull and the superstructure. He has been working on it, investing all he has, for four years.

Local gossip gives Harold's boat a strange history. He is a keen amateur astronomer, with a strong astrological bent. It is said that when the planets aligned two years ago, he predicted a disaster, a new biblical flood. The San Andreas fault would open causing a huge tidal wave that would cross the Pacific, drowning most of the eastern seaboard of Australia. The boat was his 'Noah's ark'. The planets aligned, nothing happened.

Harold – now anyway – says he plans a great voyage around the islands of the Pacific, and to become a prawn fisherman.

FANS

Everywhere – living room, bedroom, kitchen, bar, hotel – the huge fans waft the air. They are of infinitely varied make and antiquity and varying speeds and effectiveness. Only the richest have air-conditioning in their houses. Falling asleep, the visitor dreams of great fans, stretching away into infinity, rotating slowly in the night.

STUFFED UP

'We've got a stuffed up industry,' says an angry cane farmer.

THE MILL'S DARK SHADOW

'How much we can grow, how much we can get for it, how much you can harvest, they control it all.'

'You mean the mill?'

'Talking about the Cane Central Prices Board in Brisbane.' A pause. 'Same thing, ay? Know what I mean?'

ZONES

The mill controls 'zones'. Originally owners of a harvest machine (there are two types, one for cutting burnt cane, one for cutting green) could operate in up to three 'zones'. Anyone buying a harvester after 1976 can only operate in one 'zone'.

FARMER'S GRIPE

Molasses used to be ploughed back into the land. It was included in the price the farmer was paid for the cane. Now the molasses is sold by the mill to health food and other markets – the profits do not go to the farmer, and he has lost the benefit of the molasses on his fields.

THE MILL AS OGRE

The relationship of a farmer to the mill is complex. By some the mill is hated and feared: 'The mill can break me, no worry. I'm already a leper, far as they're concerned.'

FLAT FIELDS

A field should have a slope of no greater than 11 per cent for growing sugar cane. In what is now widely seen as the reckless expansion in the sixties, fields of 25 per cent were cleared and cultivated.

A GOOD POM

A North Queensland saying: 'If you find a good Pom, shoot him, 'cos he's sure to turn bad.'

SHAREHOLDERS OF THE MILL

Only shareholders can vote at the Shareholders Meeting, which, in practice, rubber-stamps decisions made by the Directors Meeting (there are five directors of the mill). Half the farmers bound to the mill are shareholders. The others have a Non-Shareholders Meeting – it can be attended by shareholders and directors. But non-shareholders cannot go to the other meetings. A share is nominally priced at $2. There are small and big shareholders. The mill is a private company, but its control over shareholders and non-shareholders alike is described by dissident farmers as 'feudal'.

FEUDALISM?

Later, a powerful mill director describes to the visitor the relationship between all the farmers and the mill as 'one family'.

A MAN AND A WOMAN

Talking of a five-year courtship between her son and a local girl, which had just been broken by her son, a farmer's wife said – 'If a woman has not got a man in five years, by rape or by feeding him, she's never going to get him.'

FIGURES

700,000 tons of sugar a year are consumed by Australians. 320,000 tons are produced.

'STRUCTURE'

The institutions of the cane industry work through a complex series of 'meetings'. 'That meeting', 'the meeting', 'that meeting in '82' pepper farmers' conversations about the industry. (Oddly, the visitor is reminded of the quasi-democracy of a non-conformist church, which has an endless round of interlocking meetings attended by more or less the same people all the time.) The visitor tried to unscramble the structure. Informants more or less agreed it is . . .

1. The Directors Meeting. 2. The Shareholders Meeting. 3. The Non-Shareholders Meeting. 4. The Cane Growers Meeting (i.e. The Cane Growers Association). 5. The ASPA (The Australian Sugar Producers Association). 6. The Harvest Operators Meeting (for the owners of cane-cutting machines). 7. The Mill Suppliers Meeting. 8. The Local Board Awards Meeting.

Farmers grumble about 'Strangled by bureaucracy, but'. (Sounding like farmers the visitor has talked to in Wales and in Kent – and probably the world over, faced with government quotas and legislation.)

'BUT'

NB. Many of the verbatim remarks written down by the visitor end with a 'but'. It is common in the Queensland dialect. It is used as a forceful full-stop to a statement. In full flow, some Queenslanders use it at the end of virtually every other sentence.

POWER

Dissident cane farmers say 'the power clique' who run the mill can take action against them in many ways.

You have to get your burnt cane to the mill, at the time allocated to you. You can find that the bins owned and moved by the mill do not arrive at your fields until two in the afternoon, rather than eleven in the morning. You find yourself paying your workers to go on late.

If your farm is below a certain size, calculated by its yield of tons of cane, you are allowed to burn your fields every other day. But if you are a dissident you can find, during the crushing, that the yield is suddenly judged by the Awards Board to be just over the limit, so you have to burn every day. But you have been allocated time in the mill every other day . . .

The scope for byzantine manipulation against you, because of the 24-hour necessity to get the burnt cane crushed, is endless.

For a stranger, it is impossible to judge whether the wrath of the farmers is justified or not. That it is fierce there is no doubt.

APOCALYPSE

'The foundations for self-destruction were laid long ago,' says a cane farmer. 'The Mossman Mill didn't bring the non-shareholders in. Other mills, yes, but here no.'

A bitter man, but with an overview, he predicts that the industry will have to contract to supplying the protected Australian market and to exporting 10% of the yield abroad. He says market forces will bring this about anyway – but if it were planned, then there will be fewer bankruptcies, fewer ruined lives.

But nothing will be planned. 'We're peasants, with a peasant's mentality.'

The visitor asks what he will do if his farm is wiped out. Unexpectedly he cheers up. 'Get out and go North,' he says. 'Go into fruit, timber, something else, no worries.'

MILLIONAIRE PEASANTS?

The visitor reports the comment, 'We're peasants, with a peasant's mentality,' to his companions. The Australian, from Sydney, pauses then says, 'Mm. Millionaire peasants? ' .

DYNAMITE

The cane farmers speak to the visitor with the glee of born trouble makers. One leans toward him and says conspiratorially, 'What do you want to write about here, Howie? It's like dynamite, but?'

TOM THE POM

Asked about Englishmen who have come to the Mossman area, which is largely settled by families of Italian extraction, there is laughter in a farm kitchen. Stories are told, with affection, of 'Tom the Pom', who is 'fucking crazy' and 'accident prone'.

DIALECT

Any meeting is called 'a party', as in 'Who brung you to this party?'.

STONE FISH

A farmer tells of being stung by a stone fish, which he kept as a pet in a tank. 'Being stung by a stone fish is like having your skin ripped off by a fork.'

FESTIVAL BANANAS

In November at Mission Beach there is a Banana Festival. It features 'the longest banana split in the world', which is made in a trough of split bamboo. There is also the straightest banana competition. Bloomfield holds a Mango Festival: they have to bring in the mangoes because they don't grow any.

THE VENETIAN

In the main street of Mossman, an old Italian farmer sits in his car with all the doors open to keep cool. In his eighties, he is talkative and cheerful. He emigrated in 1923, was some time in Melbourne before coming to Far North Queensland. His accent is thickly Italian but his grammar is North Queensland. The first thing he says is that he is 'from Venezia', the second is to ask if the visitor has been there. He has not, since he left as a young man. 'What is it like?' he asks.

W.C.

A white painted, breeze-block public toilet has been built just off the main street of Mossman. It is used exclusively by aboriginal families.

THE TRAGEDY

A Daintree resident, Beryl Wruck, was killed by a crocodile on Christmas Eve at a barbecue party. It was reported internationally – the visitor heard of it on BBC radio before he left England.

Beryl Wruck had lived for three years at Daintree and worked in the only shop, the general stores, which also doubles as the local pub. Daintree is a hamlet of some ten buildings. It is very remote. But she was widely known in the area and liked. Indeed everyone seems to have known her. In any Mossman or Port Douglas pub, one of her dearest and closest friends was to be found, propping up the bar.

Local stories about how she died have become myths. Mystery has been spun. Was it her bra hanging on a tree, on the opposite bank? Any resident knows the danger of the creeks of the Daintree River – the salt-water crocodiles, the sharks that swim up the estuary into the creeks – it is an absolute shibboleth never, ever to put hand or foot in the water. The visitor saw the creek where she died. It is a sinister place, the water black, the banks overhung. To swim in that seems an act of folly.

THE MYTHS

These are the stories told to the visitor about Beryl Wruck's death. They had all 'gone skinny' – i.e. they were swimming in the nude . . . She was 'rooting' on the opposite bank, having left her bra hanging on a tree. Her husband saw her, she argued with her lover, was swimming back to her spouse . . . They were drunk. The Minister of the Environment, Martin Tenny, was with her in the water. The crocodile that killed her was named Martin, after a publicity stunt a few years ago by the Minister of the Environment. She and two men were playing 'dare', rushing in and out of the water, drunk, shouting, 'Where are you crocs? Barby time!' – and a croc came up for the barby . . . The most bizarre story and the cruellest for her family to bear, is that she is not dead at all, that the crocodile incident was a fabrication, and she is now in the Philippines with a lover (this from several sources).

It is said she disappeared beneath the water without a sound.

LITTLE SYDNEY, LITTLE MELBOURNE

A local saying – 'Mossman and Port Douglas never agree about anything.'

PORT DOUGLAS

The visitor stays a few nights in Port Douglas. It is a small, shabby seaside resort, on a sandy spit, ten miles from Mossman. It is poised for massive and reckless expansion, there are speculators' dreams of making it a great resort. For now, it is pleasantly seedy, off-season – a little bit of 'kiss me quick' in the jungle.

'THE MAYOR'

The lush vegetation of the Port Douglas peninsula is due to the herculean efforts of recent settlers, the most famous of whom are Max and Diana Bowden. For years he was undisputed 'mayor'. The visitor is given fruit juice cocktails in their immaculate, clean-as-a-pin living room overlooking their madly sprouting and blazing garden. The room is an odd amalgam of a Surrey sitting room and a tropical collection of shells, plants, snake-skins. The Bowdens have struggled for years with a major disease of whites in the tropics, alcoholism, of which they speak openly. He has a mysterious past in the Foreign Office. Hints are dropped about the Zinoviev letter. They came to Queensland in the thirties and tried to farm bananas at Bandaberg. They 'just walked off' the property when it failed and came north to Port Douglas, then a fishing port. The town was a gold rush town in the nineteenth century – '81 pubs, each a brothel'. Max speaks of its past lovingly. They bemoan the coming development by the Quintex company – 9,000 condominiums on virgin land – in apocalyptic terms. Max speaks of 'the ruin of the earth'.

Later, the visitor is told that Max Bowden became a rich man by buying and selling plots of land . . .

THE MILL'S MUSIC

The Chief Engineer of the Mossman Mill lives in a house in the shadow of the mill. He only has a hundred yards to walk to work. It is an old, traditional Australian house of weatherboard and galvanised iron. During the crushing, with the mill working 24 hours a day, the noise is constant. His wife says, 'We can be sitting here, at dinner? He hears the row change note – and he's up and out of here. I can't tell what he's heard. It's all a great noise to me.'

REEF LORE

A local doctor advises 'no swimming on the reef if you've got infected or broken skin' (sores from prickly heat, tropical ulcers, infected mosquito bites etc.). Invisible fragments of dead coral are floating in the water. They can cause terrible infections. They don't know how to treat them anti-biotically. 'We don't know much about diseases from the sea,' he says.

FAILURES' PARADISE
A Mossman resident – 'Everyone who comes up here is running away from something. We're all failures. The first settlers were running away from something. Failures' paradise.'

HEAVIES IN THE JUNGLE
The latest influx of white immigrants in the Port Douglas, Townsville area are white South Africans, fleeing their country because of the unrest there (and, one suspects, what they see as the 'liberal' policies of P.W. Botha's government).

MACRO-MICRO-TROPICAL
The micro-biological world in the tropics must be as bizarrely inventive as the macro world of plants and animals. Talk in a Port Douglas pub turns to the infinite variety of tropical ulcers.

HEALTH LORE
Health and remedies for minor complaints are constantly discussed. One of the visitor's companions gets prickly heat. It covers his body and looks like shingles, and is as painful. He is given much kindly advice. Have cold baths, have hot baths, do not wash at all.

Do not drink alcohol, drink alcohol. Apply nothing, apply calamine mixed with benadryl. (The Mossman pharmacy's window is given over to an entire display of creams for prickly heat.) Dry the suppurating spots with a hair dryer. Eat paw-paw in huge quantities. Cover yourself in Johnson's baby powder.

NIGHT LIFE, PORT DOUGLAS
At chucking-out time in Port Douglas, a young woman, 14 or 15

years old, of mixed Philippine and aboriginal race, slender in a
sarong, leads an old man from the pub – he paws at her; he is frail
and massively drunk; expertly she puts her hand under his armpit
and hauls him across the road.

NEWS

The rumour of Beryl Wruck's flight with a lover to the Philippines
is dealt a blow. A 16-foot salt-water crocodile has been shot.
Human remains have been found in its stomach – a few small
bones, toenails. They assume it is her.

GOSSIP LIVES

But . . . Despite the news, the visitor is told, 'It could be anyone in
the croc. Some abo, some crazy fucker up there . . . Lots of people
disappear, no one knows anything about it.'

WORDS

A despairing conservationist – 'Australians call soil, the earth,
"dirt". They call a garden a "backyard".'

DIVING TERM

'A belt and braces diver' – a diver who is over-cautious.

A DIVING SAYING

'You can drown in three inches of water.'

METHS

Meths is not kept on the open shelves of a local store, 'lest Abos
nick it'. The same store keeps bottles of meths out the back – in a
cold cabinet. The inference was clear.

DUMB PLACE

An informant says that the Mossman area has the highest
unemployment in Queensland and the worst school records, it is
'the dumbest place in Queensland'.

STRANGE WEATHER

In brilliant, stinging sunlight, mid-afternoon, half the sky is blue, with wispy high cloud. You look to another part of the sky and the black anvil of a storm towers upwards for miles. In these days before 'The Wet', the atmosphere aches. From early in the morning, the temperature is anything from 95°F to 110°F. The humidity is so high the air feels solid with hot water. At night beyond the veranda the animals and insects seem in torment. The cries of the frogs are disorderly.

The days of this weather drag on. Local people change. The fear that 'The Wet' won't come eats into conversations: 'worst ever', 'all over again' (the year of a cyclone).

The visitor is told these are the weeks when marriages are broken, when children get beaten, when vendettas come to a head. It is weather to murder by.

TROPPO (i)

In the heat, because of the sheen of sweat forever oozing from your skin, the loss of potassium impairs the brain's functions. The glasses of Staminade help, but intermittently your thoughts jam. You set out to do something – you go into a shop, you stand before the counter, say 'Gidday' – and cannot remember why you're there.

Someone begins to tell a story. Suddenly you realise they have forgotten they told you the beginning and are repeating it. Your heart sinks, for it is a certainty they have forgotten the anecdote's end and for the next half-hour the story-teller, being a tenacious Queenslander, will try to talk his or her way out of trouble by force of will.

HIND LEGS OFF A DONKEY

Is potassium deficiency an explanation for the universal garrulity? For the first few days the visitor's brain was exhausted by the spiralling, endless helter-skelter of local conversationalists. Then he took it for granted and began to talk like that himself.

MYSTICAL

Often in the kitchen of a cane farm you see an astrological chart for planting – farming by the zodiac. They are a hard, realistic people, with a profound hatred of 'bloody hippies' – but many of them have a vein of strange, mystical thinking.

WITCHCRAFT

Superstition surfaces in some drunken conversations. A farmer's wife claims to be a witch – 'No one crosses me and gets away with it'. The visitor questions her (with some care). The witchcraft she describes – usually white, she claims, herbs, the chanting of runes – has nothing to do with spirit religion.

It is straight out of seventeenth-century rural England, or Salem.

CREATIONISTS

The Jehovah's Witnesses have built an expensive, spick and span chapel in Mossman. Religion amongst non-Catholics is fundamentalist. 'Creationist Science' is widespread.

The manager of the Mossman Mill believes the world was created 6,000 years ago.

THE ARSEHOLE OF THE YEAR

A resident, English, calls these weeks before 'The Wet' 'the arsehole of the year'.

THE MILL (ii)

For an afternoon Graham Jorgensen, the Chief Engineer of the Mossman Mill, takes the visitor and his companions around – and over – the mill's mighty machinery.

His father was a sugar mill engineer, now his son is a fitter in the Australian Air Force. He is a cheerful, fresh-faced man, who speaks of his charges, the machines, with an innocent, obsessive delight.

As it is 'the slack', the mill is deserted and silent. The heat amongst the metal surfaces, under the high tin roofs, is intense. It is as if the furnaces, the crushing mills, the evaporators, still retain some residue of the heat they generate when they are working.

First the burnt cane is washed and put through a shredder. It is then smashed in a hammer mill, a big brute of a machine. It is then lifted by a conveyor to be tipped down onto the first crushing mill – a machine with four colossal rollers. There are five crushing mills. The conveyor switchbacking between them looks like a rusty, ugly fairground ride. Cleaning the conveyor is one of the most difficult and dirty jobs in the mill. From the crushing mills the fibre of the mashed cane, the begasses, is taken to the boiler furnaces, which it fuels.

The sugar juice is collected in great sumps beneath each of the crushing mills and cycled through a mixing tank, a heater and a clarifier, a huge vessel. The sugar juice is a mixture of molasses, what will become raw sugar and the muck, mud and scrapings from the burnt cane. A filter beneath the clarifier collects the mill mud, as it separates out from the juice by gravity. The mill mud is then distributed to the farms as fertiliser.

Next, the clear juice, which is now 16% sugar, is cycled through five evaporators. It thickens and becomes liquor, 65% sugar, still mixed with the molasses. The liquor is boiled in a vacuum pan for further concentration, then piped to the crystalliser.

In the crystalliser, another vast tank high up beneath the mill's roofs, a strange reaction takes place. A handful of castor sugar is introduced. The grains of the castor sugar set off a process of crystallisation. The wet, crystallised sugar is then conveyed to a series of huge centrifuges, which spin it – the molasses at last separating from the grains of sugar through metal filters. The 'raw sugar', the final product of the mill, is then dried, and loaded through a sugar hopper onto the great tandem trucks, 55 tons a load, which take it to Cairns for shipment to Japan.

ENGINE DRIVERS

By tradition, the machines' operators in the mill are called 'engine drivers'.

THE MOUSE GANG

The general cleaners in the mill are called 'the mouse gang'. Like the operators, they work in shifts during the crushing, round the clock. The mill aims to have cleared all of the previous day's cane by 8 am each morning. The mill stops for a few hours every Monday morning for cleaning and maintenance.

CARRIER HAND

The carrier hand – another traditional name – connects the 10-ton bins up, to be tipped into the shredder at the beginning of the mill's process. He stands just outside the main hall of the factory. It is a lonely job.

THE WORKFORCE

Including the twelve, skilled 'engine drivers', the mouse gang, the other non-skilled jobs here and there, the mill employs about 150 men during the crushing.

A DEATH

Once a man in the boiler room, where the furnaces are monitored, died. The mill's processes began to go wrong. There was a search – it was some time before they checked the boiler room.

AN ACCIDENT

And once, at night, a small piece of metal jammed a valve in an evaporator tank. The computer could not identify what was wrong. For four hours the factory was in peril. They found the fault by trial and error. If the mill has to stop its process, there is a danger of bacteria in the liquor getting out of hand.

THE MILL'S SWEET SMELL

The visitor is told that during the crushing, over Mossman and for some miles around, the mill gives the air a smell – 'of sweetness and ash'.

THE CASTLE

The visitor ends the tour of the mill high up on a gantry over a big water tank, sixty feet deep. Mossman is a map below – the single main street, the few back alleys. The tramways are a network, a toy railway, through the cane fields. Here and there, behind palm trees, are the big white houses of the wealthier farmers. Down the hills, the tree line, Graham Jorgensen says, is encroaching again.

The impression of the mill as a great edifice of rusty iron, an industrial medieval castle, dominating the landscape and the lives of the people below, is strong.

SHY SNAKE

Walking in a wood at the back of a beach on the Port Douglas peninsula, the visitor sees a snake. It is four feet long and thin – a black yellow-bellied snake. It appears to be moving at lightning speed to get out of the way – and disappears beneath a bush.

The speed of snakes is illusory – they can move at about five miles an hour.

The visitor is told by one resident that the black yellow-bellied snake is one of the most poisonous in Australia – by another that it is a harmless tree snake.

CONTRARY TALES

Why are facts about plants and animals so contradictory? In any rural community you must take what you're told with a pinch of salt, they enjoy teasing visitors.

But the different accounts of animals come from personal

experiences, passed around the community, not from natural science books. So little is known about much of the FNQ flora and fauna (they don't really know how a rain forest works) that the local people have built their knowledge over the years from stories of personal encounters. It is not natural science, it's not necessarily true – but 'local lore' is a practical code, by which you cope with nature in the tropics as best you can.

TROPPO (ii)

'Troppo' is what a white man from a temperate climate goes – it can mean 'going native', wearing sarongs, eating islander food, babbling of the Earth Mother etc. It can mean being under the delusion that you are living in paradise. In FNQ it usually means 'going fucking crazy' – a state of mind the visitor at times easily achieves.

PERVERTS ETC.

Queenslanders are obsessed with 'child-molesters'. Cases of child abuse saturate the media. Queensland parliamentarians give impassioned speeches against the molesters. It is an obsession.

ILLEGAL IMMIGRANTS

Illegal white immigrants are known and often helped to hide and make a life in the Mossman and Daintree areas. It is a ticklish subject – the visitor's questions are answered warily. He learns of four Americans who, some years ago, arrived illegally. They were liked, hidden and helped. One was discovered and arrested in Cairns. The other three are still in Australia, 'real Aussies', though no longer in the Mossman area.

CUT YOUR HAIR, WORK LIKE STINK

Another informant, asked if two illegal immigrants from England would make it, said, 'If they cut their hair. Dress right'. A pause. 'And get productive. People who get productive are respected round here.' The visitor exchanges a glance – and knows his informant is talking about someone he knows.

A RACIST MYTH

The visitor is told that illegal immigrants, often Indians, are smuggled in by prawn trawlers and private yachts, landing on the deserted beaches he has seen north of Cape Tribulation.

There is a common and bizarre tale of Indians being landed in a giant biscuit tin at Cape Trib. 'Can't see that can you?' says David Thompson, pouring scorn. 'Twenty Indians walking into the main street of Mossman announcing they are cane farmers?' He says these stories of illegal immigration on the deserted beaches were put about by the Queensland Government, to win support for building 'the road'.

RACIST OPINIONS

A Port Douglas resident tells the visitor that aboriginals should not be given 'free money'. They blast themselves on booze. They should be given food tokens. The visitor had encountered this opinion a few days earlier, more foully expressed – 'Don't give the niggers money, why give them free booze? Give them free food. Mind you, d'you mind me saying this? Give a nigger good food, he'll wipe his arse on it?'

SUNSHINE PLATES

'Queensland – the sunshine state' – on the number plates of cars registered in Queensland, like American plates.

DEATHLY SEMANTICS

If someone is killed by a shark, it is 'a shark attack'. To be killed by a crocodile is 'to be taken'.

THE WALLABY

A Mossman farmer's wife has a baby wallaby. It lies, looking out with big brown eyes, in a wicker basket by the open living-room door. It is swaddled in a cloth.

She picks it up and fondles it. The animal seems to make a move to her breast – embarrassed she puts it down.

The wallaby, an orphan, should be in its mother's pouch. It has to be fed from a bottle at human baby hours, once every four hours. Later, the wallaby hops across the floor, at each hop dropping a small, sheep-like turd. The farmer and his wife ignore it.

The visitor is fascinated by the animal's movements, the hydraulics of his extraordinary limbs. He is as friendly as a purring cat and likes to be scratched behind the ears.

GAMMY

'Gammy-handed' – left-handed (like the visitor).

CYCLONE LORE

If a cyclone hits your house, the drop in pressure is so extreme that if your doors and windows are closed, the house can explode – like an aerosol can in the hold of a jet plane. Therefore the instinct to close yourself in to survive is the opposite of what you should do. Open all windows and doors.

SOCIALISM?

'Cane farmers work in a highly socialised industry, it's all controlled, what they plant, the sugar content, how they make their money, it's all government regulated, and they carry on like they're free and fucking pioneers, bushwhacking.' (A bitter, non-farming resident.)

'DRUMSARA'

'Drumsara' is the house of Carey and Elizabeth Phillips-Turner, The visitor meets them one evening at dinner on a neighbour's veranda. They invite him the next day to afternoon tea. He sits with them on the upper veranda of the two-floored, large white house, drinking tea and eating chocolate cake. The boards of the veranda are white. The house breathes coolness, its elegant proportions, its wide eaves, its balustrades and external staircases make it the most beautiful building the visitor has seen in Australia. It was built in 1908. Its wooden structure is embedded in concrete, massive bolts secure the roof – it has withstood cyclones.

Seen from the veranda, the cane fields stretch away across the alluvial plain of the South Mossman River. With the increasingly heavy showers, the cane is a fresh and brilliant pale green. Almost everything in sight, the Phillips-Turners own. Behind 'Drumsara' the rain-forested mountains soar into the rain clouds, dwarfing the great house. Carey Phillips-Turner looks up at the mountains. Wisps of cloud finger their way down the gulleys. Waterfalls through the rain forests are streaks of silver. 'Very Chinese, don't you think?' he says.

THE PHILLIPS-TURNERS

The Phillips-Turners have none of the Queensland garrulity. They speak softly and succinctly and with care. They have the good manners not to show their local power and authority. The visitor's first meeting with them over a dinner table was clearly an exercise to which they had given some thought. She wore an 'haute-couture'-style sarong, designed by herself, he was in light, pristinely pressed trousers, sandals and a raw silk shirt of his wife's design. They were circumspect, quietly alert, trying to judge the visitor. Being unused to the ways of millionaires, and certainly to the ways of sugar-mill millionaires, the visitor used all his tact to get shown over the Mossman Mill. He did not get a straight answer. Next day he was telephoned – a full afternoon in the mill, with the Chief Engineer, had been arranged. Carey Phillips-Turner had conferred with his fellow mill directors and a decision had been made.

STRANGLER FIGS

The visitor walks with Carey Phillips-Turner through his vast garden, an exotic parkland. Two huge milky pines, the great rain forest trees, are encased by strangler figs.

The figs have been throttling the pines for many years, their leaves mingle with those of their 'hosts', their branches twist up in strange contorted fingers, like a distorted twisty candlestick, around the trunks of the pines. On one of the pines the fig's branches hang down to the ground, fluted like a church organ. Eventually the strangler fig kills the milky pine, which rots away. The fig then stands in its own right.

POWER AND PESSIMISM

The visitor asks Carey Phillips-Turner how he sees the state of the sugar industry. The reply is quiet, with a shrug – 'People round here would be lost without the mill.'

The visitor presses – is there a likelihood of that?

'Oh yes. Mills have closed. The Mossman Mill is fortunate, it is not in debt. But many of the farmers . . . '

He walks for a while, then says – 'It's the market. It's much easier to make sugar from sugar beet, and the French are very good at it.'

And then, a little later – 'Cane was planted here to open the country up. That doesn't mean it will be here forever.'

The visitor is chilled by his eerie pessimism. There is something sepulchral about his acceptance of the very real prospect of the ruin of his industry.

He was born in Australia, of English stock. A gently spoken man, of a retiring, almost shy nature, there is an undertow of emotion in him particularly when he asks about England. He was pleased to hear about the visitor's excursions to the Kent coast. On parting, he is suddenly very warm in wishing the visitor a good journey 'home'. His eyes are moistened with feeling. The visitor finds it difficult to remind himself that this is the most hated man in the area, the mill director the dissident farmers talk about as a little Hitler.

THE MILL AND THE MILKY PINE

The visitor cannot resist the metaphor . . . the milky pine is the old order of the mill, the strangler fig is the new economic order of the world sugar market.

SILK SHIRTS

Elizabeth Phillips-Turner is a tall woman, taller than her husband. She has a startlingly beautiful face, in profile like a renaissance Florentine, with prominent forehead and chin. Her maiden name was Johnson, a family that came to the Mossman area in 1885, the very first settlers. (Before meeting her, the visitor has heard gossips say that the Johnson's near-aristocratic claims were nonsense, that they came in the 1920s. Not true, since they built 'Drumsara' in the 1900s . . . There is also the common remark that 'She wears the trousers, she's got the money . . . ' Something that farmers' wives say about each other. A common drift of gossip is to prove that what seems a wholly male-dominated society is in fact a closet matriarchy: the malice directed against the statuesque, calm Elizabeth Phillips-Turner is an example of this.)

She runs a business, making raw silk shirts to order, in a 'Drumsara' outhouse. It is her hobby and her interest; it is also, clearly, highly efficient and profitable.

FLYING ANTS

For a few hours one evening, flying ants have their life. The air is thick with them. The visitor cannot avoid swallowing one. The next day they are nowhere to be seen.

THE TAKEN

Beryl Wruck's death was the fourteenth recorded attack by a crocodile on a human being in Australia. Of the fourteen, eight were fatal.

WHAT CROCS DO

At a 'crocodile farm', an alarmingly ill-run and run-down establishment, a mad red-haired young North Queenslander in a leather hat cavorts with crocodiles in their pens. He is expert but horribly reckless.

Two salt-water crocodiles, an old male, 64, named Charlie, a 16-footer, and a young female, called Di of course, are the first to be fed. Charlie lies in a pool utterly still, Di is frisky and dangerous. It is the mating season (something that made Beryl Wruck's entering the water even more foolish). The mad keeper feeds her first with raw meat on the end of a strong nylon rope. The meat clamped in her mouth, he ties the rope to a metal stave stuck in the ground. He throws another lump of meat on a rope to Charlie so fast you almost miss it, there is a loud dull clap, and the meat is in the croc's mouth. But Charlie is 'tame', he lets the meat go and lies with his head on the end of the pool, his great jaws open. He has bad teeth.

In another pen, you look down on a patch of swampy water. Nothing is to be seen. The mad keeper enters, leaving the gate open. He throws a piece of raw meat on a rope above the muddy water. From nowhere a crocodile rises with speed – 'clap' and the meat is in its mouth. It then thrashes in a 'death roll', a terrifying spin – and is back down in the water.

Crocs rely on their prey being animals of habit. They notice you coming down to a creek with a bucket. They do nothing. They see you come a second time, there is a flicker of interest. Next time you go down to the creek, same place same time, the croc is there waiting for you. They can rear up out of the water to take you at shoulder or head height. The 'death roll' spin stuns the prey. The croc then gets it under water quickly, to drown it. They eat little – being cold-blooded, a great deal of their energy comes from the sun's heat. A fully grown salt-water crocodile will eat maybe 15 lbs. of meat at the most in one go – and then won't eat again for two or three weeks. They eat only fresh meat, though they will store a carcass for a while beneath the water, lodged under a sunken log, and go back next day for more. At the back of their mouths a flap prevents water entering their lungs. They can stay under water for up to 90 minutes. A curious eyelid can fold over their eyes to protect them under water. Their armoured backs are nerveless. They can live to 100 years or more. Besides shooting, and even that is not easy, the only way to kill them is to drown them by forcing a stick or rod down their throats, opening the flap at the back of their mouths. In a famous and fabled incident, this was once done by a thirteen-year-old girl (said the mad keeper).

REVENGE

After Beryl Wruck's death, carloads of furious men dynamited the creek indiscriminately.

'NOTHING HAS EVER COME OUT OF THE TROPICS'

David Thompson, editor of the local Mossman newspaper, came to FNQ from Melbourne 14 years ago. He is a fit, clear-headed but careful man, carefully pacing himself. A man of moderate opinions, he gave up drinking six months ago and looks well, though he has the appalling teeth of anyone in the area over 30. He was a farmer in Victoria but hit financial problems and – like so many – decided to build a new life 2,000 miles away in the tropics. His paper has a circulation of 1,500 – not bad as Douglas Shire, a huge area from Cairns to Bloomfield (as far as the visitor can find out, for some reason good maps are hard to come by locally) has a population of only 4,000 (it has doubled in the last ten years).

David is slowed by the tropics but is aware of it. He says that stress is a major problem for people living around Mossman. Tempers – and minds – snap easily.

The fate of many is to become lost in the blessed inertia of drink and ganja. The forcefulness of the cane farmers I met is an exception – the other residents, the sprinkling of the retired rich, the seasonal cane and mill workers who hang about the area during the slack, fall to dreaming. 'Nothing has ever come out of the tropics,' he says. He means invention, 'head work' as he puts it, 'that's for temperate zones, engineering, writing. You want to do any of your stuff up here, get into air-conditioning,' he says.

THE STUBBYHOLDER – A SOCIAL SURVEY

In working men's pubs and in pubs patronised by aboriginals, the stubbyholder is polystyrene, chipped and grey with sweat from many hands. In pubs that are predominantly white, with a few women drinking, the stubbyholder is of imitation leather, sometimes embossed with the image of an indigenous Australian animal. In the home of a wealthy cane farmer, with pretensions to the life of an old-style plantation owner, the stubbyholder is of the finest leather with a plastic interior, even a thin vacuum wall. In the homes of smaller, non-shareholder farmers, the stubbyholder is often home-made, non-vacuum with a polystyrene core but coated in the skin of an animal. The visitor has seen one made of turkey feathers. The rock-python-skin stubbyholder is, however, a favourite.

TROPPO (iii)

It only takes five days for the North European temperate zoner to be caught 'thinking troppo'. Simple decisions, making phone calls, arranging meetings, minor business matters which in London would be done without a moment's thought, in the tropics flower into a maze of difficult vegetation in the head. When after Machiavellian debate you have decided to do something, you have forgotten why you wanted to do it in the first place. So you don't do it.

This is a landscape of forgetting.

Throughout his fifty years as a hermit in the Daintree rain forest, Reginald Laird has codified everything. He wrote down what he wanted to do, then when he did it. Everything he built or planted is labelled with the date of its doing. At first sight this mania for listing and book-keeping seemed quaint and eccentric, but it is neither, it is hard common sense. Memory and the past are under constant threat. If you have to do 'head work', put it down on paper, at once. Then you can live with the climate, the place. You can live with memory under threat by nature.

The tradition of whites coming to the tropics to forget (Conrad) makes total sense in FNQ.

PARADISE

Two Port Douglas T-shirts – 'I'm bored with paradise' and 'Ho hum. Another shitty day in paradise'.

VICIOUS GOSSIP

A gossip tells the visitor that the wife of a well-known cane farmer was 'a tart' – that when young she and her sister were the only prostitutes in Mossman. The respected farmer caused a great sensation when he married her. The gossip, with Queensland garrulity, fights to draw a moral – that this is why the farmer is now so successful and so widely honoured.

The woman in question had previously shown the visitor her wedding photographs. She was beautiful in her wedding gown and veil.

'DRUMSARA' LOO STORY

The Phillips-Turners used to have Chinese servants at 'Drumsara'. These servants were always finding snakes in their lavatory. They came in under the door. When the Phillips-Turners ceased to have Chinese servants, they put a new door on the lavatory and decorated it in snakeskin wallpaper.

CAR STICKER

'Grow dope – plant a Pom.'

CHUCK OFF

'To chuck off' at someone – to argue with them.

IDIOM

'They was that wound up' – they were very angry. 'Stinking of grog' – drunk.

HALEY'S COMET

'After the comet's gone over, 'The Wet' will come, right?'

POISON

Dildren is an insecticide sprayed on the cane. With a perverse edge of pride, a cane farmer says it is 'banned everywhere else in the world'. Cane tops are used for cattle feed. The Dildren has shown up in milk.

OPERATION NOAH

'Operation Noah' – informing on dope traffickers and dealers.

OPERATION BLUDGER

'Operation Bludger', introduced after the success of Operation Noah, to inform on dole frauders.

THE LAST GASP

One afternoon, the visitor and his companions feel very ill. They suspect food poisoning. The heat and the humidity reach a level that a temperate zoner finds like the almost science-fiction atmosphere of another planet. The air has a sulphurous taste of bad eggs. If the visitor had had a barometer it would have been falling before his eyes for . . .

'THE WET' (i)

Two hours later and 'The Wet' has begun. It is 4 pm and like night. The roof above thunders. Frogs are drumming out a wall of sound. A conversation has to be shouted. The psychological release is enormous. The visitor and his companions are exultantly happy.

'THE WET' (ii)

Twelve hours later. The torrent still falls without a break. At midday, the Mossman Post Office Hotel pub is full of men, drinking happily. Visibility in the downpour outside is down to fifty yards. Cars drive with their headlamps on. Children in swim suits play happily on the pavements. The talk in the pub is of 'one of the latest ever' (though, by Reginald Laird's records, it is exactly on time), 'going to be a big one' and 'be a cyclone this year'. A pause. 'Only takes one.'

'THE WET' (iii)

Within hours of 'The Wet' beginning, the road to Daintree, along which the visitor travelled on the way to Cape Tribulation, is reported impassable. Telephone contact has been lost with Daintree and is erratic with Cairns.

CYCLONES (i)

The Americans call them hurricanes, or typhoons – they are the same phenomenon. The first of the season appears off Darwin and is named 'Hector'. Deep depressions form in the Coral Sea. The radio says they are being 'watched closely'.

Simple phrases often escape a stranger's comprehension. The phrase about cyclones the visitor hears again and again – 'one is enough' – is loaded with obvious meaning.

ONE IS ENOUGH

The visitor encountered a similar sang-froid in California, when he discussed the inevitable major earthquake to come. In all other ways North Queenslanders are half a world apart from Californians (an understatement), but they have the same stance toward a potentially murderous natural disaster. 'One is enough' – 'If you're gonna go, you're gonna go' – 'If it is God's will . . .'

THE LOOK OF IT

Now 'The Wet' has come, when for a while the rain stops and the grey, charcoal sky seems to be calculating which reservoir next to empty upon your head, you can see the rain-forested mountains again. They are a simple, clear cobalt blue. The flat cane fields beneath them are a shining pale green. The complexity of colours before 'The Wet' has been simplified into a contrast between a pure blue and a pure green.

MYSTICAL SANDALS

The visitor finds that his English holiday sandals have rotted in 'The Wet'. Also his toothbrush melted some days ago into a strange shape (for some obscure troppo reason he had left it on a stone in the sun – local advice about ultra-violet light). In Cairns he goes to a pharmacy to buy a new toothbrush. The shop is like a genteel Boots. He asks if they sell sandals. The respectable shop assistants light up with missionary fervour and talk the visitor into buying 'acupuncture sandals'. You walk on hard rubber spikes. A booklet explains how massaging different parts of the foot benefits the kidney, the pineal gland, the eye-ball etc. The pharmacy has a wall of these sandals, they do a roaring trade. The visitor wears them for a day. They make his feet sore.

THOSE ADS AGAIN

In motels, toward the end of the journey, the visitor is depressed by turning on televisions he encounters to be greeted by Queensland TV adverts plugging the 'Daintree Freehold Rain Forest'. In one a man of sixty says he is going to retire there. He has the tone of a bad methodist lay preacher, saccharine and insincere. (Is this history – the pioneering spirit – repeating itself as commercial farce?).

MOULDY

David Thompson tells a story about the 'Daintree Freehold Rain Forest'.

A very respectable and conservative English couple are given the full sales pitch, then driven up to see the rain forest block they are to buy. They listen politely to everything they are told. Then suddenly the woman turns to the man and says, 'I can't live here darling. My cunt would go mouldy.'

MAGNETIC ISLAND

The visitor holes up with his companions on Magnetic Island for a few days, hoping to get a swim on the Great Barrier Reef. Magnetic

Island is five miles off Townsville, the 'capital of North Queensland', two hundred miles south of Cairns.

The island, seen from the ferry, is beneath rain clouds that sit on the forested west coast like a black hat.

MOTEL BLUES

The visitor drifts south from Mossman and Port Douglas staying in off-season motels, one or two nights at a time (mid-summer is 'off-season' in the Australian tropics, because of the monsoon weather). Often he and his companions are the only customers. It is a world of a sea of tables set for dinner, glass cutlery and napkins gleaming, for which no one arrives.

One motel is baroque. The swimming pool has a swim-through jacuzzi in an artificial cave. The visitor and his companions swim 'skinny' in it at midnight. Afterwards the warm monsoon rain washes the chlorine away, and the mosquitoes go to work. This motel, between Port Douglas and Cairns, is Joh Bielke Peterson's dream – the jungle tamed as a back-drop for a restaurant upon a terrace. The rain forest as wallpaper. The staff say 'have a nice day' and try to speak mid-Atlantic American. With a little friendly prodding it slips – they are local Cairns people, trying to hold down a good job.

Another motel is bankrupt and the management resents travellers turning up, disturbing their misery.

The saddest motel was, ironically, opened by 'Joh' himself as an example of Queensland tourist progress. It is run by a family with two young children who have come from Sydney – the classic migration to a new life. They have been running the place for ten months and this is their first 'Wet'. They have been sick with the gamut of tropical ailments since they arrived – the husband's back is scarred with burnt-out ulcers – and he and she are desperately worried about their children's happiness and health. The rooms – the 'units' – of the motel are fetid, the air-conditioning pumps 'cold humidity' over the bed at night. But the family is determined to 'stick it out'. They are ambitious.

A CYCLONE WARNING

Magnetic Island, 23 January. 11 am. A cyclone warning is given on the radio. The tone is authoritative, the message ambiguous – it may come, it may not. The pressure goes down. You find yourself swallowing to clear your ears. The rain powers out of the sky, which seems to be black cloudy soup just twenty feet above your head.

STORM DIARY (i)

An hour later. The depression is now near Innisfrail. The warnings continue that it could become a cyclone. An official from the Brisbane Meteorological Bureau gives an interview. The depression could become a cyclone, he says, but it will take 24 to 48 hours to do so.

STORM DIARY (ii)

1.30 pm. There are two depressions, one inland near Cairns, one over the sea near Innisfrail. The visitor is told by a local resident that 'the one off Innisfrail is the one to watch'.

Palm trees bend and flail. The visitor thought he was in 'a tropical storm' when he woke last night. Clearly he was not. He also suspects he has still not been. The visitor says to his informant that he has no idea what the weather is doing. 'I tell you mate,' is the reply, 'neither do any of us.'

STORM DIARY (iii)

Half an hour later. It is difficult to know which storm is where. On the radio ('Station 4-T-O') an official of the Meteorological Bureau warns that the 'depression system off Cairns' is strengthening, could become a cyclone and is due to come ashore late this afternoon.

Meanwhile on Magnetic Island, 200 miles to the South, the downpour is as thick as ever and the wind is increasing. A 'strong winds warning' has been given to boats at sea in the Townsville area. Streets of the town are flooded. The radio gives traffic diversions.

The radio begins to play an advert from the National Building Society. You can go to any of their offices and pick up a free 'cyclone tracking chart'.

STORM DIARY (iv)

Evening news. The depression off the coast has claimed its first wrecks. The army has rescued four sailors by helicopter.

The near-cyclone giving Magnetic Island this storm is christened 'Clayton's' by the local people. Clayton's is an Australian non-alcoholic beer, 'not quite the real thing'.

STORM DIARY (v)

Next day. After the night and day of violent weather and bulletins on the radio, the depression changes track and heads out into the Coral Sea. It sucks the rain clouds after it and today the sky is brilliant blue. The temperature is 35°C. In the distance over the sea's horizon high clouds are in strange, pale shapes.

The visitor takes the ferry off the island to Townsville. On the seafront of the small port no public bench can be sat on, it is so hot. The pubs are full of silent men before their beers watching a one-day international cricket match on TV. The streets are deserted.

REEF SLANG

A 'Noah' – 'Noah's ark, shark'.

AN EX-TRAWLERMAN

Bill worked on the prawn trawlers out of Cairns. He would sometimes be at sea for five months at a time. The trawlers offload their catches to and are supplied by a mother ship. He is slight, wiry and rather camp. He says you can make a fortune sailing on the trawlers, but gives two reasons for coming off them – the isolation and the ugliness of the work. It is ugly because the trawlers rip the seabed to bits.

'HIPPY' FISHERMEN

The visitor is the guest at the house of fishermen on Magnetic Island. The house is wooden. His hosts have few things – there is a hunt for odd cups and glasses to drink wine from.

His host was a marine biologist who 'went troppo' and took up fishing some years ago. All the money he and his wife earn goes on their boat, which the visitor is told is magnificent. They have built it. It is laid up for the cyclone season in a Townsville creek.

All the company at dinner are lean, deep brown, almost emaciated. One, hairy as an Old Testament prophet, is a bankrupt. He had had a big old boat for some years and took supplies along the coast, Townsville, Cairns to Cook Town. The recently improved roads knocked his business out. Now he and some friends are trying to make seaworthy a wrecked boat beached up near Daintree. It is a dream.

They have all been living this life for ten years or more. If they were once 'hippies', they have become hardened. Underneath their thin almost black-skinned poverty-stricken appearance, there are still educated, student manners from Sydney and Melbourne. There is no Queensland garrulity. They are good, middle-class children transmuted in their early thirties into something else. They are the ones who have stuck it out up here.

PRAWNS

Four years ago there was a great expansion in prawn fishing. A lot of boats and trawlers went over to it. In the last year the price has dropped, people have got stung. There has been an unusual number of sinkings – there is laughter amongst the fishermen about insurance payments.

GAOL STORY

On Queensland TV there is a report about a tax official now in gaol. He is in an open prison outside Townsville, a 'state farm'. The bent revenue man had, the report said, more or less run the gaol. He ate regularly at local restaurants, and his cell had a well-stocked bar. Things came to a head when he was arrested with a prison officer at the races, watching a horse he owned. The horse won.

COOK'S COMPASS

Magnetic Island was named by Captain Cook. He believed the island's rocks deflected his compass. The rocks of the island are meant to be lodestones, natural magnets – the fishermen say they are there, but difficult to find.

THE DEVELOPER

The boss of Quintex, Christopher Chase, who is planning to build 9,000 chalets or 'condominiums' at Port Douglas, despite the appalling local water supply, first bought a Brisbane TV station. From that base he developed the power to speculate in fantastical building schemes throughout FNQ.

CHOIR PRACTICE

In off-season Picnic Bay, Magnetic Island, the visitor sat with the 'hippy' fishermen, soon after nightfall. Their children played around and under the wooden house on stilts. Suddenly, in the buzzing dark, a pure choir of women's voices began to sing the hymn 'Rock Of Ages'. It was the local baptist church at choir practice.

AUSTRALIA DAY

Of civilisation and its contents.

On his way out of the country the visitor is in Sydney for a few days. He drifts around a harbour district. It has been raining the last few days, but now the sun is out and so are the Australians, enjoying the public holiday. It is Australia Day, the 198th anniversary of the planting of the British flag on Sydney Point. He goes into a packed working-class pub. A huge drag artist dressed in 'country style' with a bonnet and frock off his mountainous shoulders clutches a raucous microphone. He tells a joke.

'Breakfast this morning. My husband said, "Do lemons squawk?" "No," I said. "Oh," he said. "I just squeezed the canary over my chips".'

Bright Past of Horrors and the Hazy Now

Visiting the Soviet Union in 1989

In 1988, Tariq Ali and I decided to write a play about Gorbachev, Glasnost and the Soviet Union. It was a time of confusion but also of hope on the Left; if the East reformed itself and democratised socialism, then the world would be reformed for the good. That hope turned out to be illusory, of course, and the socialist project to which Tariq and I, despite our political differences, are still loyal will have to be begun all over again.

I had never been to the Soviet Union, so I set out alone in the early summer of 1989. This is a journal I kept. The play was Moscow Gold: it was performed at the Barbican Theatre by the RSC in the summer of 1990 and, for one performance only, by three RSC actors with Tariq and I filling in, to a packed and hysterically laughing audience in the Moscow Children's Theatre in December 1990.

LONDON, 19TH JUNE

A sense of achievement! It took all day, but I've wrested – winkled out – finessed – prised – my visa from the Russian Consulate.

I started queuing by the Consulate entrance, a gate overhung by scraggy bushes and set in an old brick wall in Notting Hill, at eight in the morning. I thought I was smart by getting there early, but I was way back in the line.

Interesting, trying to suss the people waiting. There were business-men; 'boy-scouty, girl-guidey' middle-aged men and women (classic British CP members, I fantasised); a Vietnamese couple (going to the USSR for what, to visit a son studying at Moscow University? No, that doesn't add up . . .); and there were students

WELSH COLLEGE OF
LIBRARY
MUSIC & DRAMA

with that walnutty, gnarled look to their legs in shorts and bare arms in T-shirts, the look of 'principled travellers'. There was also a young woman from the strikers on the P & O Dover ferries (a bitter dispute that's dragged on for months). She explained that some of the strikers were being given a holiday by the Soviet Seamen's Union; she was there with their passports and forms to collect the visas. 'We're going because we need a rest,' she said, but turned taciturn when I tried to discuss the strike. Then I realised that some in the queue were 'runners' for travel agencies; 'professional Embassy queuer' is a full-time job. One had fifty-five passports and forms to process. My spirits sank. A small vigorous man in his late fifties turned up, described by one of the Embassy policemen as 'the Red Adair of the visa world'; what the Texan troubleshooter can do for an exploding oil well, this man can do for your visa problem. 'It's true!' he said, 'I can do Albania, you want Albania? Easy.'

After three and three-quarter hours of queuing I was inside, in a dusty room beneath a large oil painting of Lenin which hung tilted, out of true.

That inexplicably tilted portrait, which would have just taken one second to straighten but which had probably hung askew for months if not years, was the first touch of the unique sense of dereliction, of 'crazed inertia', which was to overwhelm me in Moscow.

My turn next at the counter . . . and there was an incident. A large American, in a dark silk suit which was impressive over wide shoulders but a bit of a mess around a big bum, exploded. 'What do you mean, you've LOST my passport?' A small young Russian woman, in a light blue angora cardigan that sang of a London shopping expedition, was wringing her hands in distress. 'We are sorry, is lost.' 'You can't lose a passport! That is not a possibility! I've been all over the world with that passport!' the American boomed. 'Is lost, is nothing we can do,' said the cardiganed young woman, near tears. The American stormed from the room in a state of disorientation.

My turn. The young woman and I smiled at each other, in what I hoped was shared contempt at the piggish behaviour of one of the Lords of the Earth. I began my spiel – 'I think you've got a fax from the Soviet Writers' Union in Moscow, confirming my visa . . . ' I thought she was going to burst into tears. But her face went blank. 'Is twelve o'clock. We are closed,' she said. 'Oh. But you do have a fax from the Writers' Union . . . ' 'Come back at three o'clock . . . ' And she was gone.

But the day didn't disintegrate. I had an interview with the Australian Broadcasting Corporation about the novel. (Is *Diving for Pearls* even advertised, let alone on sale down under?) It was one of those sessions where neither interviewer nor interviewee has the slightest idea why they are there. Anyway, did that, then went to the Oxford Street Marks and Spencer's, bought a few 'shirts for Moscow' . . . and at the counter, bumped into Lindy Posner, the costume designer. We had a coffee in Dean Street and swapped theatre gossip . . . the latest RSC horror stories, the news about Hayden Griffin, who seems to have disappeared into the Italian theatre – in our contracting profession, even the very best theatre designers can only get a living abroad – then it was, 'Why the hell are you going to Moscow, Howard?' 'To write a play about Gorbachev and perestroika . . . ' 'Sounds a bit laughy,' said Lindy. And laughed.

And I was back at the Consulate by 3.30 . . . The fax had been found, the visa was ready. 'Enjoy my country,' said a big young man with a stoop, the double-breasted jacket of his suit open and hanging forlornly to his knees.

*

Red buses coming up the Bayswater Road. The number 12, once a thread of my life in this city when I lived in Waterloo and Jane lived in Notting Hill. And Oxford Street on a sticky, hot day, amongst crowds shuffling at a slow speed that gives the long-legged back-ache. And a double espresso coffee in Soho; nudging a chunky, octagonal cup that rattles in its saucer, I sat on a stool before a wall of mirrors talking to a friend, noting a punk guy with a plumed mohican hair-cut buy a cheese sandwich. Racks of slacks in Marks & Sparks, black taxis, lunchtime joggers in Kensington Gardens . . .

All day I had that heightened sensation that comes from looking at the familiar, when in a few days' time you are to leave for a country you really know nothing about. Yeah yeah, I know the iconography, the overwhelming images of the Soviet Union, I've read the history books, I've been told traveller's tales; but really I know nothing about it.

*

Maybe it's because of the Aussie interview, but I remember something Patrick White said in Sydney. Writers shouldn't be afraid of the chaos of things as they come at you, he said. Bits of people's stories, and visual anecdote, the sudden look of things . . . that's the way for writers to begin to understand the world. In the end, if you don't panic, the mosaic reveals its pattern. This drives 'commentators' mad. White was against 'commentators'; I think he meant moralists and critics, the pedlars of easy patterns. I wonder, scribbling this tonight after a long day, and the grey folded card of a USSR visa tucked in my passport, what the Soviet mosaic is going to be like? A week's time I'll be there.

White had invited me to dinner at his house in the Sydney suburbs. I found him by no means the paranoid monster of legend, nor, indeed, the bitch-bastard he made himself out to be in his autobiography. The complexity of that faked persona is beyond me. He was very encouraging to talk to, and brilliant about writing. He'd asked to see me because a film company was considering whether I should write the screenplay of one of his late novels, *The Twyborn Affair*. It was immediately apparent that I was so hetero and he was so queer, that for this playwright to tangle with his work was out of the question; so on neutral ground we fell to an evening discussing everything but the book, de-molishing a bottle of Scotch, the sexual peccadillos of my fellow British playwrights, of which he was unnervingly well-informed, and the world in general. Though I only met him once, I was grief-stricken when he died. I'd been a fan of his books since I was a boy, something I was careful not to tell him. And I was furious at the obituaries in the British press, pecking like puzzled carrion crows at the 'bitch legend'. For me, he's one of the greatest novelists in the English language, light years ahead of Burgess or Greene, and James Joyce's peer. His day will come.

MOSCOW, 26TH JUNE

I'm fazed.

Writing this at eleven at night. A room in the Hotel Ukrania.

The ceiling seems thirty feet above me in the gloom. But one of the three lamps in the room works so I'm OK.

But fazed. I've been in stranger, more 'exotic' places in the world than here . . . And what's strange about this dilapidation, what's exotic about Moscow . . . Why has it disorientated me so much?

MUST get this account going.

*

The impact of the city. It's poor, shabby, with a strange magnificence.

A smell of petrol.

And a sweet smell. A mad thought – are there molasses, running in the sewers beneath the beat-up pavements and cracked roads?

A haze in the air. The silvery, unclean air. Boiling hot, 35° C.

The city on first sight seems Cubist. Or like a Robert Delaunay painting. The colossal Stalin-era buildings lean in the pale haze. Meshed into them and into ghastly sixties-looking blocks are old Moscow buildings. A flash, gold or bright green, of the dome of a church. All crumpled, grandeur mashed up.

Met by Nikolai, my Writers' Union guide, thirty-two years old. A well-manicured beard. One smile too many that sets into a grimace.

He is a sweet guy.

He is a maniac.

I meet him the other side of passport control. The first impression is of a friendly, almost obsequious young man. A small leather bag on his shoulder. A crisp, short-sleeved shirt. Dark grey slacks, sharply creased. Dark brown slip-on shoes that are shiny.

At first he almost goes to pieces. In the dim, scruffy baggage collection area, my big bag does not appear on the creaking carousel. Distraught, he repeats, 'They steal here, they steal . . . ' I have a benumbed calm. This diary, passport and money are in the battered shoulder bag that never leaves me. The secret of travel to mad places is to be a spaceman. Wear your support systems like a space suit at all times. I was regretting my copy of *The Canterbury Tales*, though.

The suitcase turns up on a carousel unloading from a flight from Hanoi.

No, Nicky will be an excellent companion.

No, he'll be a pain in the arse.

But 'reading' him is very difficult.

Is he bitter?

In Glasnost times does the Writers' Union send out embittered, raving anti-communists to guide Westerners, the total reverse of the legendary 'our-lorry-parks-are-wonderful-tonight-it-is-folk-dancing' guides of the 'bad old days'?

'To talk of Soviet reality,' raves Nikolai, 'is like kerosene in the mouth.'

(Terrific line . . . bung that into the play.) This in a beat-up Writers' Union car from the airport. He is getting his retaliation in early . . .

The driver says something.

Nikolai translates. He is sitting in the front with the driver.

The driver is smoking. I am smoking.

'He says please . . . ' translates Nikolai, 'to throw your cigarette out of the window. Not on the floor. Please to remember, Mr. Howard, you are sitting on the petrol tank.'

Ah.

On the road from the airport we pass a memorial by the roadside. Three huge iron tank traps.

Nikolai explains, but I know what it is. The monument marks where the German Wehrmacht reached in the Second World War. It is frighteningly close. The blockish city is within sight.

Nikolai returns to the attack.

'You can see museums for spaceflights and statues of the Reds or I will show you Soviet reality! But I don't know, perhaps you will turn away! You want spaceships!'

'Don't take me to your leader, take me to your supermarkets,' I say, idiotically. His head turns. The smile is in grimace mode.

The Hotel Ukrania.

Socialist Gothic.

Built in the late forties. Nicky's grandfather was one of the architects, he tells me, sheepishly.

It's vast. Ochre stone towers soar into the smeary blue sky. Atop the towers are classical urns with hammer-and-sickle motifs sticking out of them. It's all out of proportion. The urns must be huge.

Throngs of people coming up and down the broad steps before the main entrance, Zils and Volgas and bashed taxis parked before it, taxi drivers touting for business, inside at the reception desks a rotating swirl of people, a queue in search of a queue. Nikolai negotiates my checking-in.

This breaks my heart, but . . . I learnt much later, when Nicky visited me in London and we talked of the first day we met, that he had been to the hotel twice before my arrival, to study the procedures, so he would get it right and I'd not be hassled. Tenacious timidity . . . dogged persistence. It's a great trait. Millions have needed it in the Soviet Union, for too long.

*

Nikolai has a car. After I'd booked in to the hotel, we used it for a drive round the city.

A recent Lada. The windscreen is secured by four heavy bolts. (It's Italian; Western windscreens get stolen and sold on the black market.)

I swore the first thing I'd do in Moscow was to go to Red Square.

It seemed oddly small. Lenin's mausoleum looked modest, not the gigantic, lowering block of all the newsreels, the immovable granite of Cold War newsreels. It's pink too.

I was very moved. I didn't expect to be so overcome. 'Socialism's front room.' There were 'no smoking' signs.

St Basil's Cathedral. Onions painted in swirls etc . . . The building's shut up. Through a small window on one side I glimpse an old step ladder, leant against the pane, rags hung upon it.

(A story I was told later. Stalin was leaning over a model of Red Square with his architects. This was in the heyday of Stalin's destruction of churches, just before the war. Stalin brushed the little wooden replica of St Basil's to the floor. One of the architects had the nerve to pick it up and put it back on the model. Stalin said nothing, but St Basil's stayed on the model. And on the face of the planet.)

*

Conversation with Nikolai is a confused jumble. I ask about his apartment. It's not a state apartment. A union apartment? No. It is his grandmother's. She lives with you? No, she's dead. 'It is complicated,' he says, with a wave of the hand.

My visit is very important to him. He has made elaborate preparations; his wife and two-year-old daughter he has 'sent away', out of Moscow. I fear he wants something from me I cannot give him.

'Sent away, where to?' 'To her aunts in Siberia.'

Ah.

*

Nicky takes me to an art exhibition of Siberian winter scenes which, he says, have been greatly admired. They are grand, conventional landscapes of spectacular forests, snow fields, stormy skies beneath vast distances, i.e. Siberia. But, bizarrely, the pictures are all made out of feathers, elaborately inlaid, a soft marquetry giving a *trompe l'oeil*, chocolate-boxy effect.

Appalling kitsch, I thought, peculiarly nauseous to look at . . . snow fields, of warm feathers . . . Taking a spoonful of mousse, when you think it's ice-cream, and luke-warm gooiness hitting you. I don't know why the grotesque exhibition disturbed me so much.

*

I'm enjoying the Hotel Ukrania. The corridors are vast. The 'key ladies' sit at corridor intersections in splendid isolation at desks that are little fortresses. The corridors open into deserted hallways. There is a fine, chalky dust over the carpets and the huge, chunky and shabby sofas. Coming across one of these dim, strange areas deep in the massive hotel is like discovering the set for an Orson Welles movie that was never made.

From my hotel window there is a flat roof. Last night I climbed out and walked about. The roof's paving stones are buckled with weeds growing from the cracks. From one of the hammer-and-sickle Greek urns, a whole tree is sprouting. Old whisky and beer bottles and spent Canada Club sodas lie around and there are a couple of used condoms.

Dinner last night in the hotel's restaurant. Chaotic. Difficult to tell whether the food was meat or fish, but it was baked I'll give it that, very baked; a kind of rind, congealed to a tin dish. But there were cucumbers and tomatoes and 'Champinsky' and the restaurant was a great spectacle . . . a bustle of people dressed up for a night out, banging noises from the kitchen, a hullabaloo of talk beneath the high windows and dusty drapes of the vast room. An air of confidence, near hilarity . . . or was it hysteria? A middle-aged couple on our table were eating red caviar. 'In Moscow, just order this . . . ,' they laughed. I wanted to get an evening going and find out who they were, but Nikolai froze them out.

Poor guy, he felt desperately out of place. He wanted me all to himself. He has some kind of plan, I know it.

*

Traditional scene. The traffic lights stay at red. Cars stop. The road ahead is empty. Then, very fast, down the centre of the road, swaying as they turn onto the boulevard ahead as if they were in a movie chase, the Zil limousines. 'The Government,' says Nicky, sulkily. In the back of one of the limos I catch sight of a young guy, in a light grey suit, leaning forward holding a strap on the window jamb, an eager look on his face. Power. The last ride. An ironed cuff on a snow-white shirt, a dab of scent.

*

We drove past the Lubianka. An elongated statue towered up, in black bronze, at the centre of a traffic island, flowers at its base – Dzerzhinsky, Lenin's secret policeman.

*

What I am learning about Nicky.

He is Jewish, but neither he nor his family are religious or orthodox. 'I am sovietized,' he says, I cannot tell with irony or not.

He works in a hospital. He is a software programmer – 'engineer' – working on a diagnostic programme. He uses X-rays. The aim is computer programmes that can diagnose illnesses.

Back in England, I asked a doctor friend about this. 'State of the art stuff,' he said. I told him what I could remember of the computer details. 'Sounds Mickey Mouse,' was his response.

Nicky is idealistic about the work but bitter at being 'passed over'. His wife is a medical engineer designing medical instruments. Her pay is appalling; Nicky is ashamed when he tells me how much his wife earns, commenting 'no Western woman would work for it' – 180 roubles a month. She has three years' maternity leave; her job is reserved for her. (Neither has ever been to a Western country.) Nicky wants her to stay at home and look after their daughter permanently. There are state nurseries but the children become ill. Ill? Forty children to a class, the teachers can't look after them properly . . .

Nicky, a child of this state, has an odd mixture of cynicism and idealism which bewilders me.

*

I caught a glimpse of the Soviet housing system. Once you have a flat, you stay, that's your address. What you really want is a grandparents' flat, when they die: there's a way of securing this, but the complexities escaped me.

*

A walk in the early morning sunshine haze. Down by the river lorry drivers are breakfasting beside their big truck. They have smoked fish in newspaper, a paraffin stove with a kettle boiling, and a Nescafé jar.

*

Getting some fruit juice at breakfast, in the huge dining room of the hotel. A waiter whispers to me quickly : 'We change some dollars. You want?'

*

Street. The heat, in the static air, seems to be setting solid, into a resin that will clog up the lungs. No coffee-house, no way of getting a drink but for a Pepsi stand, with a queue of what must be over a hundred. Into a shop which is selling Bulgarian preserves in jars, some cucumbers and tomatoes. I buy tomatoes. They pick out the best ones . . . 'because you are a foreigner,' says Nicky. Muscovites will buy two kilos to get a kilo that's good.

*

There is a policy to convert cars to run on gas, as a 'green' measure against the pollution petrol brings. But I am beginning to learn that the Soviet Union is 'Post-Byzantine', in which enlightened measures turn into endless difficulties. The gas is a tenth the price of petrol. But the best converters are Italian, which are high-priced and only available in the Beriozka (foreign currency) shops, from which they quickly disappear onto the black market. The Soviet converters are terrible – taxi drivers complain of poisonous fumes, there are rumours of cars exploding.

*

When Soviet cars are parked the bonnets are left open a little, so leaking petrol fumes don't accumulate.

*

'What does it mean, it's the best one?' says Nicky, pointing to a slogan on a Coca-Cola can. Suddenly this smart, bright guy, trimmed beard, smart slacks, little leather shoulder bag, seems a stunned innocent. 'It's meaningless, Nicky,' I say, 'as meaningless as the Government poster I asked you about.' (This was a poster displayed in a large bookshop: it showed a clockwork hedgehog and a slogan that read, 'Are you ready for winter?' Soviet poster art of the Gorbachev era ain't up to the heroic Mayakovsky period of the early twenties . . . !)

*

In Arbat Street there were poets, crowds standing around them. Every poet recited by heart. I heard that catch in the throat, the tone of Russian lyricism . . . the cry of 'My life! My life! My era! . . . ' Nicky explained: 'People are very sensitive to the language. Judge by the applause, you'll know whether the poet's any good or not.'

*

Later someone says to me, 'Arbat Street in the early seventies, it was unique – the crowd was a uniform, grey sea of people.' Now they are dressed as brightly as any Western crowd on a hot day, but they don't talk much. You hear the shoes, shuffling on the pavement. I think Nikolai was disturbed when I spoke – a foreigner's language and voice raised in the packed, silent street.

*

To the Central Exhibition Hall. A huge building: outside there are indifferent sculptures by a West German artist. The car park is empty, there is not a soul in sight. Inside, I stare at an exhibition of Soviet headscarves. The rest of the space was taken up by an 'Exhibition Of Western Achievements'. Had I come to Moscow to look at American tractors?

Nicky and I went under the road, by the subway, into Gorky Park. Packed and a great park, fun to be in, actually fun. Better than Central or Hyde Park. Better than my local Dulwich Park.

Overlooking the park there rises a black glass and mauve marble tower-block, adorned by attentive cranes: a new leisure centre being built for the Party, Nicky tells me. Apartments, swimming pools, shops.

That may be so. But I've lost faith in the credibility of Nicky's observations because, in Gorky Park today, I had the most bizarre conversation with him.

We walked right through the park to the river's embankment. We stood in the bright sunshine, looking down at the black water.

'Howard,' he said. 'I've got a job in the West.'

I told him I was pleased.

'It's with Siemens.'

I was about to say, oh, you mean the company who were supposed to have used slave labour in Dachau, but . . .

'See?' Nicky said, handing me a ballpoint pen. On the side of the pen was the word 'Siemens'. 'A German businessman gave it to me. He was from their London office. He promised me a job. So I have to go to London.'

'When was this . . . ?'

'Oh, two months ago.'

Nicky smiles with enthusiasm. He stands squarely in front of me, black beard immaculately trimmed, gleaming white shirt smartly laundered. Laundered by whom? Not by him, I suspect, and his wife is away; by his Mum, making sure he's well-turned-out each day to talk to 'this Englishman who may help . . . '?

A queasiness in my stomach.

'Are you *sure* he offered you a job?' 'Oh yes.' 'Have you spoken to him again, written to him . . . ?' 'Howard, it's all arranged. I just have to go to London.'

*

Nicky did get to London in November of 1989. He phoned up, out of the blue, from Liverpool station. He'd travelled by train from Moscow, on spec, without his family. It was his first experience of the West.

Much against our better judgement, Tariq Ali and I bank-rolled his stay. But despite my tours of the worst places of the capital, the Waterloo *homeless citadel, the North Peckham Estate, lunch at the Elephant and Castle, etc., my 'anti-paradise tours', London looked like a field of gold to Nicky. It was a paradise.*

Then he rang his London contact, to say he was ready for the job, to sort out work permits etc. and move his young family over. He didn't even get to talk to the Siemens guy. A secretary cut him off. He telephoned eleven times and never got to speak to the Siemens employee who had given him a ballpoint pen – I imagine on a drunken night in Moscow, a Western businessman having a terrific time, meeting a bright young Soviet man, promising him the earth, meaning the promise for five minutes and, if he remembered it, having a flicker of embarrassment the next day. Meanwhile Nicky had rearranged his life, indeed all but wrecked it, spending his savings on the trip to London.

That Siemens ballpoint pen should have a place in a museum of modern dreams. It is as cruel as a whip.

That November, after his Siemens disaster, I saw a lot of Nicky in London. I took him with my family to our neighbourhood bonfire party. The occasion bewildered him: 'So this is an annual anti-Catholic demonstration?' 'Not really, Nicky, no, it's an annual excuse for a party.'

*

Lunch in the Writers' Union. I thought the wood-panelled room, with its stained-glass window, was the dining room in Bulgakov's *The Master and Margherita*, which catches fire . . . No, I'm told, that was in another building.

'But that's the staircase President Reagan addressed us from,' says a smiling man. 'And that's the table his security men were crouching under, out of sight of the cameras.' The food is good: recognisable lamb, smoked herrings, red caviar, salad, Georgian wine. I'm the guest of Mira, a Secretary at the Writers' Union and a translator. She eats hardly anything.

*

Mira is in her sixties, always immaculately dressed, petite, tough, a Party member, sophisticated and ascetic, hard and weary. She's a friend of Tariq Ali, over many years. I guess a friend of Tariq's father, a communist of long standing and sufferer for the Bhutto cause in Pakistan. My way is being oiled in this decaying regime. I even have a car at my disposal. The car doesn't have a clutch, the driver explains, sweating over the car's innards in the Writers' Union garden, therefore the car won't actually *drive* me anywhere.

*

A commotion in the dining room. Excited people run in with news, some stand and applaud. The Writers' Union has agreed to the publication of *The Gulag Archipelago*. 'What was the voting?' someone on our table asks. 'Unanimous.' 'Ah. Just like when we banned it.'

*

The supermarkets . . . Oh, the smell of defeat, of a defeated society – the stinking sausage, the fatty cuts of livid-looking pork – the dull metal of empty freezer cabinets – and the sweat of the queues, suffering in a dim atmosphere of failed neon lighting, floors with tiles peeled away.

You feel angry for the shoppers . . . a stupefied foreigner's rage.

In two supermarkets there were piles of eggs which no one bought – a salmonella scare is sweeping Moscow. In another there were dozens of bottles of Russian champagne – 'Champinsky' – wrapped in white paper: they were selling fast. There was literally nothing else but for the unsaleable sausage, tins of fish and Bulgarian pears in jars. I learn that at many places of work there are fridges, where you can store any food you picked up on the way to work or in the lunch hour.

People are not starving, but the hassle is wearying, the petty uncertainty of where the next day's food for a family is coming from is an all-consuming preoccupation. How is anyone going to think about 'democracy', 'third-way socialism' etc.?

*

Outside a big bookshop there is a big queue. What for? Mandelstam? No, a D.I.Y. book just published, that people are desperate to get hold of.

*

Mandelstam, Akhmatova are published now, but in small editions. You'll get one from the black-market dealers that hang around outside the bookshops.

Book bartering goes on. Alexandre Dumas' books – wildly popular in the USSR – are like currency. Five Dumas for an Akhmatova . . . I was told.

*

Gorbachev's accent is very pronounced to Moscow ears, it's throaty, a 'hurr' sound, a soft 'H' for a 'G', his stress is wrong, he uses wrong cases. Educated Muscovites sneer at his speech.

*

A day of meeting people at the Writers' Union.

Natalya – I didn't get her name – vivacious, late thirties, fizzing with that brilliance that some Soviet intellectuals have.

I asked Mira about the brilliance. Is it the education? No, she says, it's the counter-education.

The counter-education, the criticism you do for yourself.

Natalya says: 'The submitting majority, the old problem in Russia.'

Mira says: 'To us the present is hazy – the past is more real, even the future.'

*

Natalya's off to her dacha for the weekend. She leans out of the window of her office, into the Writers' Union's garden, and says something with a laugh to someone passing by. I know what she's saying! . . . 'I'm doing the perestroika talk for a foreign writer . . . '

*

Sugar is rationed. The July ration is three kilos. You get coupons. The reason is illegal vodka stills: sugar is disappearing because people are buying so much.

*

I meet Lev, in the coffee bar of the Union. He says to me, 'How does it feel, coming here from paradise?'

He becomes self-lacerating: 'It has damaged me. Living the lie. I don't know how to live with myself' and 'The head and the body aren't joined; what are we? European head, Asian body, not joined, the neck is broken.'

I have a flash – hang on, didn't Gorky say that?

Lev – we're now sitting in the Writers' Union garden, by the statue of Tolstoy – goes into a spin of Russian self-loathing. 'We know what is wrong, we know the mistakes. But we don't know what to do.' 'We don't know the basics . . . ' 'To Russians, it's one extreme or the other. Black or white. It's totalitarianism or anarchy, no grey, in-between way of living.' 'Perestroika? It won't work, because they don't want it to work.' 'It has damaged me, living the lie. I don't know how to live with myself.' 'All that I wrote, before 1985, how am I to look at it? Is it contaminated? Does it mean nothing?'

A man who lived an unheroic life, perhaps. But . . . maybe he was a joker?

*

I had sympathy with Lev. His self-lacerating reflections seemed startlingly honest to me. He had the waspishness of Russians. Why we think of Russians as being, typically, clod-hopping heavies I don't know. The people I met were quick, witty, mercurial and passionate. They have a satirical spirit, sharpened by their sufferings. Not for them, Nibelungs and Fausts: their poetry is lyric and fast and cut-glass, pointed to the heart. But when, back from Moscow, I met two Leftist friends, Israeli dissidents, who live in virtual exile in London and have had a lot to put up with in their lives, I tried to discuss Lev's convolutions, saying, 'How would any of us have got through the fifties, the sixties in that country?' They exploded with anger, cursing the Levs of the world. 'You'd have gone to gaol, Howard.' Would I? We've had some lousy governments in Britain, and you can get called a loony etc. for being in opposition to them, and become unfashionable and maybe have the odd TV play turned down. But I'm talking of something on a far greater scale: how can any of us tell, in the West, how we would behave under state terror of the scale the citizens of the USSR experienced?

'Pity the land that needs heroes . . . ' Yes, and don't assume you'd be a hero, when you come to judge a compromised writer out of the old Soviet Union. The undoubtedly heroic Solzhenitsyn is writing . . . poison.

*

'Have you noticed,' says Mira, who I suspect has lived an heroic life, ' . . . have you noticed . . . we never say "I" . . . We say "we" . . . we think "our", not "my" country.' Collectivism!

*

'Who is stealing the food?' 'Stupidity. Stupidity is stealing the food.'

*

'No one has died of starvation yet. It is best that things get worse. Then they will have to listen to our new economists,' someone says around the table at the Writers' Union. Gibberish, I thought.

*

I meet Rosov, a playwright, a respected war veteran. 'I was in Germany last year,' he said. 'I asked them what are your worst problems? They said – we're very worried about our dogs.' Rosov's leathered face crinkles with weary laughter.

*

To GUM, the famous shopping mall beside Red Square. The building is unexpectedly beautiful, the shops inside are wretched. I bought badges, a Soviet speciality, and some LPs of Schnittke's music. Great quality control at the record shop: the assistant inspected the grooves and if there was a visible fault, ditched the record into a bin under the counter. Two copies of Schnittke's piano concerto were thrown away.

Into a shoe department. A lot of people stood staring at the shoes, buying nothing, not talking. The quality was terrible. The silent crowd stared on. Apparently there was a rumour that Polish sandals were going to be delivered. The crowd seemed to be . . . grieving.

After we'd left, Nicky said he felt bad. 'It upsets me, showing you such a thing.'

*

Many people will join a queue, just to see what's at the end of it. I joined two during a walk. At the end of the first, there were orange nightdresses, being slipped quickly out of boxes; at the end of the second there was coffee in small yellow and green packets (there has been some kind of coffee disaster – a consignment of muck has been bought, and they are off-loading it in the state shops. The citizenry – always in the know – are avoiding it).

Is this furtive, quick street-selling – open the box, attract the queue, get rid of the stuff – private enterprise? Perhaps not. I'm told that big stores will have a small consignment and prefer to sell it off round the corner, on the street.

*

Nothing that you're looking at is really what you're looking at.

The word that is said to me most frequently is 'reality'. 'Soviet reality' means the food difficulties, the housing shortage etc., etc.

KIEV, 2ND JULY

A train of twenty-three coaches. A twelve-hour journey beginning in the evening. 'Travelling bourgeois,' Nicky's aunt said. That is, we have a two-berth compartment. A samovar at the end of the carriage, looked after by a student who sleeps on the train – a solution to one person's housing problem. The train is clean and immaculate, a GDR coach, heavy with chrome fittings. Nothing to eat.

Dawn, silver birches for miles.

Nicky tells me his life story. He had a marriage of convenience with a Peruvian woman, who was a student at Moscow University. For four years they lived in one room with separate beds and never slept together.

He had a plan to fly to Lima with his wife. He'd found out that the aircraft would refuel at Shannon airport, where he planned to run from the plane shouting that he was a political refugee.

The tenacity! I'm appalled by Nicky's story. Now, because of Gorbachev and Glasnost, no government will want to know anti-Soviet refugees any more. And the Soviet Government is preparing a law to allow foreign travel: at a price.

*

Call him Vlod. He's my guide from the Kiev Writers' Union and turns out to be a nationalist of a most virulent type.

So my two guides have been a Jewish dissident who wants to leave on the strength of a ballpoint pen and a raving Ukrainian nationalist. A trial in many ways! On the other hand, more informative than an old-style guide.

'The Reds!' spits Vlod.

Such an innocence about both guys, a naivety. A fool can see that Nicky won't prosper in the West and that Vlod's nationalism can only end in ruin.

*

What Mira said goes over and over in my mind, as my two crazed guides rant on and on: bright past of horrors, dim hazy present, bright hopes for the future . . .

*

Vlod says that he was near Chernobyl on holiday, in a Writers' Union dacha, when the reactor blew. He lay in the sun for two days, unaware he was beneath a radiation cloud.

(Do I believe this? I'm writing down what I was told.)

For four days after the accident nothing was done.

The first sign something was wrong was when it was noticed Russian officials were leaving. There were rumours of limousines making their way to the airport, their occupants wearing gasmasks. All normal flights were cancelled in order to get them out.

The radiation is patchy, a field is free, the wood next to it is deadly. The cloud wandered, leaving an irregular pattern. Only last week they decided to evacuate fourteen villages.

Vlod was in hospital for a year. The radiation got him in his back. He eases into a comfortable chair in the Intourist Hotel with a sigh of relief. 'Any little comfort welcome,' he says. And he speaks of a cow with one eye, a pig with no legs, dandelions two metres high, deformed children.

What is the truth? The worst of the stories, no doubt, are the ones that are true. (And a Russian nuclear disaster is wonderful propaganda for a Ukrainian nationalist.)

*

The Intourist Hotel is more orderly than the Stalinist dream halls of the Hotel Ukrania in Moscow, with its chaotic dinners and breakfasts and dollar-touting waiters.

I begin to have to take care of Nicky. He is dazed by staying in an Intourist Hotel; he has never been in one before. If, he says, a Russian has to stay in a hotel, it's four men in a room, stinks and has stains of red wine on the wall. He thinks the dreary Intourist hotel is a palace. I try to explain: it's nothing like a Western hotel; it's a no-man's-land, a curious interface.

*

We go into a free market, and I see my first orange in the Soviet Union. Lines of small stalls are run by women in country clothes, broad skirts, headscarves, a tough-looking lot. The displays are the same: good new potatoes, fat radishes, garlic, parsley, bright, succulent carrots, cherries. The cherries are seven roubles for a kilo; meat is five roubles a kilo. (The average weekly wage is around sixty roubles.) These prices are way beyond what most can afford and not much trade is being done in the market.

*

In his hospital work with gamma cameras and radioactive isotopes, Nicky has to be careful. He carries a dose meter, a personal geiger counter.

We were walking along the main street in Kiev. It began to rain and Nicky's dose meter went off. I didn't know what the beeping from his shoulder bag was. We sheltered under a tree then dodged into a doorway, and hurried back to the hotel. In my room he used the dose meter to check a couple of bottles of beer we'd bought, then ran the water in the basin and checked that: nothing. Though the meter had a low setting, easily set off, Nicky was nevertheless shaken that the rain activated it. And . . . he apologised to me, as if he felt responsible or ashamed.

*

Usov, the Defence Minister, was being questioned by the Supreme Soviet on television. A bull-man, a Brezhnev face of coagulated folds of lava. He was confirmed in his position.

*

At the open air Ukrainian Museum, out in the countryside, a huge collection of country and village buildings from the past laid out, region by region, across the countryside. There's a magnificent wooden church and gardens around the cottages, immaculately maintained. It's hot. There are bees.

We sit in a reconstructed bell tower beside a reconstructed, early-nineteenth-century church. The two guides chat to each other, about life's evils, no doubt.

'What are you saying?' I ask Vlod, after a while.

'I'm saying that if nothing's done soon, there won't be any of us left.'

'Oh,' I say. 'Emigration, the death of the nation.'

Later, between a vast collective farm's field – wretched crops three or four inches high – and a private plot – luxuriant crops roaring to head height – I watch a man with a bicycle herding a flock of big, fat geese along a path, flicking a stick.

To whose table, Ukrainian goose?

Vlod is going on about his roots, how he was brought up in a village. He tells me of the priest in his mother's village being put under the ice before the assembled villagers, who were told it would be done to anyone who did not support the Soviet power.

Yes? I say.

'The Reds will pay!' raves Vlod.

'The Kremlin will fall!' echoes Nicky.

'No', I say. 'It will change. The Gorbachev reforms will work.'

They didn't seem to hear me.

Indeed, whenever I raise an objection to Nicky's anti-Soviet expressions, he doesn't hear me. No reply.

Today, was I in a hell for Western Leftists, walking through a Ukrainian village where the peasants are all on the fiddle, being got at by a Ukrainian nationalist who scores a full ten on the Ian Paisley scale of bigoted rhetoric, and an anti-Soviet, would-be escapee dissident? And all this arranged by the Soviet Writers' Union, for a visitor with Party-approved, go-through-the-diplomatic-channel status and official car, albeit clutchless. Where's the Communism, comrades?

Ah well. I s'pose it's good for me.

*

My nutter guides were, of course, right. Gorbachev's reforms came to nothing and the Red Kremlin fell. It looks like I was the nutcase by that Ukrainian hedge: for now, anyway.

*

A tourist walk around Old Kiev with Vlod, accompanied by his KGB tails – big men in light-blue, short-sleeved shirts, brown Terylene trousers, and carrying empty shopping bags as a desultory concession to looking 'normal'; they slouch along thirty yards behind us.

A huge Brezhnev-era sculpture in gleaming metal above the wooded hills, and an arch, I think meant to symbolise Russian-Ukrainian friendship. 'We call it the yoke,' says Vlod.

Sites of churches razed by Stalin, the walls marked by patterns upon the ground. They didn't build the statue of Lenin, which was to have a revolving library in his head.

I stared out over the archaeological site of the centre of the city. Abandoned for two centuries. A dim sense of this history: didn't a Ukrainian Tsar get to the walls of Byzantium?

The great church of St Sofia was spared. The story is that the French ambassador's wife was visiting Kiev and wanted to see the cathedral. It was already mined by Stalin's engineers, but the destruction was delayed for the Ambassador's wife to see it. Then war broke out and the church wasn't dynamited. It's magnificent: from floor to ceiling the walls are painted with Byzantine images. If only they had built Lenin's revolving head nearby: isn't the Soviet Union a Byzantine bureaucracy, built on that empire's invention of a 'need to know' civil service hierarchy?

*

To Mikhail Bulgakov's house: a typewriter, a White Army hat, little else. Just a writer's house and, for the first time on this trip, a stupid American voice: it was going on and on about how wonderful it was to see things the author had touched. I don't get it. I felt the same visiting Chekhov's house next door to the Writers' Union in Moscow. Houses of great writers – but they're just houses. Bulgakov's hat is just a hat.

*

At Babi Yar, the trench where the Jews were shot – no one knows how many – is yawned over by an appalling statue of twisted bodies in a grey stone. The monument was erected in 1978 after much agitation. It's a park in what is now a suburb of Kiev and an awful place. Nicky and Vlod fell to an argument in Russian, which became intense, then heated. They were both upset, Vlod was sweating, his wispy beard running with beads of water. Later I found out, from Nicky, they were arguing about whether Ukrainian, pro-Nazi troops took part in the massacre. The official line has always been that only German troops killed there.

*

In the evening I rush off, alone, to meet a couple of Ukrainian poets who, oddly, are about to set off for Edinburgh by train, to get to the Festival. I take a kilo of cherries. We get blind drunk.

They much admire Melvyn Bragg's books; drift of bright people to a metropolis, from a country backwater – it is a very Ukrainian theme.

*

I was visited by one of the poets in London, in 1992. The Ukrainian magazine he edited had collapsed because of paper shortage and, independence having been gained, no one was interested in cultural aspirations any more. No hassles from authorities, no KGB tails, but what's the meaning of poems of liberation when you're liberated with inflated coupons, not even real money, in your hands, and those fat white geese are being cooked for a distant mafia table? He and Vlod and the nationalist intelligentsia got what they wanted and at the same time their world disappeared.

*

Little heads of Lenin and Marx, mementoes, in a glass case. And a Soviet fob watch, for four roubles, what, 45 pence unofficial rate? 'Buy the watch!' says Nicky. 'They're prized, difficult to get.' I buy it, it's beside this notebook in the hotel room. It's shiny, tinny, it clicks rather than ticks, it's mass-produced but it's sought after, it's a common thing but anachronistic, it works as well as a Swiss Swatch which it ain't. And they won't make them much longer. It's my souvenir of the trip.

MOSCOW, 5TH JULY

A great crowd of people at the station. Young army recruits, in scruffy uniforms, being marched along the platform. One of my two bags is at Nicky's home: it seemed silly to take them both to Kiev. Arrangements unravel. The key to Nicky's home is at his father's house, his father isn't in . . .

To the Hotel Rossya, legendary for vastness and ugliness.

The Writers' Union car has a clutch again! Nicky and I drive up to Moscow University. There's a wedding. We go to a Beriozka, I buy Nicky some washing powder and a bottle of wine.

Out of nowhere, the Moscow Film Festival arrives in the huge hotel. Floods of people. There are boards being hammered up announcing the films. Video equipment is being unloaded. In the foyer a beautiful young woman in high heels, red blouse, grey skirt, stares out of the window, adjusting her sleeves: an interpreter, waiting for a Festival guest.

*

Dinner in a flat. Nicky's friends, all leaving the country. A children's surgeon who has cut his hand; it's become infected and he can't shake the infection off.

The flat is like a magic box, beds fold away, tables can be moved. They colonise a corridor with their neighbour, putting up a door on a landing for the two flats, making storage space.

*

Amongst the guests, Tanya, a graphic designer. Her husband is a translator.

Tanya says: 'This country is unpredictable. It's a bear. You think you're safe with it. Then it'll bite you.' . . . and . . . 'We Russians don't know how to bend a stick. Always we bend it too far and it breaks.'

*

On the last day I go to say goodbye to Mira.

She says: 'High anxiety. High hopes. Yes?'

'Yes,' I say.

'It is a revolution. Perestroika. No doubt about it.'

She pauses.

'But people are beginning to cheat, and be cruel. Doctors, cheating their patients over drugs. Little things, mean things. In the bad times no one was mean in that way. When times were at their worst, we always treated each other well.'

I have no idea what she is talking about, only that she is touching on a dreadful fear.

She turns to me. Her small face is lined, her dark eyes are full of tears. She says, 'I could never leave. Actually, never. Despite it all.'

A silence.

Then she admits what I've suspected for some days. 'I'm sorry about Nicky. I got him the job translating for you. His mother is a close friend. He wants to learn about the West. Did he irritate you too much?'

'Never mind,' I say. 'If you'd been my translator, I'd have just got the Party line.'

'Yes you would have,' she says, steel in her voice. And grins.

Rehearsing

This is a rehearsal diary of the premiere of Berlin Bertie *at the Royal Court Theatre, March and April 1992*

Berlin Bertie tells the story of two sisters. Alice, played by Penny Downie, is a social worker in London, her life in crisis. Her boyfriend, Sandy, played by Kevin Allen, and a street performer, Joanne, played by Susan Lynch, cannot help her. Alice's sister, Rosa, played by Diana Rigg, returns from Berlin after the fall of the GDR, pursued by 'Berlin Bertie', a secret policeman, played by Nick Woodeson. Together the sisters repulse 'Bertie' and flee England for a new life.

MONDAY 9TH MARCH

The first day of rehearsals.

Didn't like the article I wrote over the weekend for the Royal Court programme. Got up at 6 am and did a new one.

This last-minute writing and rewriting of the past month or so, of the TV play *Bribing God* and of the rewrites for *Berlin Bertie*, it's not healthy! But I need the 5 am adrenalin hit. Can't get enough of it. And there'll be plenty in the week ahead. I'll be in rehearsals all day, the early morning will be the only time to do rewrites.

*

10 am. Up to the third-floor rehearsal room at the Old Vic in the theatre's creaky old lift. The venerable, battered old theatre . . . walls chipped by years of good and bad acting . . .

There are mirrors. A mirror is the LAST thing to have in a rehearsal room.

The Royal Court management are all there. Doughnuts and coffee on the first morning of the rehearsal of a new play, a Royal Court tradition.

No one enjoys the occasion. A crippling, naff shyness forces the knees together. The Royal Courtiers mingle with the actors; the actors are, inevitably, guarded at being 'looked at' by strangers.

Am I going deaf? I begin not to understand what people are saying to me. It's nerves. Actors make me shy because they're so beautiful (and brave! They take on the crippling social disease, shyness, of which I still have bouts, . . . the ultimate horror of a shy person, to walk onto a stage? . . .).

Anyway, I lumber around the gathering, smiling foolishly.

Then, relief. Danny Boyle, the director, clears everyone out of the room except for the actors and the production team, and we read the play.

*

It's important at the beginning of a rehearsal not to have a fantasy about how the rehearsals will go. ('In the theatre you never, ever learn from experience . . . ,' Bill Gaskill once said to me.)

There's a rush of joy amongst the directing and stage management team at the excellent cast. If we can get the rehearsals going, we can have a lot of fun.

But in my department, the first stab of worry gets me. The first act reads well, but is too long. I have to cut. I know the actors – particularly Penny and Nick – will resist this. It read at one hour six minutes, which means it could play at over an hour and a half. It shouldn't exceed one hour twenty minutes. I think Danny and I may already be committed to a long campaign of attrition, to wrest lines from the actors!

And the second act . . . The wave of rewriting I did last week has left some good, some bad things on the beach. Alice's confession is fiercer now, and it's right to develop the scene of 'Bertie's' return. But I've dissipated Rosa's crisis.

I fear the 'second half, not as good as the first' phenomenon, which cripples so many plays (all of Oscar Wilde's, except for *The Importance*, many of Shakespeare's – *Henry V*, *Hamlet*, *Measure for Measure*, *As You Like It* – tho' 'cos it's Bill no one admits it. The only playwright who never wrote a disappointing second half is, inevitably, sodding Chekhov.)

My second worry is that Rosa's part is desperately underwritten and, as the play wears on, the text is, for her, a cascading mess of reactive lines. I'm going to have to rewrite heavily. Will Diana take the confusion, while I do that? (How does this great actress work in rehearsals? Danny B. and I are going to have get over our awe of her from *this moment* on.)

I often saw Rosa, in my imagination, avoiding eye contact, turning away . . . If you met her, you'd think she was full of disdain, even condescending. Inside she rages. The trouble is that in writing her, I became fixated with this aspect – a striking, dominant woman, trying to deflect attention from herself, to disappear . . . which, of course, is exactly what she's trying to do by leaving her husband.

There's so much that I *must* fix. Can I get out of rehearsals on Wednesday, to have at least the morning to write?

Here we go. *Hard work*. The playwright as jazz player, going through the night, improvising his text anew. Hopefully.

*

At lunch time, the poster designer arrives. The work is wonderful.

Danny and I have been trying to ban images of Berlin Wall, barbed wire and gun towers from the play. 'Flight, the play is about flight!' we rave, to the mild embarrassment, I fear, of the press office team.

I want SONG not moralising in my new plays. I'm sick of the political epic's pseudo-moralising tone . . . 'Oh look at all these silly people crawling through the play's scenes like cockroaches, let me squash one by giving him/her a stupid remark the audience will roar at.' Satire is not enough. It too easily ameliorates. It degrades into 'holier than thou' moralising. Moralising satire is clever-clever writing. I've done too much of it.

*

And now for something maddening.

At lunch time I am suddenly told that the Young People's Theatre Scheme committee at the Court 'object' to the family of the murdered baby, the case that has broken Alice's heart and mind, being black.

In a flash of anger I find myself saying to Danny, 'Where are we living? In Maoist China? Being hauled up before Red Guards?'

Danny Boyle gives me an old-fashioned look. 'Max knows what he's doing, sending you that guy's pompous letter', he says, and laughs.

But I hear the loonies have got at our assistant director, Danny Carrick. Peeing next to me in the grim third-floor Old Vic gents, he says, 'I have difficulty with the dead baby . . . ' (Discussions about art and ideology in England are so furtive!)

I relax. This could become wonderfully farcical.

*

After this spate of nonsense the afternoon is wonderful, as Kevin Allen digs into his long sequence at the top of the play, breaking it down with actorly skill and elegance. I cut one line, change another at his request.

At 5 pm I met a young journalist from *Plays and Players*, Nick Curtis. He was interesting on German theatre. I rode a bus back to Camberwell with him, thus breaking a prime rule for artists talking to journalists: don't socialise with the carrion crows!

It's strange with the first press interview on a new play . . . You work on it for over a year, then you open your mouth and find out in a split second how you're going to talk about it! You're often stunned into silence by the first obvious question, 'What's the play about?' It's tempting to adopt the Samuel Beckett manoeuvre. There's a Royal Court legend that, during a rehearsal of one of his plays, Billie Whitelaw advanced to the end of the stage and called out to Beckett, who sat at the back of the auditorium: 'Sam! Sam! What does this line mean?' A silence, then out of the darkness came the reply, 'How can we tell?'

*

For a playwright, rehearsals are about delivering the play to the actors. Turning it over to them. You should aim to become redundant by the last week of rehearsal, when the text is set and they know it by heart – which you don't. Give the play away to them: it's that simple and that difficult . . . Particularly when the last twenty pages collapse in the first read-through!

*

Back home, Corinna Brocher, my German agent, has left a message calling for the new version of the play for the German translator to start work . . . Aie aie! Tonight *Berlin Bertie* seems like a building site, with scaffolding and unfinished walls, unglazed windows and mess everywhere! My brain? A small concrete mixer, that can't churn fast enough . . .

*

I ring Danny to chew over the day's work. We look at possible cuts for tomorrow morning's rehearsal, between Nick and Diana.

Length, length. *Determined* not to have an over-long first half. Danny and I know we must hit it hard, now.

The *Moscow Gold* lesson. I was so worried about the second half of the rehearsal draft of that play, that Tariq and I gave it a thorough rewriting. As a result, the second act ended up tight and rather good. But then it was too late in the rhythm of rehearsal time – and of writers' exhaustion – to do anything about the looser, over-long first act, which wasn't bad but had flaccid moments that should have been nipped and tucked. Twenty minutes should have gone. It was a technical, a craft failure, nothing to do with politics or higher thoughts. (I loved the radical, reckless show though, with David Calder's marvellously complex Gorbachev, and with its aching, big heart, its attempt to make the design as articulate as the spoken word.)

So we must cut. Before the text and the acting begin to set.

*

We must remember that we all know each other, or are familiar with our 'new play' world, but Diana does not. We mustn't seem intimidating, 'cliquey' to her. We need a good, happy three hours, which is why, I think, Danny B. has called a rehearsal of the big scene first thing tomorrow.

TUESDAY 8TH MARCH

Up at 4.30 am. An hour and a half on the text, achieving little.

I get to the West End by 7 am, for a breakfast meeting with David Aukin, Michael Kustow and Jack Gold in the Ramada Hotel in Brewer Street, to discuss a first draft of a TV script called *Bribing God*, about the BCCI scandal. I'm early, so I go to the Star Café nearby (oil cloth tables, Sky-TV coverage of the cricket World Cup) to look over the script and prepare a little for the discussion to come.

A grand breakfast under a high, baroque ceiling, the sausages sticking to their hotplate . . .

Kustow keeps the project alive, just.

*

Meanwhile outside, the streets, empty at 7 am, had become jammed. A small bomb had gone off at Wandsworth. Mainline stations were closed and because of a suspect package in Lillywhites, Piccadilly was sealed off. The police were very nervous; the public, approaching them with questions like mine: 'Is Leicester Square open?' etc., seemed sullen, quite unconcerned.

I got to the Old Vic just in time for the beginning of rehearsals and . . . whoosh! A wonderful morning rehearsing with Diana and Nick. Lines taking off, the characters suddenly present for whole tracts of dialogue . . .

What I feel is – relief.

I've been aware that I knew where Susan, Kevin, Penny and Nick were coming from. I know Penny, both she and Nick have been in David Hare's plays, they know how my generation of playwrights scuff around in rehearsals . . . Kevin and Susan, though I don't know them, are onto the wavelength . . . I didn't know whether Diana would even take rewrites. Stupid of me! 'I got Tom [Stoppard] to change 60 pages out of a 90-page script!' she laughed. We rehearsed the second-act scene between Rosa and 'Bertie'. Some bits fell to pieces, not a lot. (Not like the last two-thirds of Act III . . .)

Lunch time, Danny Carrick brought letters from the Court about the 'dead baby issue'. Oh dear oh dear. I lose my temper and shout at Danny C. Unpardonable of me. I apologise to him as we go down the stairs to get sandwiches. I try to joke with him, I was shooting the messenger. He takes it very well. Watch it, watch it, Howard . . . this ire . . . like a lava of bad breath . . . goes with being nearly fifty, which is old for a playwright to be still functioning. It's an 'old man in a hurry' syndrome.

*

In the afternoon there is a return to the peace of trying to make a scene work. Alice and Joanne, waking in the flat at the beginning of the play. I trawl for cuts. Danny B. is insistent, we *must* boil the first act down, protecting the climactic scene between Rosa and 'Bertie'. Penny, who was in Adrian Noble's RSC production of *The Plantagenets*, famous for its bloody cutting sessions, fights her corner like a veteran. But the scene tightens. More may have to be done.

Afterwards, Danny B. tells me he is very worried about the budget for the set. It is being squeezed. The awful truth about the Court is that there is no money to do anything, it's a miracle of stinginess and 'winging it' that the theatre is still open for new plays, and anything that is done is by sleight of hand and conjuring tricks. It's been like that for ten years.

Back home after a long day, I can't take in the TV news. I've been in my own balloon all day long . . .

I try to ring Max, but he is out, so I write him a letter about 'the dead baby' and the budget problem.

Wearisome. Also I've got a chest infection.

WEDNESDAY 10TH MARCH

Up at 5.30 am. I have the morning free to work on the script, as they are doing a scene we've already touched.

The rewrites of the first 'Bertie' scene just . . . arrange themselves before my eyes. I've little to do but just copy them out.

Inspiration? Now ya see it, now ya don't . . . Why is being able to write so unpredictable?

I can understand why they used to believe in 'a muse', perched like a parrot on your shoulder, whispering the lines into your ear. It's great when she's there. When she's not it's impossible!

*

I take the rewritten scene in at midday, and in the afternoon Nick and Diana rehearse it. A few knobs fall off the writing (knobs of baroque phrasing . . .) but the actors get up from the table onto the floor for the first time and begin to play it. Sweet, very sweet . . . I'm elated.

*

After rehearsals I look up Andrew Leigh, the manager of the Old Vic, and take him out for a drink. He tells me the news that John Major has called a General Election.

Andrew is the best theatre manager in the world, I know that because he managed my reading tour of *The Romans in Britain*, way back in 1982. (Oh, if only Andrew would run a New Plays Theatre for us all to work happily in . . .)

We catch up on gossip – particularly Bogdanov's epic confrontation with the Hamburg Schauspielhaus, which he ran for two years and got the boot from last year. Hamburg's artistic history is like an endless production of *Julius Caesar*. The average tenure for an Intendant since the last war is eleven months. It is a theatre notorious for being out of control and ruining new plays with ludicrously pretentious productions, during which directors and lead actors resign, die etc. etc.. They wrecked *Pravda* a few years back. I tell him how Corinna Brocher blocked a production of *Berlin Bertie* there because the theatre, after Michael's departure, is once again in chaos.

*

A General Election. Some of the worst theatre imaginable, all over the television screens. And *Berlin Bertie*'s first preview will be on Election Night. So it'll be me, the two Dannys and Max, sitting alone in the auditorium? Or a knot of violently depressed, drunken Labour supporters?

*

I didn't get to bed until 2.30 in the morning. I tried to work on Act III and made a pig's ear of it.

THURSDAY 12TH MARCH

11.30 pm. I've the day off to rewrite Act III, and have comprehensively blown it. Over the week I've got behind with the proofs for the playtext, due into Nick Hern Books tomorrow. If they don't get them the printer's schedules will be messed up. Because there are already so many changes, from the rewriting I did in the week before rehearsal and from what's bubbled up in the last few days, the proofs became a massive job and took all day. So I've not written anything for Act III.

Telephone calls were a work surrogate . . .

Corinna rang from Hamburg. I told her the rehearsal news. She tells me the Deutsches Theater in East Berlin are considering the play for performance. Ten dramaturgs are having heavy discussions about it this week. *Ten* dramaturgs? Phew! I see them, like a Kafkaesque jury filmed by Orson Welles, rising steeply above me in wooden pews . . .

My agent, Tom Erhardt, rings to say that Barbara Brecht has read about our play in the German press and is under the impression I have written a play attacking her father. Tom and I laugh. Is there something about the play that is going to make everyone lose their temper about everything? Tom says he'll reassure her.

*

And on the phone in the evening, Danny and I draw up a new game plan. I'll go into rehearsals tomorrow. I must be there when the actors hit a scene for the first time.

Then I'll write over the weekend and deliver the new Act III without fail on Monday morning. (That means I won't be able to do any *Bribing God* rewrites until later next week . . . but that is a problem in an alternative universe.)

*

I'm trying to get the play out of the net, the trapping net, of easy moralising.

*

I'll delay giving Nick H. the third act of the proofs until Monday morning.

FRIDAY 13TH MARCH.

Another great day. A lot of it really does seem playable and to work. There is a breathtaking wonder when superb actors 'get on their feet' and go slowly about the rehearsal floor, scripts in hand, and you see the shape of the scene form in the air for the first time. It's so much about the pursuit of a sense of gracefulness.

Even though they may be saying to themselves about your text, 'What a load of bananas.'

*

'Blame.' 'No one shall escape calumny' – is that The Bible? Then Alice says, 'Go on, blame me.' The point is, of course, in no way can Alice be blamed for the sufferings of humanity. It's the tragedy of the train driver in the accident who did, or did not, see the signals.

*

Lunch time. Another letter by hand, from Max. No more 'dead baby' aggro. As for the set and the budget, that's up to Danny B. now. But it was Danny who put me up to writing to Max. 'We need to do a pincer movement,' he said.

*

I rang Danny B. at 8.30 pm and asked him for a *big* note about rewriting Act III. He laughed. 'You're going to have to do what Chekhov can do, and no one else can,' he said. Boyle is a hard man.

He meant that I must complete the mental and the physical journeys of the characters, so they end all together, at the same point . . . as Chekhov does, with such mastery. Good. Right. That's that decided, then. A doddle.

FIRST WEEKEND

Saturday was lost. The chest infection worse. No chance to get to a doctor, so I took some penicillin that was lying round the house. Mid-afternoon I gave up trying to write. My sister-in-law and her man came round. I cooked cous-cous and we all had a lovely, 'no one talks about the theatre' evening.

On Sunday, I began writing at 7 am and went on for thirteen hours, before watching some soothing nonsense on TV. A long, sustained adrenalin hit. This has GOT to be unhealthy! It wasn't all effortless surf-boarding, but it wasn't a bad, day-long ride.

*

My agent, Peggy Ramsay, used to say, telling you she was quoting Ibsen (whether she was or not I don't know!) . . . Peggy used to say that every play has an obligation scene. It is the scene that you have to write. She also said that because playwrights are 'so bloody-minded', often a first draft has no trace of the essential scene. (I hear her voice. Since her death I've been bereft. I miss her so much.)

With *Berlin Bertie*, I think I've misidentified the 'obligation scene'. I thought it was the appearance of 'Bertie' in London. But it's not, it's the scene between the two sisters at the top of Act III. It's when Alice tells Rosa what has happened to her, and turns the play on its head: Alice's attitude is: So you think, sister from the East, you have experienced the worst. You haven't, I have. I know all about tyranny, fear and death, from working in South London.

Yes! That's it. *Yes*, that's the expectation the play has set up. If I satisfy it, the act could take off.

Rewrite! Do it now!

*

Odd how you finally come to the obvious by the most obscure routes! But the twisting about is necessary. When writing you must 'kick against the pricks' of every received notion about form.

You embrace a 'stage convention' only when the form has dragged you by the hair, screaming, to its embrace.

*

Max rang on Sunday afternoon. The theatre is looking again at the cost of the design. Running costs, because the flying and the effects all happen at once in Act II, are a problem. I fear the trucking of the set downstage is under threat. But he is, it was clear, going to do all he can to give us what we want.

He went on to tell me that he's having his own arm-wrestling match at the RSC. Adrian Noble is protesting that Max is making far too many changes to the old seventeenth-century text he's directing. The word 'authenticity' hovers in the air, north of the Thames . . . ! Max's attitude is: Sod academic questions of text and legitimacy, any show has to be for our time whether the text be old and honoured, old and knocked about, or brand new.

MONDAY 16TH MARCH

I got up at 5 am and began writing at once, not brushing my teeth, washing or shaving because I was in a rage to have another go at a section of the Act III 'Bertie' scene.

The 'rewrite-of-a-rewrite' was done by 7.30 am. Light-headed with glee, I brushed my teeth, shaved, had a bath . . . Then I spent two hours getting copies of rewrites out of the printer and stapled together. (The ink in the printer's cartridge ran out, I wasted paper and time, I collated the pages wrongly on the living-room floor, crawling about with staples etc., and at the same time I was getting the rewrites into proofs. An inky and grubby trade!)

No time to work the buses, so I rang for a mini-cab, dropped the proofs off at the publishers and made it to the rehearsal room, a direly ugly Methodist Church Hall in Pimlico. It was satisfying, after the morning's rush, to be there early – though Diana, the immaculate professional, was there before me, champing for the new scenes.

Worryingly, Kevin is off sick. Food-poisoning.

They sat in a corner looking through the rewrites for half-an-hour. I walked about the hall, very nervous. (What a horrible environment to rehearse in, after the ease of the first week at the Old Vic. Awful yellow glass jaundices the light.)

'Don't know about the scene with the sisters,' Danny Boyle whispers to me when they've finished. My heart sinks.

But after it's been read aloud, Danny confesses his doubts are allayed about the 'obligation scene'. I put a few cuts in and field the first, minor objections from the actors. More will follow no doubt, this cast is remorseless!

I'm OK about the new 'Bertie' scene. Nick seems pleased. But I don't know if I've animated the scene between the sisters enough.

Penny likes the new writing around 'the dead baby'. The lines I have added for Alice have probably made it even more 'politically incorrect' to the YPTS Thought Police Committee. I used the anger I felt at their attempted intervention last week, to try to dramatise Alice's personal responses to the child's murder.

There were no changes in Susan's part, though she may have to stand on her head for a minute or two less . . .

I *think* Diana is confident about how we are progressing.

Kevin is becoming thoughtful. I think he realises suddenly, it's a big part. And he has to kick off with a very tough routine, a long, complex speech.

Nick is friendly, likes to talk, but not about the part. Politics, music, the southern Germans . . .

I made a few cuts on the spot. Nick resisted one.

Then Danny called a discussion about the end of the play. It wasn't of much help. A social move on his part, I suspect. Part of a director's job is to be a good 'social secretary'. And in a small-cast play, with all the cast on the stage together in just one scene, it's important that we are all aware of each other's 'state of play'.

*

Then we went back to the Berlin scene in Act II. I made three small changes.

Diana, Penny and Nick are a demanding trio! Their attitude is, 'If I'm going to act this, I want to know it's right, and know it *now*!' And why not? *They* will do the play, after all, not their playwright. On opening night he'll be in the bar . . .

I am 'their' playwright. They are not 'my' actors.

*

You won't read about it in the high-minded manifestoes of playwrights – Brecht's 'Short Organum', or even in Artaud – but the truth is that the relationship between playwright and actors is riven with sexuality.

You hire them. They parade their talent before you and you choose. Auditions, at their worst, are a 'meat rack'. (I remember auditions for a play of mine in New York. The actors, dressed up to the nines, male and female, pouted and abased themselves in the most provocative ways. They were such a floorshow, I couldn't judge who could act and who could not.)

*

The trick when actors call for rewrites is not to be fazed, to keep your instinct sharp and say 'yes' or 'no' at once if you can, and 'I'm lost' – if you are. You have to put a line on ice sometimes, and promise to think about it – but I've found that is not a good idea.

The danger is that actors' ideas can be too logical. Good theatrical writing makes mad leaps, that actors sometimes fear until late in the rehearsal period.

But you must put paranoia aside and get up and dance with the actors. If you don't love actors, don't try to write plays.

Diana, Penny, Nick are a delight to rehearsal-dance with – the salt of the theatre.

*

Though I must admit, I am anxious. The play seems formidable.

I have never known whether I am in control of this writing, from day one, version one. It has always seemed just beyond me. As if my fingers are not quite long enough to touch it, as if my breath is just too short to speak its lines out . . .

I'm over-reaching with this play and I think I've always known it. Great! If I topple flat on my face, so-be-it. (Who called Marlowe 'The Overreacher'?)

*

I keep on reminding myself – a playwright's job in rehearsals is to deliver the play to the actors, and deliver it in the best state, even if that means some hairy rewriting at 5 am and scratching in the odd new line on the hoof.

And I do believe . . . the text of *that scene* is fine now.

*

Danny B. sends me away for the afternoon and he's not calling me until Friday morning. The idea is I finally write the end of the thing, the last three pages, quietly over the next few days.

Back home at my desk, I stare at the last five pages, dumbfounded. As they stand they are dreadful. 'Pump it up' writing, unearned, wrong-footed and embarrassing.

I blame myself.

Every time I've come to the end, I've been worn out. And it doesn't help to joke, as I did with the actors today, that the end of *Measure for Measure* was clearly dashed off by an exhausted writer . . . (after he'd written the three great scenes, the confrontations he really wanted to write, earlier in the play).

The 'dashed-off-last-scene' syndrome . . . . If I don't do something about it, it will sink our play.

*

But nothing occurs to me.

And the telephone does not stop ringing.

Corinna wants the latest version for the ten dramaturgs of the Deutsches Theater to chew over. I promise to send it.

Michael Kustow rings, twice, about this and that, delivering *Bribing God* to his office on Monday. He's off to Vienna. Something to do with a scheme he's trying to sell the RSC . . . At least Michael K. keeps on trucking. Enthusiasm! It's so rare, these 'receded' dog days. Enthusiasts take risks, and risks can lose you your job.

*

But writing isn't a job. Job? In the arts? Was Cubism a job? Was Mozart's C minor piano concerto 'a job' – if it was, why did he write in that key?

Despite the Thatcher years, I still can't get over people in the arts thinking that what we do has anything to do with a commerce.

I've made, at times, a good living from writing. But that was Bohemian madness, luck, not a career!

How can the arts be a career? To be an artist is a reckless under-taking, a compulsion to be compared with manic gambling, or an ob-session comparable to that of the see-ers of angels and religious nutcases . . .

*

Jackie Bodley, from Nick Hern Books, rings with a few queries about the proofs. I apologise to her for having wrecked them with bits of typescript stuck in, crossings-out, and arrows all over the place. She is very tolerant. We discuss whether we can get the new end of the play in at the last proof-checking stage. She'll see what the printers say.

I'm so tired.

*

Jack Gold, who is to direct *Bribing God*, rings. I revive. We spend an hour going through the script. Jack's great – a clear, hard mind.

Bed at 9 pm, promising to myself that I'll drop this ridiculous, Balzacian 'up at 5 in the morning to write' routine now, once and for all.

TUESDAY 17th MARCH

The Royal Court leaflet for the play arrives. It is illegible. I shout and scream at the window of my room.

8.30 am. I ring Danny B. to rage about it. I wrote the copy for the leaflet, *why can't I read it?* Why are there now 60,000 illegible leaflets in the world, all, by definition, incapable of advertising the play?

Danny is calm.

10.30 am. I ring Guy Chapman to see if there's anything to be done. There's not, nor is it his fault. The printers ignored the proof, the Court are asking for their money back; if they get their money back they'll spend it on *extra* advertising for *Berlin Bertie* etc. etc.

But . . . my play ends up with an illegible leaflet. And I'm caring too much about peripheral details. ('God is in the details . . . ' Who said that?)

*

I go to the doctor at the end of the afternoon. Bronchitis, but I feel fine. I'm given a prescription for antibiotics and a big-tasting linctus in a big old-fashioned bottle. Much relief.

I wrote a draft of the end of the play but wiped it.

WEDNESDAY 18TH MARCH

A ragged day. Coughing and spitting. No adrenalin; because I've got time to do the last scene. So I waste the time.

I go down to the bottom of the garden and give myself a good shouting at. *Don't blow this!*

It always irritated me, in Los Angeles, how they really did say the cliché – 'Life is not a rehearsal.' But, dear God, that cliché gets truer year by year in my late forties, play by play . . .

*

An officer of the local Labour Party looks in. Dulwich is one of the most marginal seats in the country: the first canvassing is not all they had hoped for. 'It's patchy, better in some places, worse in others.'

The impression is that people are so indifferent to politics, or to these politics, that even apathy is too vigorous a belief to hold.

We intelligentsia and artists, who live in such a fervour about the world, trying to understand it in our work, neglect to realise that those out there in the world see things differently. I mean, they don't give a damn.

And why should they? Perhaps real democracy, rather than the electronic shadow-play we let the ruling groups foist upon us, would be a rather unforgiving state to live in. Leaders would not be easily forgiven. Athenian ostrakia, rattling in the burial urns of reputations, the dismissed leaders drinking quietly in the corners of pubs of an evening.

THURSDAY 19TH MARCH

I sat down to work in the morning, then at eight o'clock Danny rang: could I go in?

A crisis. It's the first 'Bertie' scene. The playwright as fire engine . . . A bell in my head clanging – is the scene burning down ?

I get to Pimlico early. It's nothing much, the persistent trouble of reactive lines from Rosa. I slice them out. Nick wants clarification of the nature of his confession. He has a brilliant suggestion for a transposition of passages. I accept it with gratitude.

The text is edging away from the much-revised version I gave to Jackie for publication. But it's not disgracefully distant, at least *not yet.*

*

I go from the rehearsal into London to buy ink cartridges for the computer's bubble-jet printer. And from five until midnight, I get the last scene out, at last.

I suddenly see, it's about a 'rush of blood to the head'; it's an action scene. They decide to go. No 'rounding-up' speech is possible; when you try to write one, it is immediately lead. My mistake has been a belief that a magic phrase would appear, but it is a magic action that's needed. Which I've had all along: the ludicrous, but – I hope – wonderfully ludicrous 'flying rehearsal' in the play's last moment.

Halfway through writing it, Danny rings, to tell me of Diana's confusion about her 'line' through the part . . . how Rosa's loss of faith unfolds. Serendipity! On the screen before me is an attempt at a final speech, to Alice, about the speeding roller-coaster her life has become, without her faith.

FRIDAY 20TH. MARCH

5 am again. I re-do the last scene.

Into rehearsal, first dropping off the last scene at Nick Hern's office.

First, an hour with Diana. She is excited about the 'roller-coaster speech'. We go through all of Rosa's crises in the play, and end with a discussion about the 'desecration' soliloquy, the nun's heresy.

Diana's a believer, she wants to be absolutely sure about the aside.

Tricky ground. Important to remember, OK, Diana goes to church – but she's also a forty-carat theatre pro.

I'll never *really* talk to her about what this play means. But I will talk to her about its sexiness, what I hope is its beauty.

'Workability', beauty and meaning, are one and the same to a great actor.

'I've taken my clothes off in plays, I've stripped at the end of a first act, I'll do anything . . . ,' says Diana, pausing with majestic grace, 'as long as I know it's *justified*. I mean, as long as it . . . ' her voice goes down an octave, with force and menace . . . 'as long as it *works*.'

There speaks John Dexter's favourite actress.

We go through the heresy speech. I find it very, VERY difficult to explain what, line by line, is going on in it.

Then she reads it so very, very beautifully that writer and director are for a moment, stunned.

*

Inarticulate writers . . . I suppose that if I could explain what a play meant, what I wanted by writing it, I wouldn't write the play. I'd say 'love the world', or whatever.

*

So. A rehearsal when the playwright had to sing for his supper, the most crucial so far. Rosa's part finally put to bed and the end cracked, with some cuts done 'on the hoof'. I was paranoid about 'magic phrase' writing.

Diana – remorseless today – suggests lifting Rosa's 'amoeboid' vision of her loss of faith in the last 'Bertie' scene, and working it into her confession to Alice at the end.

I can't decide about that 'on my feet' at the last minute, so I promise to have another look at the end over the weekend.

Not much to do. A few more accurate lines. Hopefully they'll pop into my weary head.

THE SECOND WEEKEND

Saturday.

Tried to fix a lavatory cistern. Replaced the whole thing. Felt horribly like Sandy: the simple difficulties of banging a nail in a wall, of fixing a loo that won't flush . . . *The huge weight* of daily entropy, i.e., a load of bananas.

To do the job I borrow a plumber's wrench sort-of-thing from my neighbour, Mike Thorpe, a superb painter of startling abstract stuff. He is now into ravishing, dead straight, flower paintings, some huge, some tiny. But you look at 'em and think . . . *are* they straight? The flower canvases are all over his house, glisteningly new. Disturbing. Are painters even weirder than playwrights?

In the afternoon, to Selhurst Park, to watch Crystal Palace, a quasi-religious activity this family has indulged in for a very long time. It's improving for the soul . . . Goal-less draw with Aston Villa. The pits. Rumbles of discontent amongst downtrodden, shuffling fans. AND hasn't the price of a polystyrene cup of Bovril gone up 5 p? I blame the Palace Chairman, Ron Noades. Our Ron dreams of a super 80,000 seat Euro-stadium to replace the friendly but modest Selhurst Park, and vast marketing ploys for the club. Meanwhile, who are these yompers in the midfield, slicing the ball into orbit? Oh Palace, don't you love us anymore? Why are you doing this to us?

A good day off.

SUNDAY 22ND MARCH

A straight six hours in the morning writing *Bribing God*. An unreality about writing so quickly, touching about two-thirds of the scenes one way or another. Exhilarating!

Then a long lunch with some old friends, who have just returned from abroad. The afternoon becomes wonderfully cheery.

Evening, a massive attempt to sober up. Wrote a speech for *Bribing God*.

MONDAY 23RD MARCH

Another 5 am job. I get the new *Bribing God* finished by lunch time and ring Alison Carter, Michael Kustow's assistant, with the good news. A bike collects a computer disk.

Afternoon. Alison rings. The disk is corrupted, she can't print from it. I send another.

At last, I really do think it is done. Michael is giving a 'Please, David, say yes or no' sort of ultimatum to Channel 4.

TUESDAY 24TH MARCH

Michael had a telephone conversation with Aukin today, who said we were 'pressurising him'. So the 'ultimatum' hasn't worked, and it's still stuck with Channel 4.

I'm staying away from rehearsals now. It's time for the actors to take over. The writer's usefulness is in abeyance, it's the director's time now.

THURSDAY 26TH MARCH

I re-read Douglas Oliver's mighty poem *Penniless Politics*. Also the exciting introduction to the new Penguin translation of *The Iliad*. Lunch-time, I went to the rehearsal room to leave a couple of tiny rewrites that I did, late morning. Danny and the actors weren't there. I posted the pages through a gap in the locked church door.

FRIDAY 27TH MARCH

A morning looking at some scribbles for a new stage play. For now, I'm calling it *Like It or Not*. (A title theatre managers would attack to the death – 'They'll all say they don't like it at all!')

I must stop moonlighting on this production. How the hell I got a rewrite of *Bribing God* done last weekend I don't know. Looking at the clean script sent from Mike K's laser printer, I see I hammered the first thirty pages or so, cut a sequence of scenes, put in another – it's like another person was doing that last weekend. 'Oh look what he did there . . . .'

It's hard to explain just how freaky playwriting is.

*

In the afternoon, it was great to be back in *Berlin Bertie* rehearsals. I spent time in a corner with Nick Woodeson, going through 'Bertie's' line in the play, while Danny B. was orchestrating the skirmish in Act I, which calls for Alice, Joanne and an ironing board to whirl around and crash to the ground.

(An ironing board? Some subliminal salute, even after all these years, to dear old Johnny Osborne?)

I suspect Nick is an 'actor scholar', an intellectual. In a break we talk about Gesualdo's madrigals (the murderer composer! I've stolen his name in the play, for the invented Italian clown that 'Bertie' mentions). I promise Nick a tape.

Acting isn't a particularly intellectual trade, it is nearer to the gymnasium than the study. Artaud called actors 'athletes of the heart', which is very accurate about the best of them.

But I have met some 'actor scholars'; David Calder has been in two of my plays, and his political reading and grasp consistently outstripped that of his author's; and John Nettles, who was in a play of mine at the RSC, read French at Oxford and floored me in an argument about Sartre. (He's now famous as the TV detective, 'Bergerac'. I hope Nettles isn't too bright to return to us in the theatre. He's a terrific classical and 'new play' actor.)

*

An hour going through Alice's part with Penny and Danny B., its line, its crises.

Later, Danny B. says he has to watch it, to keep two very different approaches to acting working; Diana, once she's happy with the script, just wants to get on with the acting, the 'how-to-do-it'. Penny, whose acting is also technically immaculate, is nevertheless of the 'Joint Stock', experimental, 'suck it and see, spit it out and talk it through' school of rehearsal.

Then Susan performs the mime in Act I.

It's too long. The two lines I've given seem misplaced. (Can't mime and words mesh?)

I have a moment's panic. Why am I asking her to do this?

I remember Margaretta d'Arcy, John Arden's wife, attacking the first cast of my *Sore Throats*, at the RSC: she said to Ruby Wax and Paola Dionisotti, 'Why are you Brenton's slaves?'

Though thinking about it . . . Ruby? Paola? Enslaved by anyone?

That was a long time ago – 1979? But I do remember that the young Ruby Wax – now famous for a comic television show – took me out to dinner the next night, to reassure me that the actors would continue to speak the lines!

*

Meanwhile down here in a grotty Methodist rehearsal room in Pimlico, there is Susan Lynch's eerily beautiful mime performance.

And it's in character, which is extraordinary. It is like an evocation of a spirit. Susan and her teacher, Riz, embraced afterwards; it was the first time anyone apart from the two Dannys had seen the mime. The first time to strangers.

THIRD WEEKEND

I tried to write the *Guardian* article, but hated what came out – I was 'manifesto-ing'. I need another way into it.

What they want, I fear, is me slagging something or, even better, someone, off. So tedious. I wiped, electronically, what I'd done and had the weekend off, *properly* off.

MONDAY 30TH MARCH

I watched Penny and Susan rehearsing their long scene in the first act. 'To present the pretence': the simple things about the theatre always catch me out. For example, Alice is present . . . what Penny is playing is nothing like Penny, at all . . .

Great to see the scene. Three lines were sore thumbs, I thought; noted them. But, but . . .

A lunch-time meeting, setting up TV extracts for a London TV station. The usual flummery. Then Diana strode into the room, full of vigour, and buttonholed me for a tiny, tiny textual point, inside a line . . .

*

Afternoon, back home to work on the article for the *Guardian*.

Out of the blue . . . David Aukin's secretary rang to 'arrange the script meeting for tomorrow'.

What's going on? First I've heard of this . . . . I can't make it tomorrow anyway. I agree to a meeting on Wednesday.

Late, at 11.30 pm, Michael K. rings. Some notes have emerged from David. I yelp in pain when he tells them to me. Michael says, 'Please Howard, I've had a terrible day too. Don't let *us* start to give each other a bad time.' I apologise.

My good spirits sap away. In the evening I ring Jack Gold, congratulate him on last night's excellent Leavis piece, 'The Last Romantics'.

*

The trouble is if Mike K. doesn't get the go-ahead for *Bribing God* in the next few days we'll lose Jack as director to another project. And I'll have to disappear into the previews.

I think I'll write about Douglas Oliver's *Penniless Politics* in my *Guardian* article. A bracing and cheering task.

TUESDAY 31ST MARCH

Couldn't sleep. So worried, not that *Bribing God* is not going to get on, but that it's going to get wrecked, and I'm going – through exhaustion – to be a party to ruining it, to making it ordinary, to betraying its 'avant-garde TV' ambitions.

Round 4 am, I pick up the Penguin Brodsky that's lying on the floor and read a quote from Pushkin: 'The muse does not brook vanity.' No. But she sure can't get enough worry off you.

9 am. Michael K. on the phone again.

THURSDAY 2ND APRIL

Up at 6 am. I had the *Guardian* article written by 9.30 and took it into the Court.

Then to a rehearsal followed by a run of Act I. Penny is making Alice very complex, still 'doing it by numbers', but this (Danny B.'s note to her) is not a part that you can present. It has to be inhabited. Unprecedented – a play by me with a part that demands naturalistic acting (is this maturity or decline?!).

Mm. Don't let's all get carried away. I hope I've written an actable part and she – a first-class, top-division actress – hasn't really cracked it yet. Keep watching and asking – is it her fault, or yours? The simple question a playwright must always ask over and over in rehearsals: is this not working because of the acting or because of the text?

Eye on the ball, Howard.

*

And up to Muswell Hill by 4.30. A session with Mike Kustow and Jack Gold on *Bribing God.*

Michael is always expansive, hopeful; he's a generous man with a generous figure, warm eyes, a rich voice; he wants everything to work and all to be in harmony. He's voracious for notions, ideas. He's a liberal, progressive man . . . he's given to despatching me seven-page vortexes of thought about *Bribing God*, when I really want to know whether a scene is . . . too long or too short, period! But what's great about Michael is that he's an unreconstructed modernist: he hates the anti-history of fashionable post-modernism. As a Jew, he suspects anything anti-historical. He loves gossip, but hates malice. As a producer he must have borne a thousand slights, but there's no sign.

Jack is more ascetic, precise, a wiry man with an open-necked shirt. He bides his time in a discussion, then speaks in calm, intact sentences. He has a Mozartian sense of shape and good order in a script. He abhors repetition. Politically he's harder than Michael. I've always admired him and just *ache* to get this script accepted, so we can really begin to get to grips.

The three of us are tired; we relax for a moment on Michael's aggressively luxurious white leather sofas, arranged around a low table from which spill the latest books. 'Is that a nightingale, singing in your front garden?' I ask Michael. They go into Jewish humour . . . 'It's a bird.' 'Jews don't know about birds, there's just a thing, like a chicken.' 'Yes. It's a chicken in the front garden.' Giggles and laughter. Then we start at page one and keep going until we fall to bits around 10.30.

FRIDAY 3RD APRIL.

Morning, a run through of Act II.

I see hinges in the text that must be swung. Note 'em.

Nick is having difficulty, fighting private demons about the part. David Calder does that, late in a rehearsal. Danny B. and I find ourselves rather long-toothed about this. Highly talented actors like Nick and David will not want to be prepared too early, and, instinctively, find some reason for delaying really doing it. The reasons can be various; a personal crisis of confidence, a row with the director, an attack on the script . . . The director has to keep cool, be there to help, judge when to say *nothing*, and wait for the actor to come out the other side of the rapids they're swirling in.

They always do.

In the afternoon to the Young Vic Theatre, to see a one-off performance of *Bloody Poetry*. It's directed by Anna Cartaret and performed by other members of an RSC company who are touring *Les Liaisons Dangereuses* around the country. They do my play on the odd afternoon or Sunday. I'd already seen them at the Bristol Old Vic. They perform the play without decor, a few hats and coats – out of, well, ebullience, enthusiasm, love. Anna's direction is terrific.

Space, actor, audience . . . Anna's production asks 'why do we need more?' I must think of writing for 'in the round' again.

FOURTH WEEK END

Saturday 4th April and at last I see my play run through, beginning to end.

I spot four small rewrites; do two of them on the hoof, but the other two are trickier, and I promise them for Monday.

There are some small rehearsal cuts and edits that have happened in my absence, most OK, some 50-50 balls and a couple that have done damage, particularly with the 'amoeba' speech. I'll get something else in for Rosa.

Nick – predictably – takes a great leap forward. 'Bertie' appears amongst us for the first time.

Necromancy 'n' acting. Murky area there!

The production is very secure. The difficult 'don't tell till you have to' multiple revelations, all work. The punishing wave of rewriting in weeks one and two – which seem a dream now, I can't remember doing them only a little while ago – has paid off.

What I can't tell is whether the play *kicks*. Whether it attacks, or whether it is cool.

Though it was written in white heat, I suspect that it's 'cool'. Impossible to say in a rehearsal room.

Danny B. worries that the second half, Act III, is too short and the audience will feel short-changed.

I didn't feel that. But my judgement was blown by seeing these wonderful actors showing the play for the first time.

Back home, the worry that Act III ain't gonna make it 'computer-viruses' my brain.

Revived by news of a Palace victory, 2-0 over Everton, awful game, they say, but a victory . . . and by an Indian meal in the evening.

SUNDAY 4TH APRIL

I attempt some *Bribing God*, but I'm dumb-headed, incapable of doing anything, so give up.

MONDAY 5TH APRIL.

In the morning, I do the two promised rewrites and phone them through to Danny B. at 8 am.

Then I ring Jack Gold, ask for help and go through what I couldn't make work yesterday. He's terrific, he gives elegant solutions to all my troubles.

Then to the theatre for an interview with Benedict Nightingale of *The Times*. Then a German radio interview. I thought he was going to go on forever with a long speech about the German political situation. He spoke for ten minutes without stopping. When he finally turned his tape-recorder on and asked a question a mere seven sentences long, I was in such a state of stupor I had to ask him if we could begin again. Aie aie. When they come, in hell, to fix my torment, let it not be an endless interview with a German radio station . . .

*

I usually get the bus to Victoria from Camberwell Green, then tube to Sloane Square.

Standing at the Green, what is the *England* that's walking past? So many desperately poor people, so many looking ill. And then there are the derelicts, tramps, drunks. The poor, on the edge, the derelicts over the edge. Strain on every face. *What is happening to my country?*

I go from that to the chic leathered calves of Sloane Square, the latest look of the nonchalant lower lip, money dripping in ornaments from loose wrists. Two worlds, 35 minutes bus 'n' tube apart.

When I actually *look* at the city I live in, it's a shock. It rearranges itself into a cruel, social Cubism. One class passes through the other, without contact, as if each other were ghosts.

*

Afternoon, I start writing at 3 pm and by 11 pm have got somewhere.

TUESDAY 6TH APRIL

Try to sleep, can't, get up at 4.30 am saying, 'Last time! Last time I ever do this!.' I work on *Bribing God* – the 'don't shave don't brush your teeth' routine – and break off at 12.30 pm, half an hour before the Channel 4 bike is due at the door.

Into the theatre to watch the technical for a few hours. Danny is blithe, his eyes like olives in grey soup . . . that deathly look that comes with hard work in the theatre.

It's 'rehearsal room tan', a curious grey skin that struggling to write and learn imagined lives gives to us. Interesting how the women in a cast use make-up more and more to offset 'rehearsal tan', and the men become more immaculately cleanshaven. If there is a moment, during a break, of sunshine, actors sit out on the steps of a church hall, rolling polystyrene cups between their hands, their faces turned up to the sun.

I love actors. I'm in awe of them. I can't understand writers who hate actors, who think actors are stupid. The intelligence of a good actor is humanity at its best.

And look at how they live! The employment conditions . . . The *Berlin Bertie* cast are being paid £210 a week at the Court. Can that go on? We are trading on actors' love of their art. The Court management – of which I'm a part when they do my play – preen themselves on their history and principles. But how much do they pay Kevin, Susan, Diana, Penny and Nick?

Something is out of kilter here with actors' pay, even in the best theatre in the land.

All through the Thatcher years, when I was more out of fashion than halitosis, I stayed out of debt and earned a fair living.

But actors . . . some are wealthy from past films, but the public would be amazed at how many very well-known actors are hard pressed. (The only time I met Laurence Olivier, he told me he was stony broke. I bought him a drink.)

WEDNESDAY 8TH APRIL

To rehearsals, now on the stage. Into the theatre! Everyone sees what we have. The word – good or bad, never ask – goes round the theatre's workers, offices and stage crew.

*

Dress rehearsal. They are always *sepulchral*. No one laughs at the jokes. People you don't know are dotted about the auditorium. You control the paranoia as best you can.

Penny was 'internalising' as Alice; she had brought the rehearsal room to the stage.

Kevin as Sandy had a nightmarish time, hit by the terrible, glaring eye of the Royal Court's stage. I felt for him! I'm confident he will be excellent. A 'frightener' is no bad thing – for all of us!

Susan as Joanne was terrific, but she slipped and hurt her ankle.

Diana was steely as Rosa.

And Nick as 'Bertie' walked away with the show.

*

Max was there, having nipped back from his rehearsals with the RSC at Stratford. He gave us masterly notes, a micro and a macro view of play and show. A man who knows his own mind and is comfortable with what he thinks.

THURSDAY 9TH APRIL

General Election Day. First preview day.

Out to vote. A beautiful sunny day, fresh spring warmth.

*

To the theatre for notes at 2 pm. Danny calls a second dress rehearsal.

I go home to sleep – I had a restless night.

*

I return at 7. The theatre's three-quarters full, not bad for Election Night. Stephen Daldry, Max's successor at the Royal Court, comes to see the show.

And . . . Penny is right up. Kevin gets a grip and is funny and moving. Nick is brilliant, but there's something not firing in the big scene with Diana. Diana told me last night she would do the first two previews 'down', to see 'what it's like'. Maybe, but I love the wit of her playing as Rosa. (I think she's said to herself all along, 'How do I play a quiet woman?' Which, technically, becomes the acting question – 'How quietly dare I do this?')

*

It's just great to see the play for the first time. And there's the wonderful ignorance of early audiences. They have no idea what the play will be – long, boring, funny, po-faced? And moment by moment they think – is there going to be an outrage? (That's my bloody reputation – too many guns going off in my early plays!) There's a great tension between the first audiences and the play, a concentration. The journey's made, inventing maps of the route as we, the performers, and our audience, make our way through the evening . . . (romantic notion! But why not?)

But then, soon the 'word' is out, then the reviews, the play's known as success, failure or curate's egg – and the magical insecurity of the early audiences never returns.

*

Afterwards I see the actors then go to the pub with some of them. Penny and I spin, it's the adrenalin and beer.

We both live in 'Sauf London' and share a taxi back together. 'Not too Aussie is it?' she suddenly says (she's Australian). There's no way people will think that, but it suddenly strikes me that Penny's fabulous stage career in England – wonderful work with the RSC – has been in a half-foreign language. Kate Nelligan, who's Canadian, told me how living in a different English began to disturb her. I don't know if Aussie actors get that – Strine's nearer to us, or to London dialect, than any North American English.

This isn't just about the sound of words. There's some kind of cultural grammar, that shifts. I remember rehearsals of a play of mine in Los Angeles, which I attended. There were constant and sometimes comic misunderstandings. California came to feel very, very foreign . . . same words, different language . . .

*

Election gloom at home as the Tories secure a working majority. My teenage sons are very upset. They want the world 'to be different'.

*

Neil Kinnock's concession of defeat was very moving – 'I am fortunate in my personal circumstances, but there are many who are not. I feel they deserved better on April 9th.'

FRIDAY APRIL 10TH.

Second preview, a good, appreciative house.

Not the usual, flat, second preview; on the contrary, it was wildly up and down.

Kevin made a great leap with Sandy's huge opening 'playlet'. The audience laughed.

Then Penny hit silence from the audience. It was a hard pounding. She regressed to the dress rehearsal performance, internalised – the 'blazing' of the character came out as a kind of snarling . . . But come Act III she was wonderful.

Nick launched into the Berlin scene with a magnificent portrayal of a dangerous man. This very much out of Danny B.'s notes.

Dangerous, a quick-moving man, confident in the terror he creates. But then, I think, surprised by this radically new performance of the first five minutes of the scene, he lost concentration, nearly dried, dropped lines. 'Your line,' Diana said to him, at one point, very, very quickly.

At the beginning of Act II there was a classic preview cock-up. Sandy/Kevin has a lot of D.I.Y. comedy, hanging up curtains on two nails. The curtains weren't there. 'No curtains,' Diana says to Kevin, unheard by the audience. We sitting on the production row in the dress circle go to pieces; the author invents lines in his head. Kevin cuts, with great elegance. The scene goes well, without the curtain gags I'd worked so hard on!

Act III (the second half of the show) sang. My fears of not delivering, of being mute by oversight – I've always been paranoid about underwriting – do you have enough for two minutes on a stage, let alone two hours? . . . All that was laid to rest.

The only false note was a mysteriously exploding Carlsberg lager can, which sprayed the front two rows. ('Why do they take it?' Danny B. said to me, 'They pay eight quid and get soaked.' He paused, then added, 'I s'pose they think it's part of the show.' Hard nut Danny Boyle! Sometimes he looks at the theatre so . . . innocently. Perhaps that's what makes him so good a director.)

SATURDAY 11TH APRIL

Third preview. Penny much more interesting, vivid, attacking in Act I. Nick seemed great at the opening of the big 'Bertie' scene but then he and Diana dipped, seemed to be going down and down in the centre of the scene. I cannot for the life of me see what is wrong. We've not yet had this scene really run – except for the crude first preview version. When Nick loses the threat, she responds with a quiet line, he then goes quiet, the scene spreads flatly – cowpattishly – and lies there (smelling, steaming a little!).

It lifts, late, when he gets on to the bugging of the pastor and Rosa's house.

The only note that occurs to me, is that the centre of the scene is a history play; the news of the street, what has happened, is burning hot news. It's 'The King of Navarre is dead!' It's amazing stuff; the KGB has saved Rosa and her husband's cause. It puts them in a brand new, unprecedented situation, which 'Bertie' explores and defines, in desperation as he does so.

Now, *why doesn't that play?* Where is the spontaneity of a new situation, being invented, as they move and speak? If it's my fault, it's too late for me to do something about it. If it's their fault, it's getting dangerously late for them to do something . . .

And Nick is sending out signals, as an excellent actor will, that he will listen to no more notes; it's just his way, as the rehearsal period reaches its end, to work on parts outside rehearsal and bring them in.

I guess that by instinct he's a character actor. The two outer scenes, in London, he has no trouble with at all – and the Third Act 'Bertie' scene is, I'd have thought, potentially far more difficult than the big set-piece in Act II. But in the two outer scenes, he is playing 'The German abroad' – he has a fastidiously observed German accent (praised by German friends who were in on Friday night). He has the clear gestus a character actor needs. But in the Act II scene, he is 'straight'; naked; he has to 'be real as that man', not present 'Bertie' with acting as observation. Is that the difficulty he is struggling with?

There was some cutting and rearranging we did of the text in rehearsal. Was I properly on top of that? I thought the scene was as clean as a whistle, straight through . . . did I not keep a grip on the text as I should have?

I'm reminded of Wittgenstein's weird remark, which was something like, 'If anything true can be said about the philosophy of logic, you will be able to say it *all at once.*'

Is that it with the scene, in some way? It *has* no structure for the 'Bertie' actor. It *has* no rise, climax and fall. It is all there all at once . . . So the actor can blaze at once, on his entrance, fall off, return to the heat . . . as it takes him. It's timeless.

This meeting will, for the two of them, always exist out of time; it's like a lover's meeting, frozen in memory. An event that's *all at once.* Searching for a note here, but I'm disappearing up my bum . . .

Oh God. Have I asked an actor to do something utterly impossible?

*

Just read the scene three times. Can't for the life of me see anything wrong with it. It looks great. Get on the blower to Danny tomorrow about this.

*

And . . . a nearly full house but a sticky one compared to Friday's . . . Act II was ordinary. 'It didn't blaze, the play didn't blaze,' Danny B. said afterwards, biting his nails, looking like death.

It's a good thing it's the weekend. Danny has been very good, taking care not to tire them out. But he should take care of himself. One note session on Monday then the talk on Tuesday, and that is it.

I feel about tonight's show . . . OK, that was the bummer – there's always a preview that shows you what the show will be like on a bad night. But, if that's the marker for the show when it's 'down', it's pretty good.

*

I put my head around Nick's dressing-room door. Friends of his glared at me. I said thanks etc., then 'It's not as bad as you think – if you can take an author's note like that!' When I closed the door, there were guffaws of derision. Oh dear oh dear.

*

Diana blazed yesterday, tonight she withdrew. When she's not confident, or distrusts a line, she speaks with an odd husk in her voice. When she thinks she's got a line, she's clear as a bell.

*

This tiny theatre. We are pouring concentration and energy upon this show, which will run for six weeks – with no prospect of a transfer, given its difficult nature – and to us it is more important than love, or being a good person, or health, to *get it right.*

When Sandy protests, why doesn't anyone do anything for love any more . . . I think he's speaking for us!

*

Kevin was terrific yesterday. I admire his guts. He's taken on a difficult role – opening the show with a five-minute monodrama – and having to stand up on the stage in a long comic scene with one of our really great actresses. He's worked hard, he's been through crises of confidence, and come out the other side, hard and confident – and capable of 'walking away with the show', as they say. Good luck to him.

Susan, a consistent fire. I wish she could 'pull' two of the laugh lines, I'll ask Danny if he can find a note for her that will help. But she's real. And in the tricky scene – the very end – she does a great service to the play, skating over a potentially 'eggy' moment, that I've rewritten what, five, six times, but is still a pitfall. (Its final version – 'Let's get the ferry . . . .'). If she has the luck, and can stand the life, she could give wonderful performances.

*

Penny Downie and I were walking past the pseudo-French café, the Oriel, next door to the Court, which was heavily populated with 'Sloanes', sitting out having their coffees and mineral waters in the warm weather. 'Why,' Penny said, 'do the rich look so beautiful?' 'It's the food they eat', I joked.

Camberwell Green, Sloane Square . . . I am beginning to finally lose my temper about my country.

*

Walking in a side-street away from the theatre, to give the actors time to change before going round to see them, and to avoid the audience (didn't feel sociable this evening), I overheard two women who had seen the show. 'Politically he's lost,' one said to the other.

The delusions of the Left persist. Of course we're 'politically lost' That's what Alice is on about! That's her predicament!

'Penniless Politics' has it – 'Our ordinary political failure.'

When are we going to pay the penalty, to each other, for the neglect of each other during these wretched, shallow decades? Aie, aie, rage 'n' rave.

MONDAY 13TH APRIL

Into the theatre at 11 am. A TV crew are setting up to do some extracts. I do an interview for them, perched high up in the gallery with interviewer and camera crew.

Danny Boyle gestures to me from the lighting box, blowing rude faces.

He's been in Belfast. The traffic was jammed because of road blocks and searches. They're expecting violence because of Gerry Adams losing his Parliamentary seat. 'Over there,' he says, 'they look at our politics and say, 'You're crazy over there – we know we are – but your politics are crazy too.'

He wants my notes. We sit in the stalls bar, then because of a vacuum cleaner's noise, we go up to Max's office. We tell each other our concerns. 'I'm going to note 'em, note 'em hard,' he says.

*

Danny engages with Nick in the notes session (all of us, as usual, sprawled about the front of the stalls). Nick is interesting – he doesn't think 'Bertie' has come to confess, he's come to *confront*.

*

The difficulty with the 'Bertie' role is that he's 'evil' all right, BUT he's *not* a Richard III villain, no audience can love him. It's a *leper*, not a villain part. The unloved are always difficult to play, because of the old truth about us that, deep inside, no one thinks they are a shit. The fictional 'Bertie' thinks he's justified and good. The actor has to struggle to believe that . . . or (pace Diderot!) know how to pretend that he believes that.

*

I wander over to Peter Jones in Sloane Square and buy presents for Sally Emmet and Mary Wester, who are leaving the Peggy Ramsay Agency today. I worry about what I buy in a Sandy sort of way. Scent bottles. 'These fucking beautiful or are they fucking not, know what I mean?'

I'm hopelessly imprinted by the play now.

*

Early evening, to Peggy's old offices, for the last time. A farewell to Sally and Mary, a farewell to an era.

Disturbing. All the files and records have been cleared out to be taken over to the Soho offices of the new firm, Casarotto Ramsay, in Soho. There are empty shelves with all our names on them – Ayckbourn, Bond, Brenton, Churchill, Hare etc., through the alphabet.

David Hare said to me once that Peggy knew how to clear out the emotional gutters in her life, and move on.

I know I know, the Dylan song's right: 'What's done is done, what went down in the flood . . . ' Nevertheless I'm overwhelmed with sadness.

*

Oscar Lewenstein is at the party, now old but still clear-eyed, and still given to teasing me. His hair is still full and white, in a vaguely Bohemian quiff, his eyebrows also white, bushy, swept upward . . . He's a smaller man, I am a huge man . . . characteristically, he tilts his head downward, then darts his clear-eyed glance up at you, it's odd . . . as if he's suddenly thought of something and is trying to flash it, by a look, rather than words, which I don't think he likes.

'I'm writing my autobiography,' Oscar says, 'I've just reached *Magnificence*.' (My first play on the downstairs stage at the Court, when years ago, Oscar was running the theatre and I was the resident – and very green – playwright. He was very indecisive about the play; as an old CPer, I think he found the 'new Left' politics difficult to take – but in the end he put it on.)

The clear eyes shoot at me, he grins; he's teasing again!

I tell him of a memory I have of being in a small room, back then, in the Court's poky 'power corridor', listening to Lindsay Anderson shouting in the main office: 'It's shit! Never in this theatre! It's shit, shit!', and suddenly realising he was talking about *Magnificence*.

'Yes', says Oscar, 'We always encouraged you.'

*

It was a 'concessionary night' at the Court, that is five pounds for any seat. These audiences are usually wonderful, full of life and laughter, engaging with the play. Tonight's audience was no exception. The theatre was alive, everything was heightened, the molecules of the air itself over stage and auditorium seemed to shine . . .

Opening night tomorrow may be the usual dowsing in cold porridge, but I'm happy. I've delivered the play as best I can and tonight it worked.

TUESDAY 14TH APRIL (OPENING NIGHT)

In the back of The Fox and Hounds, the only pub in the Sloane Square area that isn't, yet, wrecked by loud music.

The show has just started. I don't see opening nights: what can I contribute, short of standing up and shouting 'new line there!'.

Friends there beforehand, critics to avoid etc. etc. David Aukin's in; he's come with Patti Love, who's sparky and wonderful as we stand, a little sheepishly, on the pavement before the steps of the theatre. David wishes me good luck. Since our professional relationship over the last few weeks has hung on a fraying thread, I'm pleased he's come. All's fair in love 'n' war 'n' TV . . .

Half an hour into the first act. I remember Nick Wright, fellow playwright and the National's literary manager, saying to me, 'There's only one rule for a playwright on an opening night. Don't fall over. That does create a bad impression.'

Bearing that in mind, I close this diary.

Sources of Essays

1 *Masks and Us*
Based on the T.R. Henn Memorial Lecture at St Catharine's College, Cambridge, 23 January 1994.

2 *Tea and 7-Up*
Based on an article published in *The Times*, 6 August 1982.

3 *A Crazy Optimism*
Based on an article published in the *New Statesman*, 3 July 1982.

4 *Writing in Thatcherland: Five of My Plays*
Taken from the introduction to *Brenton: Plays Two*, published by Methuen Drama. Used with permission.

5 *The Spaceman amongst the Tower Blocks*
Based on an article published in *20/20* in 1989.

6 *Democratic Laughter*
Based on an article in *Drama* magazine, No. 3, 1985.

7 *For Mickery, with Love*
Based on an article published in *City Limits* in 1990.

8 *The Unbearable Heaviness of Being English*
Based on the 1990 Cheltenham Lecture, published in the *New Statesman*.

9 *The Best We Have, Alas: Bertolt Brecht*
Based on an essay published in *Theater*, XVII, No. 2, Spring, 1986.

10 *How Can We Do It, Vsevolod*
Based on an article in *The Independent*, 1990.

11 *A Cheery Day: Margaret Thatcher's Resignation*
Based on an article in *The Guardian*, 29 November 1990.

12 *Shakespeare: Playing in the Ruins*
Based on an article published in *The Independent*, 1993.

13 *Hooks and Eyes and Plays and a Poem*
Based on an article in *The Guardian*, 1992. A version of this
article makes up the introduction to *Penniless Politics*, by
Douglas Oliver, published by Bloodaxe Books in 1994.